Parent's Guide to College Football Recruiting

Dan Lueders

An

Exsidious

brand publication

Exsidious, LLC

Cover photo by Grace Lueders

Copyright © 2015 Exsidious, LLC. All rights reserved.

Legal Notice: The references in this book to persons, organizations and trademarks are factual, and there is neither affiliation with nor endorsement by them.

First Edition

ISBN: 978-0-9862927-0-5 (paperback; First Edition)
ISBN: 978-0-9862927-1-2 (e-book; First Edition)

DEDICATION

I dedicate this book to Mary, Blake and Grace with whom I experienced Blake's journey through the world of football recruiting.

CONTENTS

LIST OF TABLES AND FIGURES

Table 1: Available Spots on College Teams (Chapter 1)

Table 2: D-1 Recruit's Size (Chapter 2)

Table 3: D-2, D-3 & NAIA Recruit's Size (Chapter 2)

Table 4: D-1 Recruit Agility & Explosiveness (Chapter 2)

Table 5: Coaching Skills (Chapter 7)

Table 6: Film Clip Notes Worksheet (Appendix E)

Fig. 1: High School Coaches (Acknowledgements)

Fig. 2: Speed is the Basic Currency for the Next Level (Chapter 2)

Fig. 3: Timely Making Film is Critical to Recruiting (Chapter 5)

Fig. 4: 20-Yard Short Shuttle (Chapter 6)

Fig. 5: Spoils of War: Player Rings and Souvenir Pins from Two Rose Bowls, Orange Bowl, Fiesta Bowl and U.S. Army All-American Bowl (Chapter 10)

Fig. 6: DVD Label on Highlight Film (Appendix D)

ACKNOWLEDGMENTS

My wife and I give special thanks to our close friend, Coach Jeff Collins, who gave Blake a great start down the road of the greatest sport in the world. We also thank state championship coaches Larry McWhorter and Gil Speer (all shown below) for an outstanding job completing that journey through high school. All three men helped Blake learn to, "do the right things, the right way."

We also give special thanks to Cynthia and Ron Lynn for their support and caring.

Fig. 1: High School Coaches

CHAPTER 1

INTRODUCTION, START EARLY AND BE PROACTIVE

"Dictionary is the only place that success comes before work. Hard work is the price we must pay for success."

- Vince Lombardi, legendary football coach

My son is a (former) All-American high school football player. He ultimately chose among sixteen (16) full ride scholarship offers to go to Stanford University to play *PAC-12* football as a linebacker and defensive end. He was the leading tackler for his East team in the 2010 *U.S. Army All-American Bowl*, the prestigious high school all-star game. His first year at Stanford he was in the two deep (second string) on a great team that went 12-1 and, led by Andrew Luck, won the Orange Bowl against the ACC champs, Virginia Tech. Throughout his college career he experienced the Fiesta Bowl, two *PAC-12* championships, a Rose Bowl championship, a Rose Bowl loss, surgery on both shoulders, and a degree in engineering with a concentration in finance. After Stanford he took a position as an investment banker with a major firm. I learned a lot watching his journey, both during his recruitment and afterwards playing college football. I have also read every book that I could find about college football recruiting. The purpose of this book is to share what I have learned so you can help your high school son in football recruiting.

It was a blast to sit in the offices of Jim Harbaugh at Stanford, Pat Fitzgerald at Northwestern, Charlie Weis and Brian Kelly at Notre Dame, Butch Davis at North Carolina, and others and talk football. In addition to my experiences during my son's D-1 recruitment, my researching for this book included interviewing college head football coaches at D-2, D-3 and NAIA programs. I have also added helpful information and war stories that I heard from scouts, players and fellow parents along the way.

First and foremost, you need to start early. A detailed month-by-month timeline of what to do and when is set forth in Chapter 3. For D-1 recruiting you should start getting organized typically by about February-April of your son's sophomore year in high school, and arguably earlier. However, do not panic if it is already later than that. Few people start that early, (even though they should), so you are in good company.

Second, be proactive. Do not sit back and wait for your son to get discovered. Get out there. Get in the car *now* and go visit a program! Make college coaches aware of your son. It does not guarantee anything, but his odds will improve. There are over 15,000 high school football teams, and each year in the U.S. there are about 250,000 to 300,000 high school football players who are seniors. If your son is in the top 1/10th of one percent (*e.g.* top 250 players in the country), then maybe you can sit back and coast and just let him be "discovered" by college coaches. But even if he is that rare, why risk it? You will not get a second chance. You should work to maximize his odds by being proactive. Also, even if he gets some scholarship offers just based on college coaching finding your son on their own, by being proactive you might help him get an offer to an even better school. Do things like create highlight film (Chapter 5), write letters to coaches, visit campuses, improve speed, strength, flexibility and footwork, and attend camps and combines. Your son just showing up and playing for the high school team is rarely enough.

There are two harsh realities that you should not ignore in football recruiting. They may help your son or hurt him, depending on where you live. The first reality is, like it or not, there is a stereotype of high school "football states" and not. You can group states into the following four (4) tiers of D-1 scholarships (listed alphabetically within each tier):

1. CA, FL and TX.

2. AL, GA, OH and LA.

3. AZ, DC, HI, IL, IN, MD, MI, MS, NJ, NC, OK, PA, SC, TN, VA and WA.

4. Each state not in categories 1-3, above.

Category 1 states tend to be large population states. The category 1 and 2 states get most of the D-1 recruiting attention. Every recruit should be proactive. However, if your son plays high school football in a state in category 3 or 4, you must *really* be proactive. D-1 college football coaches have limited time and simply focus less on those states. Also, the quality of competition, particularly in category 4, can become more of an issue, requiring your son to play far better than everyone else on the field.

The second harsh reality is big high schools vs. small high schools. If your son attends a small high school he will have a harder time getting recruited, particularly by a D-1 school. This is especially challenging for linemen at small schools. A top level lineman at a small high school is rarely challenged by a comparable opponent. This, combined with the fact that linemen are generally more difficult for college coaches to evaluate, makes the coaches gravitate to the "safe" choice – a recruit at a large high school who has a track record against tougher competition. Again, if this (a smaller school) is your son's situation, you and your son will simply have to be more proactive with recruiting.

To my knowledge there is only one *objective* measure of how good your son's high school football team is compared to other teams around the country. It is at the website:

http://www.usatodayhss.com/massey-matchups/.

It uses a distributive mathematical model of the type used by the former BCS for ranking college football teams. You can fictitiously "play" a high school team from California against a team from Ohio to see, mathematically, what the score would have been. Teams are also ranked nationally, state by state, and class by class. Everything else about how good a high school team is on the national level is subjective opinion or hometown arrogance. You will see that there are some great teams in Texas and some lousy teams in Texas. Go to that website to get an objective idea of how good (or how bad) your son's high school team is compared to national competition.

While perhaps extreme, it would be remiss not to mention that by moving where your son lives you could improve your son's chances in football recruiting. Moreover, if you can afford it or if high school financial aid is available, enrolling him in a private high school known for its football prowess may improve his chances as well by placing him in a school where college football coaches pay more attention. Changing schools is admittedly extreme and we did not do this. But I mention it in the interest of completeness. Changing schools *could* lead to better exposure and playing against better competition. But it also could make things worse. Consider that the competition at that bigger school will be greater and he runs the risk of not even starting varsity until his senior year, in which case his prospects for being recruited, especially at the D-1 level, would be hurt. They tend to offer junior stars. Also, changing schools may uproot him from his friends and is putting an awful lot of pressure on a kid.

In being proactive there is a key NCAA rule that you MUST understand. Until spring of your son's junior year, (*i.e.* the spring following his H.S. junior season), which is *after* most D-1 FBS scholarship offers have already been extended, the D-1 coaches cannot call you or your son. They cannot even return phone messages. They cannot text message. They cannot reply to e-mails. They are not being rude; nor are they ignoring your son. They are simply following NCAA rules. You may phone them, you may email them, and you may visit campuses on your own dime. What this means is that when trying to call them, you must be persistent. They are rarely in their office. Thus, you have to politely keep trying before you will reach them. I detail this and other rules in Chapter 4.

Have your son live by the following creed during his time in high school: "I play football for [XYZ] high school." Do not let him look ahead too much or get too distracted with college football recruiting. He has to take care of business on the high school field. The person who is second in importance in recruiting, behind your son, is his high school head coach. Virtually every college coach that is interested in your son will talk to his high school head coach. He should be your son's biggest fan. A less than enthusiastic response from him will likely have the college coaches looking elsewhere. Hollywood's version of this football recruiting nightmare is the movie *All The Right Moves* starring Tom Cruise and Craig Nelson. Your son needs to continue to earn the respect of his high school coach(es). He must give them 100% effort and not only follow the rules, but should be a positive leader both on and off of the field.

Start the recruiting process by reading Chapter 2 of this book. It gives specific guidelines and stats on how big, fast and skilled a high school player normally needs to be to play D-1 FBS football as well as at other levels. It helps to know what the college coaches are looking for. You should be realistic; and, it can be depressing to see the level of competition that you are up against. Statistically, VERY few kids are big enough and fast enough to play D-1 college football. If that is the case you should be honest with yourself and your child. An honest assessment early is important. It will help inform you on how strong the need is to also start the recruiting process for D-2, D-3 and NAIA football schools. There is a delicate balance between pursuing a D-1 football dream (his, not yours), and setting him up for heartbreak that could result if you are not realistic. A powerful tool to help you focus and realistically match your son with college football programs is the website: https://www.playced.com/. It is a fee-based online database of college programs (including D-1, D-2, D-3, NAIA and JUCO teams). You input academic factors (*e.g.* GPA, SAT, possible major(s)) and several athletic factors (*e.g.* 40-yard dash time, height, weight, etc.) and it generates a custom report of up to 40 schools for your son. I tried it (after the fact since my son was already at Stanford) and it was remarkable how it pegged most of the schools that ultimately had been of greatest interest to him during his recruitment. The report lists several schools that are realistic matches and provides the name and contact information for the recruiting coordinator for each team. It is like an online dating service for recruiting.

There are seven (7) categories of college football (not counting some club and community college football, such as California's non-scholarship CCCAA football (about 70 teams)). Five (5) of the categories of football below are within the NCAA, and two (2) are not. The 650+ schools in the NCAA who sponsor football drew over 50 million fans at home. All seven categories (as of 2014) are in Table 1 (below). That table shows the approximate number of football team playing for each category currently, (this varies a bit from year to year), and the team scholarship limits (set by rule) for each. The terms "head count" and "equivalency" scholarships in Table 1 are explained afterwards.

Shorthand Name		Formal Name	Approx # of Teams in USA	Max # of Scholarships per Team	Max. Theory Scholarship Totals
Division-I (D-1)	D-1 (FBS) (Formerly called Division I-A)	**NCAA Division-I Football Bowl Subdivision** *Major Conference*	65	85 head count (25 per year)	5,525
		NCAA Division-I Football Bowl Subdivision *Mid-Major Conference*	63	85 head count (25 per year)	5,355
	D-1 (FCS)	**NCAA Division-I Football Championship Subdivision** (Formerly called Division I-AA)	124	63 equivalency (30 per year)	7,812
	D-2	**NCAA Division-II**	170	36 equivalency	6,120
	D-3	**NCAA Division-III**	244	No athletic scholarships allowed	0
NAIA *Not part of the NCAA*		**National Association of Intercollegiate Athletics**	89	24 equivalency	2,136
NJCAA or "JUCO" *Not part of the NCAA*		**National Junior College Athletic Association**	64	85	5,440
Totals:			819		32,388

Table 1: Available Spots on College Teams

The above Table 1 includes upperclassmen. Note also that such scholarship limits are the *maximum* theoretically possible; however, some conferences and/or schools impose even *lower* limits for the number of football scholarships. Thus, there are not actually 32,388 football scholarships available. Additionally, most scholarship programs will also have a number of "walk-on" players who are full members of the team but are not paid a scholarship. Normally, they have to try-out, or were close to being offered a scholarship. Sometimes, if they earn a playing time, they may be eventually awarded a scholarship (rarely before finishing two years on the team). However, walk-ons receiving a scholarship is challenging and rare.

If you assume an average of about 80 players per team, then with about 800 total teams at all levels there are about 64,000 college football roster spots (for all five years, freshmen through fifth-year senior). Of those, about 30,000 are the theoretical maximum number of scholarships allowed by rule. But since among that some conferences or schools do not provide football scholarships, the real number of actual football scholarships is probably closer to 25,000 (freshman-senior). Thus, for incoming freshmen, there is potentially about one*fourth of those each year: about 16,000 roster spots (including D-3 with no scholarships) and about 6,500 potential football scholarship equivalents each year.

Of those five (5) NCAA categories, the FBS is further split into two: the "Major Conferences", (ACC, Big-10, Big-12, Pac-12 and SEC), and the rest, known as "Mid-Major" conferences. The FBS "Major Conference" football is the one with the best known teams that you see on TV every Saturday in the autumn. Most, if not all, of the 85 scholarship players on both of these two (2) categories of FBS teams receive a full ride scholarship. Those are also known in NCAA terminology as "head count" scholarships whereby each individual scholarship player receives a scholarship that is not divided among other players on the roster. The walk-on players do not receive a football scholarship, although they may otherwise qualify for some other type(s) of aid through the university. However, the "Major Conferences" were granted some autonomy by the NCAA to offer additional scholarship benefits, including an additional stipend of up to a few thousand dollars per year, plus other perks. The "Mid-Majors" cannot offer that.

To add further confusion, in D-1 FBS football, there is the "CFP" which stands for "College Football Playoffs" . It replaced the "BCS" which stood for "Bowl Championship Series" (now defunct). The CFP is *not* part of the NCAA. Rather, it is separate and facilitates team invitations to the holiday season bowl games (Rose Bowl, Orange Bowl, etc.) and to the D-1 FBS championship playoff. While not part of the NCAA, however, the CFP and the NCAA's Football Bowl Subdivision (FBS) are related in this respect – it is the FBS teams who are the ones that are eligible to play in the CFP's championship and in bowl games. The other schools are not. Instead, the other teams (D-1 FCS, D-2, D-3) may qualify for and play in their division's respective post-season tournament.

The second category in the NCAA, Football Championship Subdivision ("FCS"), gets confusing because, like FBS, it also is considered "Division-

I" (*i.e.* D-1). It is another *sub*-division of Division-I. Years back this was also known as Division I-AA. Note that in the NCAA, football is the only sport where D-1 is split into multiple subdivisions.

Regarding such FCS teams, as well as D-2 and NAIA teams, scholarships vary from school to school. However, rather than a full ride "head count" scholarship (used in D-1 FBS), those three categories have what are known as "equivalent" scholarships. "Equivalent" means that a coach may split the dollar value of a scholarship between two or more guys on the roster. He could split the equivalent of one scholarship 50-50 between two players. Thus, for example, a coach of a D-1 FCS team (which can give up to 63 equivalent scholarships) might have 50 guys on a full ride scholarship and 26 guys (2 X 13) on half scholarship.

Regarding football scholarships, (whether head count or equivalent), they are not all equal and there is a very important distinction that you need to understand. Some scholarships are guaranteed 4-year scholarships, and this is growing; whereas, others (most) are less, typically only 1-year scholarships. Such 1-year scholarships are renewable for following years or *not* at the discretion of the college head coach. This is detailed more in Chapters 7 and 9.

Note that the Ivy League is in the NCAA's Division-I "FCS" subdivision. Yet it, like some other D-1 FCS conferences, namely the Pioneer League, prohibit football scholarships altogether. The D-1 FCS Patriot league only recently allowed football scholarships, but only 15 equivalent scholarships per year, capped at a total of 60 per team. The Northeast Conference is D-1 FCS with football scholarships, but limits the number scholarships to only 40 equivalents per team (less than the NCAA's FCS limit of 63).

The three service academies (Annapolis, West Point, Air Force Academy) play D-1 football. Every cadet there is on a full ride scholarship, including those on the football team.

Division III (D-3) of the NCAA is not allowed to give any football scholarships. As a general rule, D-3 schools tend to be smaller schools in terms of their total enrollment. However, because there are far more D-3 schools overall, it offers the most playing opportunity.

Even if your son is too small and/or too slow to play D-1 FBS football, he could have a great time playing D-1 *FCS*, D-2 or D-3 or other college football. I have several friends and acquaintances that played D-3 football and the time demands were less than those who played D-1 football. The D-3 game is less about big money; it is played primarily for the love of the *game*. The major differences between D-1 football and these others is the size of the crowds at the games and the associated budgets and media hype. The difference in the players, however, is not as much as you might imagine. There are three very useful websites that list each D-2, D-3 and NAIA team, with links to each team's own website where you will find their coaches' email addresses and phone numbers:

www.d2football.com

www.d3football.com

http://www.naia.org/SportSelect.dbml?SPID=96219

The NCAA rules for D-2 football have a wrinkle. They allow for one tryout (no pads; no games) per college during your son's senior year in the offseason. D-1 and D-3 are not allowed to conduct football tryouts. However football camps (*see* Chapter 6) at D-1 schools seem a lot like tryouts.

Thus, while D-1 is harder for your son in terms of pure football, the other levels are harder in terms of other things. Grouping D-2, D-3 and NAIA together, numerically there are far more colleges from which to choose. Thus, it can be overwhelming. Also, the other levels (D-3 in particular) may require assembling an overall financial aid package from multiple sources. This can get complicated. This may include loans, Pell and other grants, non-athletic scholarships from the school, and scholarships from local, regional and national organizations. Having the football coach wanting you on his team, however, can help a lot with those other funding sources since he can offer guidance and perhaps influence.

Since the NAIA and NCJAA (JUCO or Junior College) schools are not part of the NCAA, the NCAA's rules do not apply to them or their football recruiting. Many NAIA colleges tend to be smaller in enrollment, similar to the NCAA's D-3 schools. Yet, unlike D-3 schools many of them can and do offer athletic scholarships. Also, currently NCAA academic eligibility minimum requirements for D-1 football are tougher than the NAIA minimums. Note, however, that individual NAIA *schools* may have academic requirements that are higher than those NAIA minimums. Of the NJCAA (JUCO) schools, roughly half of them offer football scholarships of some type, but also have other financial aid. The California CCCAA offers no football scholarships, but other financial aid may be available. Both JUCO programs are two-year programs, meaning there are no juniors and seniors. Thus, playing time is more available for younger guys.

Also, while our son began the very early phases of Ivy League recruiting, he stopped this process after he got a full ride scholarship offer from Stanford. Unlike the Ivy League, Stanford gives full ride scholarships to play football in the *PAC-12* Conference to compete to play in games like the Rose Bowl. That made the Harvard's less attractive. The Ivy League, by agreed rule, prevents its member schools from offering any athletic scholarships. However, if your son is a very good student and is possibly interested in playing football at an Ivy League school, I recommend reading a book by Chris Lincoln, entitled, *Playing The Game: Inside Athletic Recruiting in the Ivy League.* It is a very helpful guide through the process, but is not specific to football. Another book by Scott Britton, a former Princeton football player, entitled *The Best Book On Ivy League Football Recruiting* is more targeted on football. These books show how Ivy League football recruiting is very unique as compared to other football recruiting (D-1, D-2, D-3 or NAIA). For Ivy league recruiting, you should understand the Ivy's "Academic Index", discussed in those books. One common misconception is that Ivy League recruiting is analogous to D-3 recruiting. It is not. Unlike a D-3 school which cannot give sports scholarships but *can* give your great football player-son a "leadership" scholarship or some other form of aid, the Ivy

League schools cannot even do that. They can, by agreement among the Ivy League schools, award money for one, and *only one* thing: financial need. In the Ivy League the same limitation is true even outside of sports. For example, if your son is a world-class violin player, it does not matter. No Ivy League scholarship for that either. The Ivy League is only allowed to give scholarships for financial need. However, the Ivy Leagues do grant a lot of financial aid generally, making it accessible to most who are admitted. Thus, football is very relevant in the Ivy League in at least one respect – it can open the doors to admission. The Ivy League admissions office is looking for an "X-factor", something that sets you apart or makes you a special addition to their incoming class. Also, apart from the school itself, financial assistance may come from other sources such as the "XYZ Wealthy Alumni Association" in your area. They might just want to give one of *their* scholarships to a stud football player going to their Ivy Alma mater. If an Ivy League football coach wants your son, and he can meet their academic requirements, this can get him admitted to a great university that he otherwise might not get into. That book details the complexities.

Heed one warning if your son is a potential Ivy League recruit. Do NOT let the Ivy coach think that your son is using football *mainly* as a means to gain admission to an Ivy school. You may scare them off. Instead, have your son show them his true love of football. Ivy coaches are professional *football* coaches; most did not graduate from the Ivy's. Their teams have huge rosters (30 new players per year); yet, they also suffer huge attrition from players after their freshman or sophomore years that are discontent with their lack of playing time. In the Ivy's, there is no football scholarship to keep him on the team. The Ivy coaches are well aware of and sensitive to kids and parents using football to merely gain admissions to a prestigious Ivy school, only to quit the team a year or two later. Make sure that they know your son is committed to the game of football.

In addition to all of that, there also are a few post-high school football programs. These are one or two year programs after high school but before college. They are at private schools and military academies. Hargrave Military Academy is an example. They can serve as a school for a player to get his GPA and/or SAT scores up to qualify for college. Junior College (JUCO) can serve a similar purpose.

However, in this book I start your strategy with D-1 FBS Major Conference football (rather than FCS, D-2, D-3, NAIA or Junior College (JUCO)) recruiting for a reason. If you prepare for D-1 FBS recruiting, you will already be in great shape for the other levels. Aim high for FBS. Do the basics set forth in this book for D-1 FBS football recruiting (*e.g.* highlight and game film, among other things) and then *also* send that information to the D-1 FCS, D-2 and D-3 and other coaches. The main differences between those programs in terms of recruiting, (as compared to D-1 (FBS and FCS) football), are: (a) the recruiting normally starts later; (b) the coaches have smaller staffs and much smaller recruiting budgets (*e.g.* they can travel to you less, if at all); (c) the recruiting rules are different (generally more lax than D-1 football recruiting); (d) the size, speed and ability of the players is lower; (e) they have less money available for scholarships; and, (f) due to (e), it is more complex than D-1 in terms of financial aid. In the case of D-3 in particular, by rule they are not allowed to give any money for athletic scholarships. However, the D-3 schools, often with interaction with their football coach, will often work with you to put together various other forms of (non-athletic) financial aid. The same is true for NAIA, D-2, and JUCO.

I also suggest that you read other books about recruiting. The more you learn, the more you can help your son. I read and recommend a book entitled, *Football's Second Season: Scouting High School Game Breakers* by Tom Lemming. Tom Lemming is regarded by many as the Godfather of high school football recruiting. Indeed, he was recognized in the book (and later made a cameo appearance in the movie) *The Blind Side*, a story about the high school recruiting of a future *NFL* first round pick lineman. Starting in the 1970's, and living mainly out of his car for months on end, Tom Lemming would drive all over the United States each year meeting and scouting high school football players in person. Obviously, this was before the internet recruiting websites and highlight films on *YouTube*. Few, if anybody, has been so committed to spend their lives travelling the backwaters of America in search of the next generation of players. Mr. Lemming's *The Second Season* is interesting and insightful. Mr. Lemming met with my wife and son during his recruitment. They were very impressed with Mr. Lemming's expertise.

Another book that I read and would recommend is, *Meat Market – Inside the Smash-Mouth World of College Football Recruiting* by Bruce Feldman. The author, Mr. Feldman, is a seasoned sports writer and recounts a year embedded in the Ole Miss Rebels football program when

Ed Orgeron was the head coach leading up to their 2007 National Signing Day. Coach Orgeron has also been a coach at USC and Tennessee. The author recounts recruiting from within the belly of the beast, a major D-1 FBS NCAA team, from the coach's side of recruiting. For that reason alone it is a unique and useful perspective. It is not a how-to book, but rather gives insights that are otherwise hard to find.

Sometimes, when you think your son is being recruited, actually he is not, not yet anyways. There are six (6) levels of recruitment:

1. The college coaches are not even aware of your son. He is a so-called sleeper or under the radar.

2. The coaches are aware of him, but are not interested.

3. The coaches are aware of and interested in your son, but not enough to offer yet.

4. The coaches offer your son a place on the team (with or without scholarship), but are content with taking other kids in his place.

5. The coaches offer your son, and really want him on their team.

6. The coaches offer your son, and want him so much that they will hold a spot open for him on the team right up through National Signing Day.

The vast majority of kids never move past Level 1 or 2. Regarding Level 1, your son may be in their computer database, and thus receive mass mailing invites to their multi-day commercial camps, but that does not mean that the coaches are cognitively "aware" of your son. Levels 3 and up will get your son form letters and a questionnaire. Hundreds, if not thousands, of kids get the form letters at Level 3 and it is easy for them to mistakenly think that they are being recruited. However, they still have a ways to go. They still need to get at least to Level 4, and most do not. Many players stuck at level 3 (with respect to D-1 schools) are the guys that eventually play D-2 or D-3 or NAIA football. Level 4, obviously, will get him an offer. These higher Levels 4-6 will also lead to handwritten notes, calls, emails and visits from the coaches. The higher the level your son achieves on their recruiting board, the more of that type of attention he will receive. Also, the higher the level, the better his chances of being offered a guaranteed four (4) year scholarship rather than a year-to-year scholarship.

You really want to help your child. There is only a limited amount that you can do to help him actually become a better football player. That is more up to him and his high school coaches. If you are a "would-be coach", and you think that your job is to over coach your kid, or yell at your kid, or criticize his technique or play, to make him into a stud player, then you are probably doomed to fail. By now, like it or not, that is the high school coaching staff's job. And, the football drive must come from within your son.

Instead, you should plan to do a lot of work. You can help with all of the behind the scenes letters, communication, highlight film creation, contacting schools, researching schools, trip scheduling, etc., and if possible paying for travel. In short, become your son's football recruiting secretary and travel agent. It will take a lot of your time (and money) and is a lot of work; but, if you really want to help, that is what *you* can do. There are several Appendices at the end with some sample forms, lists and letters that I used to keep organized.

Also, it has been said that football and football recruiting is a Tower of Babel with its own terminology. It is helpful to know this language so you can understand what is being said during recruiting. There is an extensive Glossary at the end of this book to help.

There certainly are no guarantees. The competition is fierce for college football scholarships. However, do not reduce or eliminate your son's chances by starting too late by being too passive. At the same time, be realistic. In addition to striving for the highest level, D-1 FBS football, honestly evaluate his size and abilities. Make part of the plan the possibility of his playing at lower levels of college football. The following Chapter 2 can help you evaluate his chances for D-1 FBS football or otherwise.

CHAPTER 2

SPEED, HEIGHT AND OTHER QUALITIES

"We may be small, but we are slow."

- Howard Buckwalter, head football coach, describing my 1976 high school team.

The odds of getting a D-1 (FBS or FCS) football scholarship are very slim. That is why your son should keep other options like D-2, D-3 and NAIA football open as well. In round numbers, each year there are about 300,000 high school senior football players. FBS is the top 128 college programs. Each year, at those highest levels there are only about 2,500 to 3,000 D-1 FBS football scholarships for incoming freshmen. That is one scholarship for every 100 high school senior players – *i.e.* about 1% of them get a D-1 football scholarship at a FBS school. Table 1, in Chapter 1, itemizes the number of teams and scholarships at each level.

The NCAA publishes statistics that about only 1 out of 16 high school senior football players will go on to play football at an NCAA school at any level (D-1 (FBS and FCS); D-2; and, D-3). Thus, adding in NAIA and JUCO roughly 6-8% of high school senior football players go on to play college ball (with or without a football scholarship). However, even if your son is not in the top 6-8%, do not lose heart. Many extremely good high school players never even go to college. Or, even if they go to college they do not go out for college football for a variety of reasons. Thus, in round numbers, if your son is in about the top 10-20% of high school football players in the country, and he has the desire, he has a shot at making a college football team at some level.

For every 10,000 high school football players, only eight, or approximately 0.08 percent, will eventually be drafted by an *NFL* team. Many college players that get drafted do not even make an *NFL* roster. And even if your son beats those odds, while the *NFL* may be awash in money, not so for most rookies. Even if they make a roster, the average

NFL career is only about 3 ½ years long. And rookies contracts are capped in the first four (4) years (even though a team can drop a player any time without further payment). If a college player makes an *NFL* roster and is not cut, for the first four years the median annual pay is quite good, but normally not the lofty "set for life" salaries that you read about for the high profile veterans. Most *NFL* players still need a career after football. If big money is your son's goal, his odds are much better becoming a computer programmer.

It's good to have dreams, but bad to live in a fantasy world. In assessing if your child has a realistic chance to play D-1 football, I address two aspects, physical and mental. Of the two, the physical (size and speed limitations) eliminates most high school players from recruitment.

A. PHYSICAL

1. Speed, Height and Weight

The three most import things are speed, speed and speed. Did I mention speed? There are no hard and fast rules. However, in Table 2 (below) I have compiled from various sources typical numbers for speed (40-yard dash, hand stopwatch timed), height, and weight for D-1 recruits that are high school seniors. I list them according to what I call the "speed food chain", from fastest to slowest, for both offense and defense.

D-1 Position	40 yd. dash (sec.)	Height (ft. in)	Weight (lbs.)
Offense:			
Receiver	4.3 – 4.6	5'11" – 6' 4"	170 - 210
Run. Back	4.4 – 4.6	5'8" – 6' 3"	170 - 230
QB	4.5 – 4.9	6'2" – 6' 6"	180 - 230
Tight End	4.6 – 4.9	6'3" – 6' 7"	210 - 240
Lineman	4.9 – 5.8	6'2" – 6' 8"	260 - 320
Defense:			
Cornerback	4.3 – 4.6	5'10" – 6' 2"	170 - 200
Safety	4.4 – 4.7	5'10" – 6' 2"	180 - 210
Linebacker	4.5 – 4.8	6'0" – 6' 4"	200 - 230
End	4.6 – 5.0	6'3" – 6' 7"	210 - 260
Tackle	4.8 – 5.2	6'2" – 6' 5"	250 - 320

Table 2: D-1 Recruit's Size and Speed

In terms of position, a player-recruit can move *down* the speed food chain, but rarely can he move up. A similar Table 3 a few pages later shows the typical profile of non-D-1 recruits (*e.g.* D-2, D-3 and NAIA).

Yes, there are exceptions to what is in those tables. For example, if the college team's offense is based on a spread run-option, then for quarterback they would place a comparatively higher premium on speed and a lower premium on height. Conversely, if another college team's offense was based on a pro-style pocket passing QB, then the opposite is true. Take that into account in targeting which schools would be best for your son. But, if your son falls outside of one or several of these values in Table 2, your son is probably fighting the statistical odds for D-1 FBS ball. Also, if he is low in one range, he should be better in another range. For example, if an offensive lineman is comparatively slow, then he ought to be comparatively large on that scale.

Also, for linemen, obviously open field speed is far less critical than for other positions. No team is going to run a guard 40 yards up field to catch a pass. However, some (not all) coaches never-the-less consider the 40-yard dash a useful indicator of athleticism in general, even for lineman. A retired head of scouting for an NFL team told me that the 40-yard dash was the most important NFL combine test, even for defensive linemen (but not for offensive linemen). The "shuttle run" (also known as the "5-10-5" or "pro-agility" test) (see Figure 1 in Chapter 6), or a 10-yard time split within a 40-yard dash, are more direct indicators of quickness. So are vertical jump and standing broad jump since they correlate to explosiveness which is key to short burst quickness. Typical values for D-1 football recruits are shown in Table 4, below.

What matters second to speed (at least physically) is height. It is what it is, and there is nothing you can do to change it. You can see from the above table which positions it seems to matter the most. However, if your son has true wide receiver speed (4.3 – 4.5 second 40 yard dash time) *and* is 6'5", that is a very rare combination, and your son should be in great shape. However, one reason that height is important is that tall people tend to have long arms. This is important for linemen, especially offensive linemen. This is discussed more below. Also, height is particularly important for quarterbacks. This is because they need to see over the linemen (offensive and defensive) in order to see the pass receivers and pass coverage. College offensive and defensive lines are typically much taller than in high school. As such, some D-1 college coaches have a hard time giving serious consideration to a shorter high school quarterback, even if he is a passer with great accuracy and outstanding high school statistics. In college if he cannot see the receivers, it does not matter how accurate a passer he may be. If your son is a super-fast, great athlete that plays quarterback in high school, but he is less than 6'2" tall, in terms of D-1 football, he should seriously consider trying to get recruited as a wide receiver, defensive back, and/or linebacker instead, or at least as an alternative.

Also, of the three categories in the Table 2, (speed, height, and weight), weight seems to be the *least* important. Every D-1 program can and does add weight to their players once they arrive on campus. They have professional nutritionists and eat at the team "training table" (translated: more and better food than normal dormitory food). They also do a lot of weight lifting which adds bulk and weight.

However, your son's *future* weight is relevant. D-1 football has big guys. One term that you hear a lot is a kid's, "frame". He has a "big frame". Or, we can, "hang a lot of weight on his frame". By 'frame', they mean the size of his skeletal structure. This includes height of course, but also includes shoulder width, hip width, bone thickness, hand and feet size, and the like. If it sounds like sizing up cattle at a meat market – well it is. I have even been told that some coaches also look to the "frame" of the mother and father to help guess the future growth/body type of a football prospect. If mom or dad is small in stature, you might consider having him or her stay home on recruiting visits, at least until *after* your son receives a scholarship offer.

Fig. 2: Speed is the Basic Currency for the Next Level

Another measurement that you hear from time to time is something called a player's "Speed Score". It relates to the combination of speed and weigh, derived from the following formula:

$$SS = (200 \times weight) \div (40\ time)^4$$

The weight is measured in pounds (*e.g.* 221 lbs.), and the 40-yard dash time is measured in seconds (*e.g.* 4.63 sec.), then taken to the fourth power. Thus, a kid who weighed 221 pounds and ran a 4.63 40-yard dash would have a speed score of: (200 X 221), divided by (4.63 X 4.63 X 4.63 X 4.63), which equals 96.2. In the *NFL* a speed score at or above 100 is considered pretty good for a running back. That is the position that Speed Score seems to be used the most. Speed Score also seems relevant to other positions where impact is important such as linebacker, speed rushing defensive end and strong safety. However, in college recruiting the Speed Score has not gained widespread use.

The speed and height at "non-D-1" football programs (*e.g.* D-2, D-3 and NAIA) are set forth below in Table 3 (below):

Position	40 yd. dash (sec.)	Height (ft. in)	Weight (lbs.)
Offense:			
Receiver	4.5 – 4.7	5'8" – 6' 3"	150 – 220
Run. Back	4.5 – 4.7	5'7" – 6' 1"	150 – 210
QB	4.6 – 5.0	5'11" – 6'3"	150 - 210
Tight End	4.7 – 4.9	6'1" – 6' 5"	190 - 240
Lineman	4.9 – 5.9	6'0" – 6' 6"	230 - 300
Defense:			
Cornerback	4.5 – 4.6	5'8" – 6'0"	140 - 190
Safety	4.6 – 4.7	5'8" – 6' 0"	150 - 200
Linebacker	4.6 – 4.8	5'10" – 6' 2"	170 - 220
End	4.8 – 5.0	6'1" – 6' 4"	190 - 240
Tackle	4.9 – 5.6	6'0" – 6' 3"	230 - 300

Table 3: D-2, D-3 & NAIA Recruit's Size and Speed

That table combines D-2, D-3 and NAIA because there is enough overlap in size and speed between those programs that it is hard to meaningfully distinguish them within those ranges. As a general rule, the D-2 players will be a bit faster and more skilled as players. However, just as with D-1 the differences are not always great and there are many individual exceptions. There are D-3 or NAIA players that are bigger and/or faster than D-2 players and vice versa.

2. Agility, Explosiveness and other attributes

In addition, two other very important qualities are agility and explosiveness. While pass receivers and defensive backs run longer distances, most players run in mainly short bursts from 5 to 20 yards per play. The agility and explosiveness of a player are evaluated by a coach by watching game film. Below, in Table 4, are some typical ranges for high school seniors that get D-1 FBS offers.

D-1 Position	Shuttle Run (sec.)	Vertical Jump (ft. in)	Bench Press Max. (lbs.)
Offense:			
Receiver	4.2 – 4.6	28 - 40	NA
Run. Back	4.2 – 4.6	28 - 40	220 - 350
QB	4.3 – 4.9	26 - 36	NA
Tight End	4.4 – 4.7	26 - 38	250 - 325
Lineman	4.8 – 5.4	22 - 28	275 - 450
Defense:			
Cornerback	4.0 - 4.5	30 - 42	NA
Safety	4.1 - 4.6	28 - 40	NA
Linebacker	4.3 – 4.7	26 - 36	220 - 350
End	4.3 - 4.8	25 - 32	250 - 400
Tackle	4.8 – 5.4	22 - 28	250 - 425

Table 4: D-1 Recruit Agility and Explosiveness

Reliable data for those attributes at the D-2, D-3 and NAIA levels is not readily available.

A *SPARQ* score is a *Nike* trademark which is an acronym for speed, power, agility, reaction and quickness. The score is a single number calculated using a formula. For football, it takes into account five numbers: (1) 40-yard dash time; (2) 5-10-5 shuttle run time; (3) vertical jump; (4) body weight; and, (5) distance throwing a 3 kilogram *SPARQ* medicine ball. The formula to calculate the *SPARQ* score is not published, and unfortunately *Nike* discontinued its website where you could enter data and calculate a *SPARQ* score. Thus, apparently you must attend one of their combines to get a score, likely relegating the *SPARQ* score to marginal relevance. It had been useful because it gave you a realistic indicator of where your son's athletic abilities measure compared to nationwide competition.

I received varying opinions from college football coaches about the criticality of a high school kid's strength. One coach we met during recruiting would pat our son on the back, shoulders, etc. and horse around and mock-wrestle a bit. We later learned that he routinely did this to check out how solid and strong a kid's muscles were. Of course, being strong always helps. If nothing else it will help your son actually play better in high school and, thus, be a better prospect. However, most of the colleges did not seem to hold it against a kid if he was not a strong as an ox. They seemed confident that if you had the right frame, their weight lifting program could make him plenty strong. However, several coaches did agree that good weight lifting numbers in high school were a good indicator of work ethic (*see* below, discussing Mental – work ethic). Also, old timers love the bench press, and the *NFL* uses it in their combine, measuring the number of reps at 225 pounds. One equation (by *Slovak et al.*) that has been used to approximately translate such repetitions of bench press (Reps@225) to a one repetition maximum (1RM) is:

$$1RM = 221.8 \text{ lb.} + 6.81 \times \text{Reps} @ 225$$

Nowadays, however, in football more emphasis is placed on squats and cleans – power cleans and hang cleans and others. Squats are particularly important for offensive and defensive lineman. They are important for linebackers and running backs too. In modern football there also is a lot more emphasis at all positions on "core" strength (*e.g.* the abdomen). Also, development of muscles along the *back* side of the legs, arms and body is very important, in part because it helps with ever important speed, as well as injury prevention. Pull ups and rows are examples. Physical training has advanced and colleges emphasize weight lifting that simulates how the game of football is played – fast, explosively and *on your feet.*

Arm length can be another important quality, particularly if your son is a lineman. Indeed, if he is an offensive tackle, arm length can be extremely important. For lineman, one reason that coaches like tall players is that tall people tend to have long arms. The reason that long arms are important has to do with blocking. A defensive lineman with long arms can do a better job in keeping "separation" between his torso and the man that is trying to block him. In such case, the offensive lineman struggles to even get his hands on the defensive player, making him difficult, if not impossible, to block. Conversely, an offensive lineman that has long arms can neutralize that advantage. Moreover, if the offensive player's arms are even longer than the defender's arms, the tables are turned and that advantage goes to the offense. In this situation, it more difficult for the defender to use his hands and arms to get the offensive lineman's away from his torso (called "hand fighting" or "disengagement"). The defender with shorter arms has a harder time getting off of the block so as to make a tackle on the ball carrier. Thus, in D-1 football recruiting, there quite literally is an "arms race" to get the best (longest) arms.

If you doubt its importance, then ask yourself why does the *NFL Combine* measure arm length? They measure it because they, the experts, know that it is important. Based on the *NFL Combine*, generally here are some guidelines as to what is considered good for offensive linemen in the NFL:

Excellent: longer than 35"

Good: 34" to 35"

Average: 32" to 34"

Below Ave.:   shorter than 32"

Remember, those values are for the highest levels at the *NFL*. Obviously, many college players on average will have shorter arms, but that gives you the gold standard as a frame of reference. I could not find hard data on high school or college arm length, but generally subtract about one-half or one inch from those *NFL* ranges listed above.

Here is how arm length is measured. Have your son fully extend his arms in front of him. To get arm length, measure from the tip of his fully extended middle finger to the "point" of the shoulder, which is the highest protruding bone near the outside of his shoulder. You may want to measure both the left and the right arm length because some people are not perfectly symmetric.

Thus, measure your son's arm length(s). If they are good (*i.e.* long), include those in his stats, particularly if your son is a lineman, receiver or defensive back. Arm length is arguably more relevant for a lineman than his 40-yard dash time. If they are particularly good (long), emphasize arm length in cover letters to coaches, football resumes, and highlight film (the beginning screens and the outer DVD label).

Do not confuse the term "arm length" with "arm span". Arm span in the distance from left middle finger tip to right middle finger tip when both arms are fully extended to each side. Two players with identical arm length could have different arm spans if one of them had broader shoulders than the other.

One thing that many college coaches *love* is "loose hips". This is just what it sounds like: flexible, limber hip and groin muscles and joints. They do not want tight muscles front or back, high or low. Loose hips manifest themselves in a player being able to change direction quickly and fluidly. They also help him achieve a low pad level. Its importance seems to apply to most all positions, linemen and otherwise. It is particularly important for defensive backs. Lose hips allow a defensive back to transition, at nearly full speed from running backwards (back peddling) to reversing his feet around and so as to sprint normally in that same direction.

Another measurement taken at the *NFL Combine* is hand size. This is measured in inches with the hand laid fully open, measuring the distance from the pinky tip to the thumb tip. This can be perceived as relevant for linemen, especially defensive lineman. Big hands are particularly a plus for tight ends and pass receivers in that it correlates with being able to better catch passes.

Hand size can be critical for quarterbacks. I have one anecdote unique to quarterbacks. Mind you, this came from only one college D-1 football graduate assistant; but, one of the college quarterbacks that he worked with later won the NFL's *Super Bowl*. We talked about hand size. He told me that at his D-1 FBS University they would not even consider a quarterback whose hands were too small. And they defined "too small" as requiring the quarterback's hand, when laid open, to have a span of at least nine inches (9") from the tip of his thumb to the tip of his pinky finger. He explained to me that without that, they had found that the risk of fumbling in wet conditions was too great, and that the ability to pump fake a pass was too limited. He said that their D-1 football team adhered to this 9" rule in their recruiting, no matter how great the kid's high school passing statistics were. Wow; talk about unfair. That is one example how brutal college football recruiting can be. If your son has big hands, emphasize that measurement in letters to coaches.

Another anecdote was being "pigeon toed". I had previously thought that being pigeon toed was a bad thing. However, on one recruiting trip at a D-1 school that had already offered our son a scholarship, two separate coaches remarked about my son (enthusiastically), "look at that; pigeon toed". I couldn't resist; I had to ask them what they meant and why they cared. They said that athletic, coordinated guys tend to walk somewhat pigeon toed. They said, conversely, if you see a guy that, when standing, has his feet/toes pointed or flared outwardly, the odds are he is not especially coordinated and/or does not have especially good footwork. I have no I idea if that is true or not. But I do know that at least two D-1 coaches believe it.

Another D-1 coach we met likes to look at the kid's calf muscles. "High and tight knots" is what he liked. This makes sense and may be correlated with speed. I read a speed training book that stated that for most kids, their muscles along their back side generally, and more specifically their calf muscles, (which are critical for speed), are usually the most *underdeveloped* muscles in their body. After my son got to college and into the football program's strength and conditioning program for a while, I asked him what was the biggest difference between that and what he had done in high school training. He said that in college they did much more work on muscles along the *back* side of the body.

Of course, football is a game played on the field. That is why highlight and full game film, discussed in Chapter 5, are very important. Some kids are very fast, tall and skilled but just not cut out for the violence of football. Those guidelines for speed and size in Tables 2-4 presume that your son also is a very good football player, or at least is a very, very good natural athlete with the potential to become a very good football player. Thousands of very large kids never get D-1 football scholarships. Being big is not enough. Ask yourself the following questions:

1. In little league football, was my son one of the 1-5 most dominant players in the entire league?

2. In middle school, was he one of the top three players on the team? Was he a "go to" guy when the game was on the line?

3. Did he start varsity football by the time he was a sophomore?

4. When he was a junior, was he all-conference or all-state?

5. By the time he was a junior, were people asking, "why doesn't the coach play him both ways and on special teams all the time?"

6. By the summer before his senior year, had he been receiving letters from D-1 football programs?

7. Was he among the best 1-2 players on his high school team?

8. When he was a senior, was he all-state?

9. When the game is on the line, did he want the ball in his hands?

10. Was he a team captain?

If you answered, "no" to many of these questions, you need to ask yourself, even though he might be tall and fast, and even though he is a great high school player, is my son skilled and aggressive enough to play D-1 football?

Remember too that your son might play one position in high school but be better suited for another position in college. Our 6' 5" son played fullback and later middle linebacker in high school. *Rivals, Scout, ESPN* and most teams recruiting him considered him, however, to be a 4-3 defensive end. Yet, he started his college career as an inside linebacker. Then after an outside linebacker on his team (3-4 defense) was injured, they moved him there. Later, he finished college starting at defensive end. Coaches move players around. Many quarterbacks are the best overall athletes on their high school team and move to other positions in college. Some high school tight ends become interior linemen. Keep an open mind in view of your son's body type, speed, skills, and listen to what the college coaches are indicating. Also, if he changes positions, it is likely going to be a move *down* the "speed food chain" (*see* Tables 2 and 3, above), not up it.

The Glossary to this book explains various statistics, including: pass rating, speed score, vertical jump, broad jump, shuttle run, tackles, TFL's, sacks, etc. Be sure to understand them before representing stats to a college football coach so that you are accurate.

3. Ways your son can improve

There are things your son can and should do to continue improving his playing ability and his chances of getting to play college football. First and most importantly, your son should participate fully in his high school football team's strength and conditioning program.

In addition, in planning your budget, I would place a professional speed trainer high on the list of priorities. Sprinting mechanics and run form are not natural acts for most people. And speed is critical. While high school track may help (and is free), your son will not get much individualized coaching – there just are too many kids. Thus, seriously consider hiring a private speed coach, even if just once a week. Ask around or search the internet to find ones to interview. Do not necessarily settle on the first one your son tries. Experiment with different ones to see which one seems best for your son. To save money, private speed lessons are still very beneficial in small groups of kids, such as two to four players per speed coach.

One item of training equipment that you might want to look into is a device known as a *Vertimax*. My son was introduced to this by his outstanding speed coach during high school, Brian Griffitts, and it really helped. The device is not cheap (several thousand dollars), but maybe you can find one in your area or have your Booster Club buy one for the high school. It is a platform with bungee-like cords on pulleys to create resistance when jumping and other short burst movements. The *Vertimax* increases explosiveness and first step quickness. It has been used and endorsed by several notable NFL and NCAA programs and coaches.

Another tool to enhance reaction time and other eye-based skills is "weight training for the eyes", found at www.vizualedge.com. It is a web-based product, for a fee per session, with a variety of workouts for your eye muscles tracking objects on the computer screen. It is endorsed by several pro athletes and college programs.

Yet, high priced training equipment is not the only way. Importantly, I would suggest that your son augment his training with a very exotic and high-tech item of workout equipment: a jump rope. It is the best bang-for-the-buck training device available. Every football player can benefit by better footwork and quicker feet, and jump roping is a great help. I must give credit for this simple but powerful advice to one of my son's basketball coaches, Phil Isenbarger. Phil played basketball at Indiana University on one of their national championship teams coached by Bobby Knight. Phil learned a thing or two there. Start early and often with jumping rope.

Another exotic training device that Phil put us onto was a tennis ball. Have your son face away from you, about 15 feet apart. Hold the tennis ball and say "go". On "go" he is to instantly hop around to face you -- whereupon you toss the tennis ball toward him. He tries to catch it with both hands. For football, (or basketball), it is important that he learns to instinctively move both arms and catch the tennis ball with *both* hands simultaneously. That is how you should catch a ball in a football game, and you want to develop good habits and good muscle memory. You should always place the throw randomly yet still within his reach. It will improve his reaction time, quickness and hands. As your son improves with practice, pick up the tempo. Eventually, you will not say "go" until the ball is already in flight, halfway towards him. He will be able spin and pluck it out of the air, again using both hands.

One question that comes up is, "should my son play other sports, in addition to football?" The answer is emphatically, *yes*. I literally never heard any college football coach say that participation in another sport was bad. Quite the contrary, every single one that I talked to about that subject said that it was a definite plus. Most of those football coaches even said that being a multi-sport athlete was something that they actively look for it in a prospect. They want "athletes". They want guys that are fast, coordinated, scrappy, and love to compete. Classic favorites include track (running for football skill players; throwing discus or shot for lineman), basketball, wrestling and baseball. Now do not confuse this love of multi-sport athletes by college coaches with love from your *high school* coaches. Sadly, however, there are a significant number of high school coaches that selfishly will encourage kids to only play the sport that they are coaching. If this is your case, you will have to try to work through it depending on your situation.

I read that in a recent year of the *NFL* draft, of the 32 players selected in the first round: (a) 19 of those 32 players were in high school track and field; (b) 21 of those 32 players played high school basketball; and, (c) 30 of those 32 players participated in at least one high school varsity sport other than football. Now, remember that this group of top 32 *NFL* draft picks is not, statistically speaking, a representative sample of the approximately 3,000 kids each year that are awarded a D-1 FBS football scholarship. Still, those numbers are consistent with a very high correlation of high level football players also playing other sports.

On my son's college football team, most all of the players also played another sport in high school. My son played varsity basketball throughout high school. He also played *AAU* basketball in the spring and summer for a club named *Indiana Elite*. Basketball really helped his quickness and footwork.

However, there is a risk in playing other sports. If your son gets injured in that other sport, it might risk a chance at a football scholarship. I address this more in Chapter 7.

Do not confuse a college football coach's love of *high school* multi-sport athletes with them wanting your son to be a multi-sport athlete at their college. Most do not. They strongly prefer your son be dedicated to football all year. There are a few rare exceptions, but I believe that even when that happens, the football coaches tolerate (but do not like) their players splitting their time on another team. It is usually a concession that the football coach is willing to make for a rare stud to get him to commit to the coaches' school. Thus, in my estimation, if during football recruiting your son tells the football coach that he also wants to play another sport in college, then all things being equal that will diminish the odds of him receiving a football scholarship offer.

B. **MENTAL**

Mental attributes are important to college recruiters. By mental attributes I mean the following, in no particular ranking: (a) academics (grade point average; SAT/ACT scores); (b) moral character (and the lack of a record of being a trouble maker); (c) work ethic; (d) mental toughness, competitiveness and grit; and, (e) leadership qualities. Their importance, however, seems to vary a lot from college to college.

1. Academics

I heard from several coaches that the first thing they look for are the academic minimums to qualify under the NCAA rules to play. *See* Chapter 4 for more details. This, of course, makes perfect sense. If your son cannot be admitted to college, they cannot play football for the college. Moreover, if they are admitted and take up a highly valued scholarship, but then flunk out, that is a huge wasted opportunity for the football team. Thus, while most (not all) D-1 football coaches did not appear to me to care too much if your son is a future Nobel prize winner or Rhodes Scholar, they do care a lot about both getting admitted and staying academically eligible.

Some colleges have academic standards that are much higher than the NCAA minimums. Others do not. Accordingly, some admissions offices effectively force their football coaches to find football recruits with strong academic records (although this is a minority of D-1 FBS universities). Your son's excellence at football can be a positive "X" factor that helps them gain admission, just like if they were a great musician, or started a charity, or did some other noteworthy accomplishment in high school.

Beyond the "minimums", it seemed to me that most college coaches did genuinely prefer (but not absolutely require) a kid with strong academics. This was true not only at Stanford, but also at colleges that we looked at that had what I would describe as typical college academic admissions requirements. Generally, I came to believe that the college coaches over time have come to believe that good academics are a good predictor of both work ethic (*e.g.* weight lifting, practicing hard), as well of following the rules (*e.g.* less likely to break the law and/or otherwise get into trouble). Thus, having good grades and good SAT/ACT scores seems to almost always help. Have your son, as an eighth grader, talk to an assistant college football coach about this. College coaches are good guys and want to help kids out. They will sincerely stress the importance of academics to your son. That message coming from them may be more persuasive to your son than coming from just mom and dad.

2. Moral Character

Character matters a lot to *most* coaches. If it does not, run away fast! Your son's football teammates will become his best friends. You want him surrounded by good people. If the coach recruits thugs, (and some do despite what they may tell you), your son could fall into the wrong crowd.

Most college coaches wanted to know about moral character early on, before they invested too much time recruiting. They start with the high school head coach, and may also follow up with school administrators, teachers or coaches from other sports.

College coaches want to win; and, they want to coach football. They did not become football coaches to baby sit troublemakers. Life is too short. They have much real work to do and not enough time to do it. They want to eliminate (or minimize) dealing with off-the-field issues with their team members. When deciding whom to recruit, they take character into account. However, do not be naive. There are, sadly, a number of exceptions where programs recruit convicted criminals and trouble makers. I discuss this in more detail in Chapter 9.

Good character starts at home, and you should not blame a college coach if your son is a trouble maker. Thus, your son should be made to realize that his character, as well as his reputation, will be factors in whether he gets offered a scholarship. He should strive to be a good person. He should also earn the respect of his teachers, coaches and others at school.

3. Work Ethic

Work ethic is very important. Your son's high school head coach will be the key source of information to college coaches about this for your son. Be sure that your son earns his high school coach's respect as to work ethic. Also, they will talk to your son's coaches in other sports, primarily to assess moral character (above) and work ethic. College football is very hard work. It will involve much lifting, much effort. College coaches know that it is unlikely at this late stage in your son's development that his personality will change much. If he is lazy now, they know (or believe) that he will always be lazy.

I think that work ethic is a big reason that college football coaches care about weight lifting in high school. Weight lifting is highly correlated to work ethic. Talk is cheap in the weight room and the numbers do not lie. Either you can squat 450 pounds or you cannot. And, college coaches know that the only way to squat 450 pounds is to put in many long hours of work in the weight room. Thus, while they know that they can make your kid stronger in their own weight room, if he has achieved good numbers in the high school weight room, then that is a positive indicator regarding work ethic.

4. Mental Toughness, Competitiveness and Grit

Football coaches intensely want to win. Indeed, if they do not win, then they get fired. Winning requires players who have a burning desire to win. Most competitive athletes that I have known hate losing more than they like winning. Victories are nice, but fade from memory. However, losing torments them. Some people are wired that way; most are not. Most guys describe themselves as being competitive, but few truly are. Perhaps that is best because I am not sure that it is really healthy. In any event, your son should not fake it, but at a minimum should certainly not be cavalier about losing around any coach.

Mental toughness also includes pushing on long after you do not want to. The elite *Navy Seals* have a great motto: "The only easy day was yesterday." Football coach Vince Lombardi said, "Fatigue makes cowards of us all." Great comebacks in games require mental toughness. Few seasons go perfectly. Thus to win championships, most teams will have to make at least one or two comebacks during a season. If the coach had recruited quitters, lacking in mental toughness, winning in tough or big games will not happen. In recruiting, coaches look for whether your son takes off plays when he is tired. Does he let up when the game is a sure win or sure loss? What do his high school coaches say? Does he play on while bleeding with a busted nose? In basketball, will he take a hard charge on defense and set bone crushing screens on offense? In baseball, will he slide head first into the catcher at home plate and mow him over? In football does he whine like a sissy about playing in ice, snow and freezing muck? Or does he play with a mean streak all the time?

5. Leadership Qualities

Leadership on a college football team is required at many levels, including: (a) team wide; (b) within each of the offense, defense, and special teams; (c) within position groups; (d) within classes (*e.g.* freshman); and, (e) amongst a group of guys out on the town and presented with temptation. It takes more than one or two leaders on a team. A well run football team has many similarities to a disciplined military unit with strong leadership up and down its ranks. In recruiting, college coaches will investigate objective indications of positive leadership by your son, like being a team captain, and subjective indicators such as talking with coaches, teachers and school administrators.

Those physical and mental factors are what coaches are looking for in recruits. Even if your son falls within those guidelines, that is no guarantee of getting recruited. Moreover, the further outside of those guidelines that he is, the more likely it is that he should pursue football at levels other than D-1 FBS

CHAPTER 3

TIMELINE OF RECRUITING EVENTS

"I have been impressed with the urgency of doing. Knowing is not enough; we must apply. Being willing is not enough; we must do."

- Leonardo da Vinci

Most families of high school football players get started way too late in recruiting activity. You should start about spring of your son's sophomore year.

Below is a timeline for recruiting. This will vary depending on your son's circumstances and skill level. For those (very enthusiastic) parents who are reading this book while sitting alongside their newborn son's crib, I start with pee-wee football in third grade and work my way up to college. Obviously, however, most of the action is in high school, particularly your son's *junior* year. If I had to pin-point one month in time that is most critical for D-1 recruiting, it is the month immediately following your son's junior season (normally November of his junior year). However, if he is truly an elite prospect, then it begins earlier. On the other hand, if he is a D-2 or D-3 prospect, then the critical period normally is later, typically the month following his senior season. However, each year the timetable seems to move earlier. Most major D-1 programs have given most all of their scholarship offers to high school juniors, and spend the senior year trying to recruit them to come to their university.

If you just get started your son's senior year, it is probably too late for D-1 football unless he is really great and yet is a "sleeper" -- under the radar.

As a backdrop to this time line, it is a good idea to review the NCAA's *Guide for the College-Bound Student Athlete*. It summarizes what college coaches can, and cannot, do at various points of time in your son's high school years. Those rules, and their timing, vary a lot from sport to sport.

Additionally, on the NCAA's website they have their, "NCAA Recruiting Calendars" separately for each sport and for D-1, D-2 and D-3. It sets forth the specific dates of the four (4) types of NCAA defined "periods", namely: (1) dead period; (2) quiet period; (3) evaluation period; and, (4) contact period. However, realize that for D-1 football for the most part such "periods" are relevant mainly your son's *senior* year. That is because, as summarized in their *Guide* mentioned above, the NCAA greatly limits what D-1 football coaches can do in terms of recruiting freshmen, sophomores and juniors. Also, realize there is a dead period in part of July; thus, you cannot even visit coaches on campus (unofficial visit) then.

Below is my month by month timeline (starting in August) of action items of the things that you and your son normally should be doing. I generally indicate which of the four types of NCAA "period" (listed above) applies to that month for D-1 FBS football. D-2 and D-3 coaches have far fewer restrictions. Also, for some months, in addition to what you should be doing, I add sections "What the Coaches Are Doing" (D-1) to give you a sense of what is going on from their side.

A. GRADE AND MIDDLE SCHOOLS

3rd AND 4th GRADE

Your Action Items:

1.   Sign him up for little league football, tackle if it is available. Some parents want to wait, fearful of injury. As a little league coach, I believe that by waiting, such as until 5th grade, they actually increase the chance of injury to their son. This is because, otherwise, in later years the other kids will have a 2-year head start on him and will clobber him when he does not know how to protect himself.

First, your goal with pee-wee ball is to infect him with the love of football. The key is that the experience be *fun*. I do not mean *soft*; I mean fun. The coaches must treat the kids age appropriately, but those boys want to learn to be tough. Help them do so in positive ways. Also, "fun" is not a code word for teaching kids that it is OK to lose. Realize that winning usually is a big contributor to fun. Second, help him develop "contact courage" (*i.e.* liking to hit in football). Your third goal should be for him to begin learning technique, fundamentals and terminology. However, at this age, other than safety techniques (*e.g.* keep head up; do not lead or hit with your head), perfecting football technique is tertiary; that will come later.

2.   Consider coaching him in football, at least as an assistant. Do this if for no other reason than to protect him from having a misguided or incompetent coach ruin his love of football.

5th AND 6th GRADE

Your Action Items:

1. Sign him up for tackle football, on a travelling team if possible. The game is played at a higher level and the hitting intensity is significantly greater. The game is heavily run based, but coaches will start to pass the ball with some modest to poor results.

2. Consider additional (private) speed training. Proper run-form is not natural, and most kids do it poorly. Early technique development can help develop good running habits and muscle memory.

3. Consider coaching him. This is your last chance to coach him.

4. Get him to start jumping rope.

7th AND 8th GRADE

Your Action Items:

1. Sign him up for tackle football. Parents are now merely spectators; school coaches are in charge. Puberty hits some kids but not others. As such, some kids will grow and in some cases peak disproportionately early.

2. Continue jumping rope, evermore.

3. Consider additional (private) speed training.

4. Particularly if your son would go to a small enrollment high school, consider enrolling him in (or even moving to) either a large high school or a private school known for football. Most high school athletic

association's jurisdiction, and anti-transfer rules, begin when 9th grade school starts.

B. FRESHMAN IN HIGH SCHOOL

AUGUST (Freshman) - (*Quiet period*)

Your Action Items:

1. Follow all NCAA rules. *See e.g.,* Chapter 3. Upon entering high school, your son is now classified by the NCAA as a "prospect", and thus is governed by their rules.

2. Have good study habits; keep GPA up. A D-2 coach told me that one of his big challenges in recruiting is getting kids admitted to his college due to poor grades from their freshman year.

3. Check *Facebook, Twitter* and other social networking pages to remove any inappropriate material posted by your son or his so-called "friends". Police this throughout high school.

4. Sign up for high school physical education classes for weight lifting and other sports training.

SEPTEMBER (Freshman) - (*Evaluation period*)

Your Action Items:

1. Play hard. Hustle all the time. Be a leader. Put the team first.

2. Your son should do whatever his coaches ask. As in the movie, he should be like *Forest Gump* being grilled by the Army Drill Sergeant:

> *Drill Sergeant*: Gump! What's your sole purpose in this army?
>
> *Forrest Gump*: To do whatever you tell me, drill sergeant!
>
> *Drill Sergeant*: [dang] it, Gump! You're a [dang] genius! This is the most outstanding answer I have ever heard. You must have a [dang] I.Q. of 160...."

3. Continue these attitudes and actions throughout your football career.

NOVEMBER (Freshman) - (Mixed *Evaluation and Contact periods*)

Your Action Items:

1. Play another high school sport, in the winter and/or in the spring.

2. Consider additional speed training for the rest of the year.

3. Do football team's off-season workouts for the rest of the year.

JANUARY (Freshman) - (Mixed *Contact, Quiet and Dead periods*)

Your Action Items:

1. Consider signing up for a freshman level "combine", such as the *National Underclassmen Combine* (NUC). It is best to do this if he has

already tested privately and his times and numbers are quite good. *See* Chapter 6.

FEBRUARY (Freshman) - (Mixed *Dead and Quiet periods*)

Your Action Items:

1. If planning to attend a combine, practice and perfect the combine events and how to best to perform them. Have your son go thru some private "mock" combines to see how he scores.

MARCH (Freshman) - (*Quiet period*)

Your Action Items:

1. Go out for track and field.

MAY (Freshman) - (Mixed *Quiet and Evaluation periods*)

Your Action Items:

1. Sign up for a D-1 university's commercial summer camp.

JUNE (Post-Freshman) - (*Quiet period*)

Your Action Items:

1. Attend every varsity football weight training and speed/conditioning session.

2. Attend one or more college football camps at D-1 school(s) of interest, particularly of schools that are of great interest. If in doubt, pick one close to home since local D-3 and other coaches will likely also be there.

3. Create a first draft list of colleges of interest to your son, including D-1, D-2, D-3 and NAIA schools.

4. Contact some of your son's potential higher priority D-2, D-3, NAIA, and/or Ivy coaches to start developing backup opportunities early. Visit one or more of their campuses if possible.

JULY (Post-Freshman) - (Mixed *Quiet and Dead periods*)

Your Action Items:

1. Attend one or more football camps.

C. SOPHOMORE IN HIGH SCHOOL

AUGUST (Sophomore) - (*Quiet period*)

Your Action Items:

1. Varsity team camp; earn a starting or 2nd string position in the depth chart.

2. Be sure your son is academically on track to complete the 16 "core" classes required by the NCAA.

SEPTEMBER (Sophomore) - (*Evaluation period*)

Your Action Items:

1. Play hard; never loaf; never take any play off.

2. Subscribe to at least one recruiting website (*e.g.* Scout.com; Rivals.com; or, ESPN.com) and start immersing yourself (somewhat) into that world. You will learn terminology, event dates, and a better idea of what level of player one must be to get D-1 offers.

3. Once your son is a varsity starter (this season or next):

    a. create profiles for him on websites: Scout.com; Rivals.com; and, ESPN.com (*See* Chapter 6);

    b. start collecting all game film of him (weekly if possible);

    c. start making a highlight film (*see* Chapter 5 for details).

4. You are allowed to make an unlimited number of unofficial visits to campuses.

What the Coaches Are Doing:

a. NCAA allows them to send brochures for camps and questionnaires. They mail thousands of these out, and receiving these, while positive, does not in and of itself mean that your son is being recruited.

b. You may call coaches. However, coaches cannot call you during your son's sophomore year. They cannot by rule even return your calls, texts or emails. Nor can they have any off campus contact with your son during his sophomore year.

NOVEMBER (Sophomore) - (Mixed *Evaluation and Contact periods*)

Your Action Items:

1. Play another high school sport, now and/or in the spring.

2. Do additional speed training for the rest of the year.

3. Do football team's off-season workouts for the rest of the year.

JANUARY (Sophomore) - (Mixed *Contact, Quiet and Dead periods*)

Your Action Items:

1. Consider signing up for a sophomore level "combine", such as the *National Underclassmen Combine* (NUC). Only do this if he has already tested and his times and numbers are quite good. *See* Chapter 6.

FEBRUARY (Sophomore) - (Mixed *Dead and Quiet periods*)

Your Action Items:

1. If planning to attend a combine, practice and perfect the combine events and how best to perform them. Have your son go thru some private "mock" combines to see his scores.

What the Coaches Are Doing:

a. National signing day of their current H.S. senior recruits is in the first week in February. For the following week, there is a good chance that the coaches are on vacation.

b. Starting to focus recruiting on the class ahead of your son, including hosting Junior Days for them.

c. Evaluating standout sophomore prospects and developing a list of prospects of interest.

MARCH (Sophomore) - (*Quiet period*)

Your Action Items:

1. Have your son firm up a list of colleges (D-1, D-2, D-3 and NAIA) that are of interest to him and why. Include possible academic majors and other academic considerations, football considerations, and others. *See* Appendix G.

2. On spring break, visit one or more campuses. Try to pre-arrange a meeting with someone on the football staff to give you a tour.

3. During the week or on weekends, visit one or more college campus near home, particularly for one of their spring practices and/or in connection with their spring game (inter-squad scrimmage). Try to pre-arrange this with the football office. Consider D-2 and D-3 schools of interest as well for doing this.

APRIL (Sophomore) - (Mixed *Quiet and Evaluation periods*)

Your Action Items:

1. Work on getting invited to several one-day football camps at D-1 campuses this summer. Target the ones of highest interest. Write, call and/or visit the football offices to do this. *See* Chapter 6.

2. Send highlight and/or full game film to coaches if your son was a standout varsity starter as a sophomore. *See* Appendices A and B for sample letters.

JUNE (Post-Sophomore) - (*Quiet period*)

Your Action Items:

1. Attend several one-day football camps at D-1 campuses. Target the ones of highest interest.

JULY (Post-Sophomore) - (Mixed *Quiet and Dead periods*)

<u>Your Action Items:</u>

1. Attend several one-day football camps at D-1 campuses. Target the ones of highest interest.

2. Register you son on the NCAA's Eligibility Center website.

D. **JUNIOR IN HIGH SCHOOL**

AUGUST (Junior) - (*Quiet period*)

<u>Your Action Items:</u>

1. Try to set up some unofficial visits to home games for colleges of interest during the coming season. They are allowed to give you up to three (3) free tickets for a game (5 if the parents are divorced or separated). Try to get invited to the pre-game recruiting function.

2. Sign your son up for the Fall SAT or ACT test, and have the scores automatically forwarded to the NCAA Eligibility Center by indicating code number "9999" and the NAIA Eligibility Center by indicating code number "9876".

<u>What the Coaches Are Doing:</u>

a. Conducting their teams summer training camp leading into their football season.

SEPTEMBER (Junior) - (*Evaluation period*)

Your Action Items:

1. Start gathering full game film (both sideline and end zone, if available) each week.

2. Review game film each week and start listing potential highlight plays. *See* Chapter 5; and, Appendix E.

3. You are allowed to make an unlimited number of unofficial visits to campuses (now or even earlier).

What the Coaches Are Doing:

a. D-1 coaches may begin sending your son recruiting materials, including questionnaires, but not written scholarship offers. If your son is visiting on their campus, or your son calls them, then they are permitted to extend a *verbal* scholarship offer.

b. You may call coaches. However, D-1 and D-2 coaches cannot call you during your son's junior year (except *once* in April/May for D-1). They cannot by rule even return your calls, texts or emails. Nor can they have any off campus contact with your son during his sophomore year.

OCTOBER (Junior) - (*Evaluation period*)

Your Action Items:

1. Complete highlight film through the end of the junior season. Post it on the internet, on his recruiting websites, and mail it to coaches of interest. *See* Chapter 5.

2. Select two (2) best full game films. Mail DVD's of that to coaches of interest.

3. Give five (5) sets of your son's highlight film and of your son's two (2) best full game films to your high school head coach to have on hand to give to college coaches.

4. Update your son's profiles on recruiting websites. *See* Chapter 6.

NOVEMBER (Junior) - (Mixed *Evaluation and Contact periods*)

Your Action Items:

1. If you have not yet finished film, do so now and get it distributed. See above.

2. Continue scheduling unofficial visits to campus.

3. Try to get invited to "Junior Days" for colleges of interest. These tend to be scheduled to occur the following February and March.

JANUARY (Junior) - (Mixed *Contact, Quiet and Dead periods*)

Your Action Items:

1. If invited, attend the *U.S. Army National* Combine in San Antonio, Texas.

FEBRUARY (Junior) - (Mixed *Contact, Quiet and Dead periods*)

Your Action Items:

1. If invited, attend junior day on-campus unofficial visits. If not invited, call and try to get invited.

What the Coaches Are Doing:

a. National signing day of their current H.S. senior recruits is in the first week in February. For the following week, there is a good chance that the coaches are on vacation.

b. Hosting one or more Junior Days.

MARCH (Junior) - (*Quiet period*)

Your Action Items:

1. If your son has one or more offers, take an unofficial visit (your expense) for a spring practice and/or in connection with their spring game (inter-squad scrimmage) of those schools of greatest interest. Have him spend the night with a player if possible. Do this on spring break, the week or on weekends. Pre-arrange this with your recruiters.

2. If invited, attend junior day on-campus unofficial visits.

3. If your son does not have offers, ask a coach if you can do item #1 above.

<u>What the Coaches Are Doing</u>:

a. Conducting spring practices for their college team during March/April.

b. At the D-1 FBS level, sending out the bulk of their remaining scholarship offers.

APRIL (Junior) - (Mixed *Quiet and Evaluation periods*)

<u>Your Action Items</u>:

1. Take an unofficial visit to campus for a spring practice and/or in connection with their spring game.

2. Sign up for and take SAT and/or ACT tests, if not already happy with score.

<u>What the Coaches Are Doing</u>:

a. Coaches may place only one call to your son in April/May.

b. Coaching their team for spring practices culminating in their spring game.

JUNE (Post-Junior) - (*Quiet period*)

Your Action Items:

1. Attend summer football camps, preferably one-day recruiting camps run by D-1 teams.

2. Register you son on the NAIA Eligibility Center website.

What the Coaches Are Doing:

a. Hosting summer camps.

b. D-2 and D-3 coaches can begin having off-campus contact with your son after his junior year. Most D-3 programs are starting to turn their recruiting attention to your son's class about this time.

c. D-2 coaches are allowed to start making weekly phone call to prospects.

d. NAIA coaches (who are allowed to have contact with your son as early as his freshman year) are starting to turn their attention to recruiting your son's class.

JULY (Post-Junior) - (Mixed *Quiet and Dead periods*)

Your Action Items:

1. Attend summer football camps, preferably one-day recruiting camps run by D-1 teams on campus.

2. Collect college admissions applications of interest, including all levels of football and non-football schools.

What the Coaches Are Doing:

a. Take a week of vacation with their family.

E. SENIOR IN HIGH SCHOOL

AUGUST (Senior) - (*Quiet period*)

Your Action Items:

1. Try to set up some visits to home games for colleges of interest during the coming season. Try to get invited to the pre-game recruiting function. If a program is interested, or if they have already offered, they will likely extend an invitation for an "official" visit, in which case they will pay for your son's travel and lodging expenses. Otherwise, have him attend on an unofficial visit (at your expense).

What the Coaches Are Doing:

a. D-1 coaches may send your son a written scholarship offer.

b. Conducting their college team's summer training camp leading into their football season.

SEPTEMBER (Senior) - (*Evaluation period*)

Your Action Items:

1. Contact D-2 and D-3 coaches regarding visits to their campus during their season.

2. If invited by a college team (D-1, D-2 or D-3), once classes begin your son's senior year, then he may begin taking "official" visits paid for by the college. Such invites for an official visit are, (as a practical matter at the D-1 level), normally only extended to kids that already have an offer and/or who have committed. Your son is limited to five (5) official visits to D-1 and D-2 colleges.

3. Prepare and submit college applications to schools of interest (football and non-football).

4. Sign up for and take SAT and/or ACT tests if needed still.

What the Coaches Are Doing:

a. Coaches may call your son once per week for the rest of his senior year.

b. During his senior year, coaches may have up to six (6) evaluations and contacts. However, they may only make one evaluation (such as attending one of your son's high school football games) during September, October and November.

OCTOBER (Senior) - (*Evaluation period*)

<u>Your Action Items</u>:

1. Contact D-2, D-3 and NAIA coaches regarding visits to their campus during their season.

NOVEMBER (Senior) - (Mixed *Evaluation and Contact periods*)

<u>Your Action Items</u>:

1. Contact D-2 and D-3 coaches regarding visits to their campus after football season.

<u>What the Coaches Are Doing</u>:

1. Trying to convince uncommitted senior recruits whom they have already offered to come to their college.

2. Evaluating film of the class *behind* you.

DECEMBER (Senior) - (Mixed *Contact, Quiet and Dead periods*)

<u>What the Coaches Are Doing</u>:

a. Practicing for a bowl game or playoff.

b. College D-1 coaches may have off-campus contact with you during December and January, except during Dead Periods during the holidays and preceding National Signing Day. This includes home visits by assistant coaches and one visit by the head coach. As a practical matter in D-1 football, this only occurs with kids that already have offers and/or who have committed.

JANUARY (Senior) - (Mixed *Contact, Quiet and Dead periods*)

What the Coaches Are Doing:

a. Ivy League football recruiting is culminated by hosting recruiting days or weekends on their campus.

b. D-1 coaches trying to convince, with home visits and otherwise, the few remaining uncommitted senior recruits whom they have already offered to come to their college.

c. D-2 coaches are now allowed to conduct one tryout per recruit on campus (no pads; no games).

FEBRUARY (Senior) - (Mixed *Dead and Quiet periods*)

Your Action Items:

1. Sign and submit National Letter of Intent.

2. Receive, study and follow off-season workout book from your college strength and conditioning coach.

3. If a low-income student, consult with the football staff and apply for a Pell grant.

MARCH (Senior) - (*Quiet period*)

Your Action Items:

1. Continue doing the workouts provided by your college strength and conditioning coach.

What the Coaches Are Doing:

a. Conducting spring practices for their college team during March/April.

b. Recruiting the class *behind* you.

APRIL (Senior) - (Mixed *Quiet and Evaluation periods*)

Your Action Items:

1. Continue doing the workouts provided by your college strength and conditioning coach.

MAY (Senior) - (Mixed *Quiet and Evaluation periods*)

Your Action Items:

1. Get final high school transcripts to NCAA Eligibility center.

2. Complete final amateurism questionnaire on NCAA Eligibility center.

3. Continue doing the workouts provided by your college strength and conditioning coach.

4. Prepare to arrive on campus next month for summer school and weight lifting.

CHAPTER 4

RULES, ACADEMICS AND AMATEUR ELIGIBILITY

"The most common commodity in this country is unrealized potential."

- Calvin Coolidge, U.S. President

Your son can be an all-world football player and yet if he is not eligible, then he will not be allowed to be on the team. These requirements generally fall into three categories: (1) following NCAA (or NAIA) recruiting rules; (2) academics; and, (3) amateurism.

A. <u>NCAA AND NAIA RULES</u>

The NCAA rules are long and complex. The NCAA has three (3) separate manuals of its "Bylaws", one each for D-1, D-2 and D-3 sports. Each is over 300 pages long and they get amended from time to time. They are available for free on their website. The most strict rules, generally, pertain to D-1. As such, I have reprinted in Appendix H some (not all) of those NCAA rules for D-1's "Article 13" pertaining to football recruiting. If you suffer from insomnia try reading them all. If you abide by the D-1 rules, you should be compliant with the more lax D-2 and D-3 rules as well. However, a quick reference to compare those rules is included as part of the NCAA publication entitled, *Guide for the College-Bound Student-Athlete*. It is free online at:

http://www.ncaapublications.com/productdownloads/CBSA.pdf

That guide is an excellent summary of the current NCAA rules and eligibility requirements. Of course, those standards may change over time, so always check that website for the current rules.

The NAIA rules are far less strict than D-1 rules, and have more in common with the NCAA's rules pertaining to D-3 football. The NAIA rules are available from their website for free at:

http://www.playnaia.org/d/NAIA_GuidefortheCollegeBoundStudent.pdf

The NAIA also offers there, for free, a helpful *NAIA Guide for the College-Bound Student-Athlete*. It compares its recruiting rules, stating that the, "NAIA recruiting process for both freshmen and transfers is less cumbersome, with few restrictions on the contact between a student-athlete and coach."

Even though the various rules are complex, they are pretty easy for a recruit and his family to follow. The basics are: get good grades and do not accept anything of value. However, it is valuable if you do have a deeper understanding of the complex rules, beyond the basics, that govern the *coaches*. By understanding what the coaches can, and cannot, do, then you can better position your son for their consideration within the rules. You will better understand how the process works and, thereby, how to help the coaches recruit your son.

Regarding the NCAA's rules, I have created a list of "10 Commandments" of recruiting rules for D-1 FBS football. If you follow them, you should be OK for all levels. These commandments are by no means all of the rules, but are intended to simplify some of the key rules that you should understand:

10 Commandments of
D-1 FBS Recruiting Rules

1. Neither your son nor anyone related to him should seek or accept anything of value (cash, services, job, goods or otherwise) from anyone even remotely connected with a college (*see* broad definition of "representative" at NCAA Bylaw 13.02.14) or due to his athletic ability, with the exceptions that: (a) each college can provide up to three (3) free tickets to watch a sporting event each time your son visits their campus (or 5 tickets if parents are divorced or separate); and, (b) if your son is invited on an "official visit" his senior year that college can pay for certain things for that trip (*e.g.* food for recruit and 4 family members, and recruit's reasonable travel and lodging). (*See e.g.* NCAA Bylaws: 13.2.1; 13.15.1; 13.7.2.1; 13.5.3; 13.5.2).

2. Your son needs to graduate and to have a GPA of at least 2.3 (on a 4.0 scale) for his 16 "core" classes as well as a suitable SAT or ACT score according to the NCAA's "sliding scale" (Appendix I)(*See also* NCAA Bylaws: Article 14). A GPA of 2.0 to 2.3 will make him an academic redshirt, able in D-1 to get a scholarship but unable to play in games as a freshman.

3. Your son needs to be an amateur, not a professional, in the sport he is being recruited. (discussed more in Section C, below)(*See e.g.* NCAA Bylaws: Article 12)

4. Your son or you can make an unlimited number of phone calls to coaches (NCAA Bylaw 13.1.3.2.2), but the coaches cannot initiate any phone call (even to return a message), except that they can call once during April 15-May 31 of his junior year and once per week beginning September 1 of his junior year. (*See e.g.* NCAA Bylaws: 13.1.3.1; 13.1.3.1.3). There are exceptions, allowing unlimited calls five days before an official visit, and 48 hours before and after national signing day. (NCAA Bylaws: 13.1.3.3.1.1; 13.1.3.3.2.1).

5. Coaches are not allowed to text message nor instant message with your son or you, nor engage in publicity about a recruit before he signs a Letter of Intent. (*See e.g.* NCAA Bylaw: 13.4.1.4.1)

6. You and your son can write to coaches any time; however, coaches are not allowed to write (via e-mail, fax and/or regular mail) to your son or you with recruiting materials until after September 1 of his junior year. (*See e.g.* NCAA Bylaw: 13.4.1)

7. The coaches may not provide a *written* football scholarship offer to your son until after he is registered with the Eligibility Center and no sooner than August 1 of his senior year. (*See e.g.* NCAA Bylaws: 13.9.2.2

8. Off-campus in-person "contact" (and discussion) (such as home visits) with your son by the coaches off of their campus is strictly regulated, limited to two coaches from a school at a time, limited to six off-campus contact days, and only can occur beginning July 1 of his junior year. (*See e.g.* NCAA Bylaws: 13.1.1.1; 13.1.5.2; 13.1.4.2; 13.17.4)

9. On-campus in-person "contact" (and discussion) is far less regulated, being almost unlimited during "unofficial visits" (you pay) at any age level or time as well as during permissible camps and "official visits" (except during the rare "dead periods"). (*See e.g.* NCAA Bylaws: 13.7.1)

10. The number of off-campus "evaluations" of your son's athletic abilities (with or without "contact" with your son) or a visit to his high-school (without "contact" with your son) (NCAA Bylaw 13.1.7.1) by the college is strictly regulated and is so limited (maximum of seven assistant (7) coaches travelling the entire nation during April-May; over 15,000 high school football teams) that practically speaking it leads to little, if any, chance for them to see your son perform football live. (*See e.g.* NCAA Bylaws: 13.1; 13.1.2.6.2; 13.02.7.2; 13.1.7.4-10). Hence, being proactive, visiting campuses, and providing film to college coaches is important.

For D-2, many of the similar concepts apply but some of the rules are more lax. For example, in D-2 recruiting the coaches may have off-campus contact and call your son beginning June 15 after your son's junior year in high school.

Note, that in D-3, commandments 2, 4, 5, 6, 8 and 10 do not apply. Also, for D-3 the coach can call any time and could visit you after your son's junior year. However, limited D-3 recruiting budgets are typically tiny and staff size may well foreclose much of that type of recruiting activity anyways.

If you follow those commandments and Bylaws and ask a coach recruiting your son about any other questions, then you should be able to comply with the complex rules. Importantly, you should also understand the constraints that those rules place on the college football coaches so that you can be proactive so as to give them a chance, within those rules, to learn about and evaluate your son. Help them help you.

B. ACADEMIC MINIMUMS

Regarding NCAA academic minimums, the NCAA requires for D-1 for students entering college after August 1, 2016 (*e.g.* high school class of 2016 and after) must:

A.   **Graduate** from high school.

B.   The successful completion of **16 core courses** (below).

C. **Core GPA Minimums**

(1) ***Qualifier***: Earn a minimum GPA of 2.3 in those 16 core courses, with grades earned in 10 of the 16 before the start of his seventh semester (i.e. start of senior year) to be a "Qualifier" with both a scholarship and to play in games as a freshman.

(2) ***Academic Redshirt***: Same as qualifier, but with a core GPA from 2.0 to 2.299. Unlike a qualifier, an Academic Redshirt may get a scholarship and practice, but cannot play in games their freshmen year. In D-1, you also will *lose a year* of playing eligibility, unless your son completes at least 80% of his degree requirements before his fifth year in college.

D.   **SAT/ACT Minimums**. Must meet a sliding-scale combination of grades in high school core courses and standardized-test scores. For example, if a student-athlete earns a 3.0 grade-point average in core courses, that individual must score at least 620 [2 parts- math and reading] on the SAT or 52 [sum score] on the ACT. *See* Appendix I. As the GPA increases, the required test score decreases, and vice versa."

Those "core" courses for D-1 require completion of 16 core-course requirement in eight semesters, namely:

(a) 4 years of English

(b) 3 years of math (Algebra 1 or higher)

(c) 2 years of natural or physical science (including one year of lab science if offered by the high school)

(d) 1 extra year of English, math or natural or physical science

(e) 2 years of social science

(f) 4 years of extra core courses (from any category above, or foreign language, nondoctrinal religion or philosophy)"

For D-2 football, the core 16 requirements are similar, but the mix of the 16 classes is slightly more flexible. *See, NCAA Guide for the College Bound Student-Athlete.* Also for D-2, as of the publishing of this book your son's SAT (two part) must be at least 820 or his ACT "sum" score on all four parts (explained below) must be at least 68. These are set to change August 1, 2018, applying the new D-2 "sliding scale".

For D-3, admission to the D-3 college is sufficient. Realize, however, that many D-3 (and D-2 and NAIA) college's own admission requirements *exceed* that which is required by many D-1 football programs under the NCAA's D-1 rules.

The academic eligibility requirements for NAIA have many parallels to the NCAA structure. Its rules are available on its website, mentioned in Section A, above. It also has an *NAIA Eligibility Center* (fee about $70, waived if demonstrated financial need). To send your son's SAT and ACT scores to the NAIA, you need to use code "9876". In general terms, the high school prospect must have graduated high school or be accepted as a regular student in good standing as defined by the NAIA member college. To play as an entering NAIA freshman, your son must meet two

(2) out of three (3) of the following requirements: (1) achieve a minimum "composite" ACT score of 18 or two-part SAT score of 860; (2) have a high school overall GPA of at least 2.0 on a 4.0 scale; and/or, (3) graduate in the top half of his high school class.

The academic eligibility requirements for JUCO are available by searching "eligibility" within their website: http://www.njcaa.org/. In general terms, the high school prospect must have graduated high school with an academic diploma or a General Education diploma. However, JJCAA also has a track for student-athletes who are completing high school and are simultaneously enrolled in 12 or more credits at a college, subject to other provisions.

For D-1 football, academic eligibility is more complicated. For D-1 football the NCAA has what they call a "sliding scale". The better your son's "core" GPA (on a 4.0-point scale), the lower his SAT or ACT scores need be, and vice versa. This is GPA based on his 16 core classes (see above), not on his overall high school GPA. The 2011 table showing the NCAA's sliding scale core GPA is reprinted in Appendix I. For example, if your son had a GPA of 2.100 in his "core 16" classes, then to be eligible for D-1, (and soon for D-2), he would need either: (a) 970 or higher on his two-part SAT score; or, (b) 83 or higher on his "sum" four-part ACT score.

Importantly, for core GPA calculation purposes the NCAA only uses round numbers (i.e. a B = 3.0; B+ = 3.0). It does not use fractions (e.g. B+ = 3.3).

Also, for D-1 ten (10) of the sixteen (16) core GPA class grades must be complete *before* your son's senior year. Otherwise, at most he will be an Academic Redshirt, ineligible to play in games as a freshman. Thus, he should not procrastinate taking his core 16 classes.

Be aware that those "core" classes must meet the standards of the NCAA Eligibility Center. Thus, if there is any doubt about whether there is sufficient rigor of your son's high school curriculum, either check it out yourself by checking your son's school on the Eligibility Center website (or calling them at phone: 877-262-1492) or at least inquire of the coaches that are recruiting your son.

The ACT score is a bit more confusing in terminology. You have to understand the difference between the so-called "sum" score that the NCAA uses and the more common term, "composite" score. For the ACT, the NCAA's numbers look to the "sum" score which is the *sum* of four parts: English, mathematics, reading, and science. The "composite" score, however, is a term that the ACT test folks, (and most college admissions offices), use to mean the *average* of those four scores. A perfect ACT score would be 36 on each of the four parts. That would give you a "sum" ACT score of 144 (36+36+36+36=144), but a "composite" score of 36 (the average of 36, 36, 36 and 36). Thus for NCAA football recruiting purposes, sum together the four parts of the ACT for the NCAA's sliding scale table (reprinted in Appendix I). However, the NAIA looks for a composite (average) ACT score of 18 or higher.

As a side note, while I am not an SAT or ACT guru, I have read that some regard the ACT test easier than the SAT if your son's is better at reading/writing, whereas the SAT score tends to favor those who are better at math. I have also heard that the ACT is more common sense, but requires better time management during the test. Others say the ACT measures "achievement" whereas the SAT measures "aptitude", whatever that distinction is supposed to mean. The SAT score penalizes students for making a wrong answer on multiple choice questions (to try to neutralize guessing), whereas the ACT does not. Some or all of these may be old wives' tales, and do your own researching. There seem to be a variety of opinions on the differences. I suspect that it depends a lot on your son's individual personality and skills. But if your son's scores, in view of his likely GPA, are near the borderline in terms of being eligible, then you might want to take such differences into account and/or have him try each test, the ACT *and* the SAT. Also, be wary of geography. For some reason, (at least based on a study done in 2006), more high school kids on the east coast, the west coast, Texas and Indiana took the SAT; whereas, more kids in the remaining states take the ACT. Do what is best for you son, not what happens to be trendy in your state.

Some kids that are not academically eligible go to either a post-high school prep school or a junior college (JUCO). They do this to try to get their grades up to make themselves eligible to enroll at a D-1 football university. Normally, they also play football while at the prep school or junior college. It is my perception that only a relatively low percentage makes their way back into D-1 football from this path. Many get lost in terms of major college football. You can see published data on which

JUCO players get offers to which colleges at *scout.com*'s website at http://jcfootball.scout.com/. Also, years at a Junior College (typically 2 years for an associate's degree) eat into your son's limited eligibility at an NCAA school. Anecdotally, we knew of an amazingly good football player that was offered and accepted a full ride D-1 football scholarship to a major program. Yet, he never enrolled because he was not academically eligible. He had to enroll in a JUCO school, and was never to be heard from again in the world of D-1 football. There are exceptions to this. But your son will need to get the required grades eventually, so it is far easier just to get disciplined and work for the grades that he needs the first time around during high school.

If his core GPA is below 2.0 (on a 4.0-point scale), then he is not eligible for NCAA D-1 or D-2 regardless of test scores. Thus, be sure that his grades stay up. Some kids get off to a bad start their freshman year, digging a hole for themselves. If your son is serious about college football, he should keep his grades up starting in the ninth grade.

However, the NCAA allows a college (not a recruit) to petition the NCAA for a "Waiver of Initial Academic Eligibility Requirements Pursuant to NCAA Bylaw 4.3". For example, this may be based on an education-impacting disability or being an international student.

The foregoing are just the NCAA, NAIA and JUCO minimums. In addition to that, however, your son must also get admitted to the college itself. However, for most D-1 programs the zeal to get top recruits clearly leads to admissions of most kids that clear the NCAA minimums if the football coaches want him. There are a few schools that are exceptions by having higher admissions standards, but not many. In fact, to the contrary, many D-1 programs admit kids with academic records lower than their normal college admissions standards. It varies for such schools, but this is sometimes known as "special admits".

C. <u>AMATEURISM</u>

Your son must also be athletically an "amateur". There is an NCAA required certification process for this where you fill out a questionnaire. Practically speaking, in football I have never heard of a professional high school football player. This is more relevant for sports like golf or tennis.

In any event, even for football this Eligibility Center registration is required for D-1 and D-2, but not for D-3. This can be done at the beginning of his junior year, on a website: www.eligibilitycenter.org. At graduation from high school, your son will also have to request a final certification prior to enrolling in college. That website also is where high school grade transcripts and SAT and/or ACT scores (use the Eligibility Center's code number, "9999") are collected on behalf of the NCAA. There is currently a $65 fee to register, which can be waived for low-income families. This certification process is convenient in that you only have to do it once, rather that separately for each college.

Regarding amateurism, when in doubt, do not allow your son to accept any cash or anything else of value until you are sure that it will not jeopardize his status as an amateur. The NCAA has described the amateurism questionnaire as follows:

"The questionnaire covers the following precollegiate enrollment activities:

- Contracts with professional teams

- Salary for participating in athletics

- Prize money

- Play with professionals

- Tryouts, practice or competition with a professional team

- Benefits from an agent or prospective agent

- Agreement to be represented by an agent

- Delayed initial full-time collegiate enrollment to participate in organized sports competition

The *Guide for the College-Bound Student-Athlete* contains more detailed information about initial academic and amateurism eligibility."

These rules may change from time to time, so be sure to check with the NCAA for the final word. Especially be aware of this issue if your son plays for a travel 7-on-7 football team discussed more in Chapter 6, below. Some of those teams have corporate sponsors, such as sportswear companies, that pay for uniforms, travel expenses, coach's stipends, and other things. Verify that the coach and the program both are on the up and up and are knowledgeable about and follow all of the NCAA rules. The same is true for some private trainers, so-called promoters, and others. Otherwise, they may jeopardize your son's eligibility. Worse yet, if those 7-on-7 teams evolve the way that some (not most) *AAU* high school level basketball teams have, then some unsavory characters might try to attach themselves to your son so that they can try to make money off of him. For example, make sure that they (coaches or other hangers-on) are not receiving money or other value (or worse yet giving your son money or other illegal benefits) to try to influence where he goes to college to play football. Also, make sure they are not agents, or "runners" for agents.

When you meet a 7-on-7 coach (or an *AAU* Basketball coach), try to size up *why* is this guy doing this? Is he coaching because he has a real day job and he just loves sports and kids? Or is it more that this is his business and it is mainly about the money for him? Ask the coach if he is making *any* money (directly or indirectly) from football, and if so what are the sources. That may help you avoid trouble.

Obviously, stay involved with whom your son is interacting with and why. Otherwise, they too may jeopardize you son's eligibility. The NCAA has no jurisdiction over such parasites directly, and thus cannot punish *them*. And the parasites are well aware of their NCAA immunity. As such, while seeking to make themselves some money *they* frequently have little downside in breaking the rules, whereas your son has a great deal to lose.

Also realize that the NCAA defines who is a "representative" of a college for recruiting purposes very broadly. It includes not only coaches, but even season ticket holders, donors to the school, boosters, and former players, to name a few. Thus, if your son is around any such person, keep a close watch on the situation since they might violate NCAA rules, even inadvertently and innocently. Be sure, for example, that they do not provide him anything of value, at least not until you first clear the situation with a knowledgeable and honest recruiting coach as to what is or is not permissible. Individuals with questions about their amateur status may contact the NCAA Eligibility Center at 877-262-1492.

CHAPTER 5

RECRUITING FILM – HIGHLIGHT AND FULL GAME

"When I played pro football, I never set out to hurt anyone deliberately - unless it was, you know, important, like a league game or something."

- Dick Butkus, NFL Hall of Fame linebacker

A. __OVERVIEW__

Game film of your son playing football is very important. A very common misperception among parents and kids is that D-1 college coaches come out to watch live high school football games to evaluate your son to decide whether to give him an offer. They don't, particularly at the D-1 level. Allow me to repeat, they *don't*. They come to live football games in the fall of a kid's *senior* year. And by then, nearly all of their scholarship slots have already been offered. They visit high school games not to evaluate, but rather as part of their efforts to convince a kid (to whom they have *already* offered) to sign with their team. The handful of coaches only have limited Friday nights (before their own Saturday games) to visit a small number of high school games, usually nearby. About the only exception is that if they are there watching another, older kid on your son's team (or on an opposing team) who they are recruiting, and happen to notice your son playing well. Rather, most all of D-1 FBS coach's game evaluation in deciding who to offer scholarships comes from watching film from sophomore and junior year games.

A D-3 coach told me that getting his hands on film, especially highlights film, was one of his greatest challenges he faced in recruiting. Help him to help your son my making his job easier – get the film to him.

Highlight film can be very time consuming to make, so get started early. It is one of the first things that you should begin working on, during or right after the end of his junior season in high school. It normally should only include varsity film, not JV or freshman film. Of course, when I say "film" nowadays it is all digital on DVD or published on the internet (for example via *YouTube*), or both.

There are five (5) major considerations in making the film: (1) what footage is on it; (2) in what sequence; (3) who makes it; (4) when it should be made; and, (5) how do you get it to the college coaches. Realize that there are two types of film, highlights and full games. It is understood that when you send a college coach one or two full game films, that they will be your son's *best* overall game(s). Highlight films are much more labor intensive to make since they involve selection, editing and production. However, I strongly suggest that for full game films you do nothing other than make a raw copy of all of the footage for that game. Do *not* edit full game film. College coaches want to have access to the full game without interruption. The reason is simple; they want to ensure that the "full" game film actually shows the whole game and that "bad" plays are not edited out. The D-1 college football staffs have video production people that can quickly edit and cut that full game film down if they want to do that. For example, the staff might edit out dead time to save the head coach from wasting time watching it, but in the process the staff can ensure that plays had not been removed from the film. For this reason, while you always want to be helpful to the college coaches, if they prefer to get film directly from your high school coach instead of you, let them. It is one form of quality control for them, and you do not want to interfere with that.

Fig. 3: Timely Making Film is Critical to Recruiting

If your son's high school does not shoot or provide game film, or if you want to supplement that with your own footage, then obviously you will need to shoot the footage yourself, or hire or convince someone else to do that. Here are some guidelines. First, use a tripod (or at least a mono-pod) to stabilize the video camera, resulting is less jerky footage. Second, footage from up high, looking down, is better than footage taken at ground level. Third, consider footage from the end zone. This is discussed more in Section B, below. Fourth, resist the temptation to zoom in on your son too much. Rather, keep a broad enough view that a college coach can evaluate the context of what your son is doing and how he is reacting to events around him. This is film for football evaluation, not for Aunt Nellie's home movies. Fifth, smoothly pan as your son moves while maintaining that broad enough view in the camera.

B. **WHAT PLAYS TO CHOOSE IN WHAT ORDER?**

For full game film, the answer is obvious. Include the full game. As explained above, do not edit full game film. Ideally, if you have two sets of film for the same game, one from the end zone and the other from the side view, include both on the same DVD. You can include one or two different games on the same DVD, and/or better yet, if you are finished with your son's highlight film (discussed below), also include it all on a single DVD. If you do this, however, I suggest you start the DVD with a table of contents, or at least clearly show on the outside DVD label, that the DVD includes both highlights and one (or two) full games. Otherwise, the coach may accidentally overlook one and just turn off the DVD player before it gets to the next segment. Try to make it mistake proof.

There is another thing to remember about choosing full game film for recruiting purposes. It is OK if your son's team lost that game, so long as he played great individually. Do not confuse a team win with a great showing by your son. Also, if choosing between two equally good full game films, seriously consider choosing the one where the opposition is, (or at least appears to be by reputation or otherwise), a big, fast, quality opponent. Your son's team blowing out a lame opponent may be less impressive than a hard fought loss against a great opponent.

Also, for both game film as well as highlight film, on the outside label and preferably also at the beginning of the film itself you should have an

97

introductory screen with your son's name, jersey number(s), high school name, year of high school graduation, height and weight. Most all DVD video creation software like *Adobe Premiere* allows you to create these opening screens. You might also include a few key stats, but I suggest not going overboard with stats on such screens. The reason is that the more stats that you throw at the viewer, the less likely it is that the important ones will register or be remembered. Sometimes, less is more.

Duration of a highlight film is important. Keep it short. It's a commando raid, not the invasion of Normandy. Limit its duration to about 4 to 7 minutes. Also, put your son's best plays at the very beginning. I have heard that some coaches will stop watching after 5 to 10 plays if they are not impressed right off the bat. Each year, each college staff is inundated with hundreds of DVD's. I have walked passed the large book shelves in FBS college team's football offices where the recruiting DVD's are stored, and it is staggering how many they have. The highlight film is the hook, the teaser. However, the general rule of putting the best plays first is in tension with another consideration. It is nice to group the plays by type so as to showcase particular skill sets. If your son has enough great highlights, then you can group them. When in doubt, however, err on the side of putting the very best plays first rather than grouping them by type.

Edit each play tightly, very tightly. Do not torture the coach with highlight film that shows the team breaking from the huddle, then jogging up to the line, then getting set, them running the play, then getting off the pile, and then high-fiving each other. Do you think that a busy college coach wants to watch all of that? Yet I have seen highlight film that does that. It suggests that your son does not have many highlight worthy plays, so you are filling the film with fluff. Just show the play. I edited my son's film so that each clip began about ½ second before the ball was snapped and ended almost immediately after the ball carrier was tackled. This not only makes the highlight film more interesting, it also allows you to pack more plays into a 4-7 minute highlight film.

Rarely, if ever, show the same play twice. College coaches are experts; they get it the first time. They have spent more time watching football film in their life than you have spent sleeping.

Very important - indicate where your son is on *each* film clip immediately prior to the play beginning. It is usually done by superimposing on the film an arrow, or circle, or box around your son. This is done during video editing, and for me was one of the most time consuming aspects of the highlight film preparation. It was tedious. But in my opinion, it is very important. You love your son and spend every Friday night in the fall watching him play football. Because of that, you could spot him on the field even during a blizzard. However, not everyone else can pick him out so easily. If you do not believe me, try watching high school film of a team you that you have never seen and try to keep track of the left guard, #61, during the action. It is *very* hard. When your son's dream coach is bleary eyed taking the red-eye flight back to campus at 1:00 AM and decides to watch your son's DVD on a laptop computer on the plane, try to make it as easy for that coach as possible to find your son in the film.

Another helpful feature can be to include short captions on a few clips (not each) to inform the viewer of non-obvious but relevant information for that play. This can be favorable stuff like "State Championship Game" or "Last Play to Win Game" or "Blocked Univ. of Georgia Recruit". It can also explain context, such as "Sophomore Season". In the latter example, while the play clip of your son might be great, when the viewing coach realizes that your son did that play as merely a sophomore it might be *really* great. Indeed, if the highlight film includes any plays from the freshman or sophomore season, you probably should note that on the screen.

One small point is whether or not to include music, and if so what song(s). I have been told by college coaches that it is irrelevant. Some coaches turn the sound off. However, the kids like it because it makes viewing more fun. We added music. However, we used only one song (repeated once) that my son picked out. But, although it was a current, hip, "rap" song, we used the *instrumental* version of it – no lyrics. My view was, and is, first do no harm. Some song's lyrics are pretty nasty and offensive. I thought, why even risk offending anybody or making them question character, no matter how unlikely? I expected that the colleges would delete the sound anyways. However, to my surprise, at least one university replayed our son's video while we were visiting on a recruiting trip *with* the music on his highlight DVD. Be judicious in your choice, and if in doubt go with silent film.

Amateurs like you and I are used to watching football on TV, from the *side* view of the game. By contrast, college coaches watch much, and probably most, of their film from the end zone view. They do this for a reason; it is a better vantage point from which to evaluate plays and players. D-1 football programs routinely film all of their practices, and they do it from multiple vantage points, notably including the end zone view. They meet in video viewing rooms which are separate for each position (*e.g.* all of the running backs meet together). From the game and practice film, in these sessions the coaches teach the player what they did right and what they did wrong, in excruciating and repetitive detail. Much of it is with film shot from the end zone. If your high school football program is wealthy enough to have film from both vantages (side and end zone), then when in doubt you should use the end zone view. This is especially true if your son is a lineman (offense or defense). They play in the jumbled blocking zone that is packed with bodies and action. Thus they tend to be much harder to pick out on film that is shot from the side. However, the end zone view will not always be the best vantage point. The end zone perspective is usually best when shot from *behind* your son. Otherwise, the opposing player(s) may block the view of your son on film. And in a football game, assuming that your high school uses a camera at only one end zone, then the footage will be behind your son only for two (2) out of the four (4) quarters of a game since the teams change directions at each quarter. Also, sometimes the side view simply is better footage. So use your judgment for each play clip.

One thing that you should resist is including film clips *merely* because, for whatever reason, you like the play. Try instead to consider if you were a college coach viewing hundreds of these. That is the audience and the correct perspective.

Which plays do you choose to include? Assuming your son's high school team plays a 10-game season with four 12-minute quarters per game, then there will be about 1,000 total plays per year. If he only plays one-way plus some special teams, then he is in on about 500 plays per season. You have to cut that down to about 20-40 plays on his highlight film. The obvious ones will be obvious. Pick the super-great plays and put them at the very beginning of the film. That is very important; you want to grab the attention of a college coach.

But how do you choose from the rest? Let me give you some food for thought. Do not think in terms of *ESPN SportsCenter* crowd pleaser highlights. Instead, think in terms of an intense, detail oriented, technical expert football coach looking for athleticism and hustle. Now those are not mutually exclusive, and the super-great plays will often appeal to both. But choosing between the remaining plays is tougher. Let me give some hypothetical examples below.

Example 1 – Pass Receiver:

Film clip A: Your son catches a long pass and goes 82 yards for a touchdown. However, on closer review there was man-to-man coverage. The defensive back covering your son tripped on the turf and fell down, leaving your son wide open. The quarterback throws a perfect pass, which your son catches on stride *en route* to the touchdown.

<u>Film clip B</u>: Your son catches a pass, but only for a 9 yard gain. It was a crossing pattern over the middle, he made a crisp cut, and he had to jump up high in the air, in traffic, to catch the ball which was thrown wobbly and slightly behind him. He got killed by a linebacker who lit up his ribs, but he managed to hang on to the ball for the reception.

Clip B is probably the better choice. Sure, the fancy 82 yard touchdown is nice, and it does show one easy catch on stride, and it may showcase his speed. But depending on how many other fancy touchdowns you already have in your highlight film, Clip B can better showcase your son's athleticism and toughness.

<u>Example 2 – Offensive Lineman</u>:

<u>Film clip A</u>: Your 6'4" son that weighs 280 lbs. lead blocks on a running play off tackle. He crushes the defender with a pancake block, and the running back scampers untouched for a 60 yard touchdown. However, on closer review the player that your son pancaked is a 138 pound sophomore linebacker, playing for an opposing team known to be very weak.

<u>Film clip B</u>: Your 6'4" son that weighs 280 lbs. pulls as lead blocker on a sweep around end. He shows impressive speed and footwork, swinging his hips around to hook the outside linebacker, keeping the linebacker to the inside. The running back reads this and advances for 5 yards outside of and past your son's block, but then fumbles.

Clip B is probably the better choice. Sure, the pancake block is cool, but it doesn't translate to D-1 football due to the major size advantage your son had on that play. Clip B might better showcase your son's speed, footwork and loose hips. The fumble is likely the running back's fault, and thus is irrelevant in evaluating your son. Obviously, for the running back that is not a clip that he would want to include in *his* highlight film.

Example 3 – Linebacker:

Film clip A: Your son is 6' 3" and weighs 220 pounds and is playing left outside linebacker. It is a running play to your son's right, away from him to the opposite side. He is in back-side pursuit and the running back cuts back against the grain and inside of your son. As the running back slashes across your son's chest, with his own left fist, your son punches the ball loose from the ball carrier's left hand.

Film clip B:

Your son is 6' 3" and weighs 220 pounds and is playing outside linebacker. It is a passing play. The tight end runs straight up field as a receiver on a "seam" route deep down field. Your son reads the lineman's helmets popping up, and immediately sinks his hips and back peddles. As the tight end runs past, your son takes a drop step and then flips his hips and stays very close in man-coverage on the tight end the whole way down the field. However, your linebacker-son is nowhere near the ball and is oblivious to the fact that one of his teammates sacks the quarterback.

Clip B is probably the better choice. Sure, a forced fumble is always good. However sexy, he showed bad technique in Clip A. The very reason for his back-side pursuit was to prevent the cutback by the running back. Your son nearly blew it by over-pursuing against an average high school running back, and got lucky to punch the ball loose. By contrast, Clip B is not as sexy, but better showed both good technique and "assignment football". College (and NFL) football is assignment football – each player must do their own job. They must trust that their teammates will do their jobs. The pass coverage showed good recognition, footwork, and loose hips. Sure he was oblivious to the quarterback, but he was in man-to-man pass coverage and thus was supposed to be focused on the tight end, not the quarterback. The good result showed – the tight end was covered so well that the quarterback did not even attempt to pass to him. Your son's good pass coverage (may have) contributed to the sack.

Thus, what on the surface appears to be a good highlight might not be as good as some other, less obvious play. If you are not a football junkie, then this is an example of where your son's high school coach or a friend that knows proper football *technique* (not just is a football fan) can offer some guidance.

Here are some other things to consider when reviewing his film, both in evaluating your son's chances of playing D-1 football (*see* Chapter 2) and in selecting which full game film to use or which plays to include in his highlight film:

1. Do the plays show effort and focus by your son even when the ball is not around him, for example:

a. When he is blocking on the backside, away from the ball, does he loaf?

b. On defense, does he sprint towards the ball in pursuit, even if he only has a small chance of getting into the play?

c. If he is a receiver that does not have the ball thrown to him, does he never-the-less run his routes crisply and at full speed?

d. If he is a receiver or running back, does he block on running plays or is he a prima donna?

e. If he is a quarterback, does he carry out backside fakes in earnest after he has handed off the ball, or does he just become a spectator?

f. On the sidelines is he goofing off or is he watching the game?

2. Do the plays show footwork, balance and athleticism, *e.g.* does he look coordinated and in control of his body, or is he consistently out of place or on the ground?

3. Do the plays show that he stays with his blocks on offense, and does he get off of blocks when he is on defense?

4. Do the plays show that he likes contact, hits hard and is tough?

5. Do the plays show that he commits penalties or other mental mistakes?

6. Do the plays show that his team's opponent is strong or weak?

7. Do the plays show that he does not stick to his assignment, but instead tries to make a selfish hot dog play?

These guidelines should help you make your choices. It helps to consider them *before* going through the roughly 1,000 play film clips for the season. I created a table in a word processing document where I would note the ID number of the digital film clip (end zone and corresponding side line clip). I would rate a play from 1-5, with 5 being best. I also used codes, like "T" for tackle, "B" for block, etc. I only included plays that were possible candidate film clips, and not every play from the year. It made things go faster because on the first pass I did not agonize over evaluating each play. Rather, if I thought it might be a candidate, I included it on the list. Over time I developed a better sense of what to include. I started off keeping about 15 plays per game, but as the season went on, with better recognition I only would keep about 5 to 10 plays per game on the list. Thereafter, I would go back and work from that smaller list of plays, which was much faster and easier. I have reprinted a sample of part of that table in Appendix E.

Finally, sometimes kids will include some brief footage of other sports, such a weight lifting, track or basketball to showcase strength, speed or athleticism. If you do that, keep it very limited.

C. **WHO MAKES THE FILM?**

Regarding who is to make the film, there are five choices: (a) a high school coach or other person affiliated with the high school team; (b) you (alone or with a friend or relative): (c) a hired "amateur", like a high school kid, who is good with computers; or, (d) a professional fee-based recruiting service; or, (e) a professional fee-based video company.

On the first option, I think that most high schools do not create highlight film for players. Some high school programs do, and if yours does and they do a good job consider yourself very lucky. However, do not expect this to happen, particularly of a highlight film for the whole season. Most high school coaches are paid next to nothing and already put in very long hours doing many things to prepare their team. They do not have the time, and often do not have the computer expertise, to compile a highlight film. However, they often do have full game film that was used for team scouting and/or for team self-evaluation during the season. It should be easier for the coaches to get you an extra copy or two of full games. You can then have multiple copies to give or mail to college coaches. High school budgets are tight, and most high school coaches are not millionaires, so offer to help and/or at least reimburse the cost of supplies such as DVD blanks. As discussed below, I made our son's highlight films. However, the coaching staff was of great assistance to us. They provided copies of the raw footage that I then edited into the highlights. Also, if you make the highlight film yourself, it is still a good idea to get your high school coach's ideas and feedback as to which plays to include or omit. Show him a draft copy before sending it out, if possible. Odds are pretty good that his football knowledge and experience will be helpful to improve the editing of your son's highlight film.

I created our son's highlight film on my computer at home. Our son's high school had upgraded cameras to "digital" filming of games, with digital recorders. Thus, their output was a digital computer file for each play clip. If your school uses VHS or other magnetic tape, that will still work but it will add a time consuming extra step. You will have to play the video "into" your computer to convert it to digital computer file format. Our high school team shot each game with both a side-view camera from the press box and an end zone camera. The end zone camera was mounted on a tall pole structure about 30 feet high and behind an end zone. It was remotely controlled.

Depending on what system your son's high school team uses may dictate the best way to create highlight film. For example, more teams are starting to use web-based game film and film editing. One such system is called *HUDL* sold by a company to teams on an annual subscription basis. That one is found on the internet at www.hudl.com. The nifty thing is that if your son's high school team purchases that service for their film needs, then the highlight editing and creation software is available on the website for no additional charge to players with the proper access codes from the high school team. You can create, and update your son's highlight films and full game film, and then email to college coaches a link to view that film, even if the college coach's team is not a subscriber. One downside is that they do charge about $25 per DVD if you want to get a copy instead of viewing the film on the internet.

I used *Adobe Premiere Elements* software on my home computer to create and edit the highlight films, and then to "burn" copies onto DVD's. It worked well and the software cost about $100. Other software will do fine too, and some may be easier to learn. My daughter had a small business creating highlight film and she used *Apple's iMovie* software successfully on her laptop. Indeed, many computers come already loaded with acceptable video editing software. Ask your kids; they probably know about it. Realize that video editing takes a tremendous amount of computer speed (random access memory ("RAM"), as well as processor speed), as well as hard drive memory storage. A slow computer for video editing often can lead to the software crashing, wasting hours' worth of editing and causing much frustration. Check the recommendations from your video software maker, and if possible use a computer on the powerful and fast side of what they recommend.

To store the digital video footage taken by the high school football team, buy a multi-gigabyte external computer memory hard drive from your local office supply store or online. It is an electronic box that is extra computer memory storage. Prices keep dropping, but less than $100 is typical. I strongly suggest, if compatible with your computer, that you buy an external drive with a very fast connection. As of 2015, this would be USB 3.0 (not USB 2.0) connection. The reason to get this is that a *fast* connection transmits large amounts of data much faster. Digital video files are huge, and without a very fast connection you could be waiting for hours for the video to upload. Since computer technology keeps improving, check with the store to see what can handle fast transfers of many video files for the best price. Also, be sure your computer has the corresponding connection.

Each Monday following a Friday night game, my son would drop off the external memory hard drive to the coach in charge of film, Andy Gall. Coach Gall was kind enough to digitally copy the film files to the hard drive and return it to my son. To minimize hassling Coach Gall, I shared my hard-drive with the dad of another player-recruit on the team, so that he too could copy it to his computer that week. In that way Coach Gall only had to do this once per week. Coach Gall appreciated that I invested in a hard drive with a very fast connection since that also saved him a lot of time when copying the digital video files onto it. After that, each week my son would retrieve that hard drive from the coach and bring it home to me. I would then begin reviewing and editing. It was fun, but it took a lot of time. I estimate that I spent 40-80 hours total reviewing all the game films and compiling and editing the highlight film. It was a labor of love and I had a blast.

Do not forget the label on the outside of the DVD. I always wanted the DVD to have key information (name, phone, etc.) in case it got separated from the cover letter used to send it to a college. You can buy at any office supply store DVD labels and a simple device called an "applicator" to apply the labels to the DVD. For example, *Avery* and *Memorex* each sell applicators for about $10. It comes with (or you can download from the internet for free) software to create and print out very nice customized labels for the DVD's (*see* sample at Appendix D). Include the following information on the label:

1. Your son's name.
2. Year of your son's HS graduation (this is how they group recruits).
3. E-mail address.
4. Phone number.
5. Home mailing address.
6. High school name and state.
7. Jersey Number(s), (if he has different numbers for home and away jerseys, then list both).
8. Height.
9. Weight.

10. Possibly a few other key stats (*e.g.* an impressive 40-yard dash time, if applicable).

I also bought a bunch of DVD protective plastic cases with clear lids, and bubble-padded DVD mailers so that I could easily mail DVD copies to college coaches.

In terms of cost, when you total the DVD, the label, photo ink for the label, the case, a DVD sized bubble-padded mailer, and first class postage, you will spend about six dollars ($6.00) out of pocket per DVD that you send.

One sleazy trick that you (or your hired person) should *not* do is speed up your son's film to make him look faster. If you think this is clever or novel, it is not. This trick is well known to college coaches and they have watched so much film they can spot this. This may hurt your son's recruitment by casting doubt on everything you tell them.

So go forth and be the next Steven Spielberg in the world of D-1 college football recruiting films. And even if you hire someone else to actually make the high light film, you can supply them with *which* plays to include by using a table, like the one in Appendix E, based on review of the game films by you, your son and his high school coaches.

The other option, if you do not have the desire or ability to make the highlight film yourself, is to hire someone to do it for you. There are numerous firms out there that you can find by searching the internet. The results can be quite good. However, like any business there are good ones and bad ones. You can usually view samples on their website. However, beware of good looking film production vs. bad play selection and sequencing. Do not be dazzled by glitz – the college coaches will not. Take an active and critical role in what plays are selected, and what sequence they appear. *See* Section B, above. If you do not feel qualified, enlist the help of a friend or high school coach who is qualified. I had a friend that had a bad initial experience with such a service. They put an underqualified person on the job who then lazily proceeded to merely sequence the highlights in chronological order of the football season, game by game, play by play. They "fired" him and had to start over which delayed them. So do your due diligence in hiring such a firm, including interviewing the *individual* at that firm who will be working on your son's film. Ask to see samples of his/her prior work. Ask if they ever played football. Quiz him/her about their methodology in selecting and sequencing plays and about the concepts set forth in Section B, above.

Another disadvantage of hiring a professional outside firm is the cost. You will need to get a quote from them, but it is not cheap. However, after you buy all of the do-it-yourself software and equipment that I described above, and spend all of the time, it may be better to go with such a firm if you can afford it.

Such firms also offer other services. They can help set up a personal website page. They can advise you and your son on recruiting. They can evaluate your son's chances for D-1 or some other level. One of the larger such firms is *NCSA Athletic Recruiting*. There are many others, so do your research and read reviews about them.

Also, such firms are set up for mass mailing and distribution of DVD's and letters, with databases of coaches names and addresses ready to go. If you want to do such a mass shotgun approach, that may make the logistics easier. However, this has limitations. A D-3 head coach told me that he gets about eight (8) such mass e-mails per day, and considers them "annoying". He said that he pays far more attention to an e-mail or letter directly from a kid (or his parents) since it shows true interest in that college, rather than just being part of a mass mailing blitz. Mass mailing may never-the-less work. But, if you hire a firm to do this, you should definitely supplement it with your own personalized letters and/or e-mails to the colleges that your son really wants to target. Do not worry if you duplicate some colleges with your hired firm's mass mailing. There is a good chance that the mass mailing version got discarded.

Finally, if you cannot afford to make highlight film, it may be less critical if your son is an offensive or defensive lineman, so long as you get the college coach suitable full game film. A head coach at a D-3 program told me that for lineman, he can make a reasonable assessment merely from watching full game film; whereas, for a receiver (since passes to that player were more rare), highlight film was far more helpful.

D. **WHEN SHOULD YOU MAKE THE FILM?**

The short answer is ASAP. However, there is a trade-off. You want to make the film and get it into the hands of the coaches as soon as you can. Yet, by waiting you may well be able to include some additional, better footage, thereby improving the appeal of your son. You could address this by simply updating the highlight film from time to time. However, you only get one chance to make a first impression and it may be hard to get a busy coach to take the time to review multiple, follow on highlight films.

Another way to deal with this dilemma is to send college coaches one or two full game films early, and then follow up with the highlight film. However, say that you do this early during his junior season. You do run the "risk" that that early full game film that you sent to the coach turns out to not be your son's best game. You might not get a second chance with a coach. However, you know your son and between you and him you should have a fairly good feel for when he plays a good game overall. If you feel confident that the early game in the junior season is a great one for him, send it.

I strongly suggest that you should be working on your son's highlight film, week by week, during his junior season. It will be time consuming, and so this helps break up the task into more manageable bits. More importantly, at the end of that season you will be ready to start sending it out right away. Now obviously, if your son starts playing varsity football earlier, as a freshman or sophomore, then you can push that time table up a year or two. However, most kids, at least at large high schools, will not have much, if any, freshman or sophomore *varsity* film, and do not be discouraged by that. The junior film will normally be more critical. Senior film might help seal the deal, but most D-1 prospects have been identified and offered scholarships before the senior season. Just get it done and out to the coaches soon. For D-2, D-3 and NAIA, senior film is still very relevant since they tend to do most of their recruiting during and shortly after the senior season.

Regarding timing, there is a potential big problem with most commercial recruiting services that you might hire to help with putting together your son's highlight film. It is called supply and demand. Your son is not their only client. And everybody finishes their football season at about the same time. So everyone is clamoring to suddenly have that recruiting service work on and complete *their* film at the same time. I have a good friend that experienced that log jam at the end of his son's junior season. It worked out fine and his son never-the-less earned several D-1 scholarships, but it caused stress. Be aware of it, and try to negotiate a commitment from the vendor. One way to avoid that log jam is to hire a local video production company instead of a football recruiting service. The problem with that alternative, however, is that they are less likely to have someone knowledgeable in selecting which football plays to include. You would likely need to take an active role in that aspect. Either way, (recruiting service or generic video production company), keep supplying them with the raw game footage week by week, or at least soon, so they are not waiting on you.

Also, you could just hire a local high school kid that is good with computers and video editing software. Better yet, your son may have these skills. This would be cheaper and may avoid potential delays if he is diligent. You and your son can be involved in play selection, and the hired student can do the production work.

E.   HOW DO YOU DISTRIBUTE THE FILM?

There are two main ways to distribute the highlight film: (1) over the internet; and, (2) giving out copies of it on DVD. I suggest doing *both*. They each have pros and cons, and by doing both you improve your son's chances of exposure.

Internet distribution is the cheapest, and once posted can be seen by any coach anywhere once he knows to look for it. This can be done several ways. First, some people set up a dedicated website for their son's recruitment, and include video footage (among other things) on it. Note that some commercial for-profit recruiting companies as part of the service offer to help you set that website up (for a fee).

Second, as discussed above, if your son's high school team uses a web-based film service, such as www.hudl.com, then part of that includes web-based distribution of highlight film you create there.

Third, some people post football footage on open websites such as *YouTube*. I know a family that used this as their main tool for getting film to coaches and he earned a *Big Ten* football scholarship.

Fourth, if you send your son's highlight DVD to the recruiting services (*Scout.com*; *Rivals.com*; *ESPN*) they will post some or all of it on their website as part of your son's profile for free. *See* Chapter 6.

DVD distribution provides more computer memory space, which is typically required for full game footage. For example, most *YouTube* clips are just a few minutes long. Thus, due to memory and bandwidth transmission constraints, internet distribution, such as *YouTube*, is better suited for highlight film. DVD's also allow for much higher resolution, or picture quality, than most web-based videos, although this technology is improving. Thus, with DVD it may be easier for the coach to see your son, instead of a blurry mess. It is hard to offer a scholarship to a blurry mess.

DVD's have some other advantages. You can hand them to a college coach when you meet them, almost like a calling card. It is tangible. A DVD is a bit less high-tech, and has that modest appeal. Also, college football coaches travel a lot while recruiting. This means they have a lot of time on airplanes, in airports, and in hotel rooms. Many carry laptop computers with them, and they can toss a bunch of recruiting DVD's into their carry-on bag and watch them on their flight. Make their job easy to see your son by getting them a DVD to take with them.

Also, keep your son's high school head coach stocked with 4 or 5 copies of the DVD's (highlight and full game). College coaches may stop by, even unannounced, to visit him to talk recruiting (of your son and/or other kids at the high school) and this makes it easy for your high school coach to hand a copy to such visiting coaches.

Finally, be aware that there are private, for-profit scouting companies that collect prospect film from various sources, edit it, and then sell it to college football programs as part of their recruiting search process. We learned after the fact that such businesses had done this with our son's film. Do not, however, assume that this will happen. Control your own destiny; do not hope one of these companies will save you from the work of creating highlight film.

Creating highlight film and full game film may be one of the most important things that you can do to help with your son's recruiting. It also will also be one of the most time consuming. It does little good if you finish it too late, after most scholarship offers have already been made. Try to have it finished by October or November of his junior year. That way, you are well positioned to get it distributed (via mail and the internet) to college coaches.

CHAPTER 6

CAMPS, COMBINES, 7-ON-7 AND RECRUITING WEBSITES

"Gentlemen, it is better to have died as a small boy than to fumble this football."

- John Heisman, legendary football coach

In addition to his high school football team, (and its strength, speed and conditioning workouts), there are several things that your son can participate in that may help with recruiting. These include: (a) camps; (b) combines; (c) playing on 7-on-7 football teams in the offseason; (d) creating a profile on the various recruiting websites; and where available (e) high school spring football. However, a poor performance can also hurt his chances, for example, if your son registers a slow speed at a combine. I address some aspects of each below.

A. __CAMPS__

There are three kinds of football camps: (1) one-day 'invitation' camps run by the D-1 university football programs; (2) publicized commercial camps run primarily by the D-1 university football programs (often multi-day); and, (3) commercial camps run by someone other than a college football program. Their value to your son in getting recruited at the D-1 level is in that rank order. However, for D-2, D-3 and NAIA recruiting, items #2 and #3 above may be more important since D-2, D-3 and NAIA coaches help staff those camps and use them to evaluate prospects. Most all of such camps are during the summer. If your son is injured, he should not attend; his stock will drop.

One day camps by the college football coaches are mainly for D-1 football evaluation. These one day camps often are not publicized, except by individual invitation by the D-1 college football program. However, NCAA Bylaw 13.12.1.3 ,(See Appendix H), states that a college's "camp or clinic shall be open to any and all entrants (limited only by number, age, grade level and/or gender)". Thus, it appears that some D-1 programs finesse this rule by technically not excluding kids, but effectively accomplishing this by not publicizing the camp. Thus, call the football program and asked when *all* of their football camps are scheduled. At first, they may only mention the multi-day camp that is the subject of their publicized brochure. Follow up and ask if they have any additional football camps, including any one day camps. Then ask if your son can attend. Typically the one-day camps are focused on kids the summer immediately before their senior season. Often, however, they will also include some kids going into their junior season. The colleges are required by NCAA rules to charge a fee to cover costs (*e.g.* lunch and beverages, about $25). These one-day camps are also best for your son because they take less time. Thus, he can attend more of them to increase exposure. Be forewarned; these camps are far more exhausting for your son than you might expect. I believe that this is mainly due to the emotional anxiety and stress that your son will put on himself wanting to perform at his best. Have him get a good night's sleep beforehand. If he has more than 4 or 5 camps in him per summer, he is doing well. They last a full day, and the format is typically: (a) registration; (b) weight and height measured; (c) 40-yard dash, shuttle run and other testing; (d) various position specific skill drills. Typically, the college will have their respective position coach run the drills (and evaluate the prospects) for his position specialty. These allow the coach to conduct the eyeball test on the prospects as well as see their athleticism and hustle in action. Often players can and do play multiple positions for their high school. However, give careful thought as to which position group your son goes with at a camp because that could influence whether he gets an offer. Do not lose heart if your son does not get an offer at the camp. More often, the coaching staff will meet with each other after a camp to discuss prospects before extending an offer.

Sometimes, these one-day D-1 recruiting camps are embedded as a sub-part of a much larger commercial camp run by the university football program (discussed below). They may skim off some top performers and have them off in the corner or otherwise apart from the main camp. This is usually where the head coach spends most of his time. Other times, however, the one-day camps are standalone events.

Commercial camps that are run by a D-1 university football program serve several purposes. First, they are money makers since often 500 or more kids attend. The ages typically range from 8th grade to high school seniors. They are often overnight camps (sleeping in the college dormitory), and cost several hundred dollars. Second, they also serve as a form of community outreach by the football program, letting any kid be part of the fun. Third, they teach football. They are focused less on D-1 recruiting by the host university and more on improving football skills. However, there is a significant, and underappreciated, recruiting aspect to these camps. They are mostly staffed by local high school football coaches and, more importantly, by various D-2, D-3 and NAIA coaches. With about 500 kids in attendance, the D-1 host school's 10-man coaching staff can't possibly coach everyone there. Thus, they hire these other coaches to help. The local D-2, D-3 and NAIA coaches are not competing against the D-1 host, and thus they make a natural fit. Those other coaches make some extra money over the summer by working the camp, but they are also keeping their eyes out for prospects that might not get a D-1 offer. Your son should be aware of this and work hard to impress them as well.

Finally, there are commercial camps run by someone *other* than a university football program. Sometime former NFL players, large shoe or sportswear companies sponsor these. Other times, recruiting website services run these camps. Also, there are various other for-profit businesses that run these camps. Some of them are team camps; some are for individuals, and some for both. Importantly, by NCAA rule, D-1 college football coaches are no longer allowed to work these camps. However, some professional scouts attend *some* of the more high profile camps, and then provide scouting reports to college teams. These types of camps, as compared to D-1 college run camps, overall appear to have the least value for D-1 recruiting purposes. However, these camps sometimes also have D-2, D-3 and NAIA coaches working them, and thus can have recruiting value at those levels. Even if you are targeting D-1, I am not saying that your son should not go to these camps. But understand that their main value is to improve his football skills, not D-1 recruiting. Since they are for-profit enterprises however, they may exaggerate about their D-1 "contacts" in the world of active football coaches and how they can help get your son recruited. While perhaps sometimes they can, consider also their financial bias in wanting to convince you to pay several hundred dollars for their camp.

One favorable exception is the (free) *Nike Football Training Camps*. These are invitation only, and have much better than normal recruiting exposure to sports media and professional scouts. If your son can get an invitation to one of these camps it is worth serious consideration. The invitations are either earned at a *Nike Football Combine* (open to all), and/or by sending (or better yet having your son's high school head coach send) profile information (*see* Appendix D) and DVD highlight film to the address found online.

Also, there are specialty camps for quarterbacks. That position is unique enough that specialty camps are more appropriate. The same is true for specialists such as punters, kickers and long snappers. There are a couple of specialized camps around the country. You can find these by searching the internet. An example is Kohl's Kicking, Punting and Snapping camps. *See* www.kohlskicking.com.

As mentioned, some of the recruiting website camps will feature top performers at their camps on their websites. Their commercial motives in hosting camps include creating content to write about on their website. However, while there are some exceptions, I found that in reading their articles about their camps (or combines) most of their coverage was about elite level kids that *already* had numerous offers. Not much was written about kids on the bubble between a D-1 offer and not. Thus, I am skeptical about how much real additional recruiting attention results from such articles.

B. COMBINES

Combines are good if used properly. Combines have, in my opinion, one primary purpose. They can serve as independent verification for a college coach of your son's measurable scores, such as 40-yard dash time, shuttle run time, height, weight, etc. They are like the SAT test – an independent source of how good your son is, at least as to those attributes on that day. And like the SAT test, your son could have a good day or a bad day. Again, if your son is injured he should not attend.

Typical combines emulate parts of the *NFL Combine*, testing: (1) 40-yard dash; (2) shuttle run (aka "pro-agility", "5-10-5" or "short shuttle"); (3) vertical jump; (4) standing broad jump; (5) height; and, (6) weight. Other items vary. For example, the *NUC* (discussed below) also measures repetitions of bench press (135 lbs. or 185 lbs. depending on age). At *Nike* combines, instead of bench press they measure how far a kid can throw their 3 kilogram *SPARQ* medicine ball. The "*SPARQ* score", aggregating some of these events, was discussed in more detail in Chapter 2.

I strongly suggest that your son train specifically for a combine before showing up at one. Bad scores might hurt his chances in recruiting. Most combines allow you to have a bad event "not reported". However, obviously when that is done it does not take a genius to figure out that the omitted score was bad. Some of the events, like pro-agility, have techniques that can be practiced and perfected to get a faster time. He should work on that in advance, with good coaching if available. I also suggest that he conduct one or more "mock" combines privately in advance. It will help him focus and give him a true test of whether or not he is ready. You can arrange for a mock combine at a private fitness center, or ask one of your son's football coaches to conduct it at the school.

The shuttle run is an example of an event that should be coached and practiced, and is shown below in Figure 4:

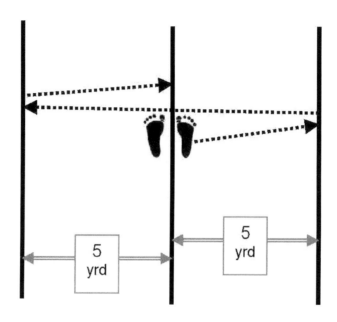

Fig. 4: 20-Yard Short Shuttle

It is a shuttle run, sprinting 5 yards to one side, then 10 yards to the other, and then 5 yards back to the middle, as shown above. It may look simple but it is not when done right. Each kid is different. Some are faster starting right; others left. The number and placement of steps make a difference. So do a host of other factors. This and other events like the 40-yard dash can be improved with a knowledgeable coach.

In my opinion, I would suggest that you *not* have your son attend a combine that uses laser timing. This advice creates a dilemma since the well-respected *Nike* combines use laser timing. Your son's times will be slower as compared to being timed with a stopwatch. This is due to stopwatch operator reaction time delay in starting the stopwatch. Normally, stopwatch times in the 40-yard dash are about 0.1 to 0.3 seconds better. In football, that can be a *big* difference. *See* Chapter 2, Tables 2-4. Some "purists" will point out, correctly, that laser timing is more accurate and for that reason is used at the *NFL Combine*. However, stopwatch timing has been just fine for most every high school track meet in history. Stopwatches are good enough for college football coaches at their camps for D-1 football prospects. NFL coaches use stopwatches at college's "pro-days". Stopwatch times are what most all of the other recruits are reporting. Do you want to be a purist or do you want to have your son receive a D-1 scholarship offer? However, if you do report a time to a coach that was laser timed, be certain to clearly identify it as such (*e.g.* "40-yard dash time: 4.67 sec. (laser timed)") since a college football coach will appreciate the difference.

Also, when deciding on a combine, investigate in advance the running surface(s) that will be present. They vary, and at some combines, different events may even be on different surfaces. Running a short shuttle is much different on loose field turf, as compared to a smooth wooden basketball court, as opposed to *Astroturf*, etc. Your son could slip a lot, losing time. Also, have him bring the appropriate shoe or shoes depending on such surface(s). This might include bringing track shoes, running/basketball shoes *and* football cleats to a single combine. If possible, he should practice in advance on the same surfaces. Also, after he warms up at the combine, he should do a few practice runs at full speed to get used to the conditions. Regarding surfaces, particularly for 40-yard dash times, try to avoid combines conducted on football field-turf. It tends to be too soft and thus will slow your son's time. This tends to affect heavier players more than lighter ones. One notable exception to avoiding soft turf is the *U.S. Army National Combine* held in San Antonio, Texas each January in conjunction with the *U.S. Army All-American Bowl* game for seniors that same week. That combine is invite only (about 500 juniors) and it is run on a notoriously slow field-turf surface. However, that fact is fairly well known among recruiting insiders and the prestige of that particular combine and the potential high level exposure far outweighs the shortcoming of a slow surface for that event.

My son went to only one combine, but it worked out well. He attended the local *National Underclassman Combine* (*NUC*) in May of his sophomore year. The fee for participating in their combine is on their website, http://nationalunderclassmen.com, and currently ranges from about $90 to $120. The National Underclassman Combine visits many cities, mainly during the months of February thru June. The results are posted on their website. When writing college coaches and mentioning your son's measurable skills, I would include the link to the *exact* sub-page on that website where the coach could go directly, without searching, to verify the scores.

In addition to the *NUC* and *Nike* combines already mentioned, other sponsors of reputable combines include *Scout*, *Rivals*, *ESPN* and *Under Armour*. You can word search the internet for "football combine" and see what cities and dates they are scheduled to be held. Normally, these are held from early spring through the summer.

Once your son has established good measurables, (*e.g. see* Chapter 2, Tables 2-4), at a combine I do not see great value in devoting time and money to multiple combines. However, some recruits seem to attend a lot of them. I perceived that often these tend to be very high profile elite recruits that already have numerous offers. Just because some elite recruits attend multiple combines does not mean that it is the best use of your son's time. Yet, it may be of some value, particularly if your son is not otherwise receiving recruiting interest or if he is trying to use the combine to qualify for some other event such as a *Nike Football Training Camp*.

C. 7-on-7 FOOTBALL TEAMS

The growth of 7-on-7 football is a fairly recent phenomenon but for skill players it has become important. It has both good and bad aspects, but is here to stay. It is "touch" football, played without pads, although sometimes helmets are worn. However, even without pads, with boys being boys, it can get rough. It is only played with "skill" players and "big skill" players, not offensive or defensive linemen. It is virtually all passing. High school and college teams play it, normally in the off-season, to practice their passing game (*e.g.* practice route timing, reading pass coverages and working on quarterback throwing accuracy) as well as to practice their pass defense.

7-on-7 has emerged like *AAU* basketball did for that sport. As such, 7-on-7 football will provide similar recruiting help, and similar recruiting violations, as are found in *AAU* basketball. Since comparatively 7-on-7 football is young, in predicting its future, it is worthwhile to understand the more established world of *AAU* basketball.

If you are not familiar with *AAU* basketball, it is the main event for college basketball recruiting. Basketball at the high school has become far less important. The main reasons are that *AAU* clubs can assemble, in effect, all-star teams made up of kids from all over the state (or even from around the country) to converge at tournaments in various states to play other such all-star teams. The college basketball coaches are in hog-heaven. They can attend a single tournament and see, in very high concentration, the best pitted against the best. Those college basketball coaches do not have to travel 178 miles to Bumpkinsville High School in the middle of nowhere to see one D-1 level prospect destroy weak opponents from the next town over. The coach can see a prospect against high level competition, and in a single trip, he can also recruit 10 other kids.

However, there are accounts of some very shady operators that are affiliated with some *AAU* basketball clubs. Big time sports bring money. Big time sports needs top recruits. Therefore, influencing a top recruit to go to a particular big time program is valuable. Some unscrupulous adults try to cash in on that value. They seek money for recruiting influence, and otherwise try to cash in on a kid. This is the exception, and most coaches are very honorable. But the sleazy also exist.

However, there are also many real virtues of *AAU* basketball, and by analogy then, 7-on-7 football. Perhaps the biggest virtue is meritocracy. First, a very good kid who happens to live in a very small town, with weak high school opponents, can show his stuff against top level talent. He just needs to try out for and make a good team. Second, opportunities for exposure are greater. Reporters or scouts can see a kid at a national or regional tourney that they might not otherwise see. Note that for football, current NCAA rules prohibit college football coaches from attending 7-on-7 tourneys, in contrast to AAU basketball. But one can image that this rule may change in the future. Third, while 7-on-7 is not true football with blocking and tackling, never-the-less it allows one to showcase actual football skills more than just running a 40-yard dash at a combine.

So if your son is a skill player and can play on a good 7-on-7 football team over the spring and/or summer, then he probably should. Just be sure that the NCAA rules are being strictly followed. It may have particular value if your son is from a smaller high school since he, individually, can show his skills against kids from bigger schools.

D. **INTERNET RECRUITING WEBSITES**

The major players in this industry are:

(1) *Scout* http://recruiting.scout.com/;

(2) *Rivals* http://footballrecruiting.rivals.com/; and,

(3) *ESPN* http://espn.go.com/college-sports/football/recruiting/index.

(4) *247Sports* (CBS)) http://247sports.com/

This is a big money business, and they receive their revenue from advertisers and from football fans that pay subscription fees to access their recruiting content. However, much of their information is available to you for free. Having said that, I found their subscription content to be both helpful and informative. I suggest that if it is within your budget, that you subscribe to at least one such service. Either way, (free or paid), you should become familiar with them.

The business model of these sites includes a franchise-like arrangement. An entrepreneur sports journalist, for example, can acquire affiliation with the national website. Each major D-1 program has one or more such sites. Take For example coverage of Notre Dame football, with *IrishIllustrated* being the *Rivals* affiliate and having an internet URL of http://notredame.rivals.com. It will interview Notre Dame coaches, prospects, players and others, and write articles viewable by their subscribers. The website also has "blogs" where the subscribers (and the website's "moderators") dialogue with each other on a wide variety of topics, normally pertaining to their team. Some of the content is shared with *Rivals* nationally, which in turn makes it available on the national website and in some cases is also carried on other team's websites. The latter usually occurs if the article is about a recruiting prospect that is also being recruited by that other school. By being an affiliate, they also have access to the national site's huge database of all high school recruits nationwide (past and present).

This database is made up of profiles of each kid. You should set up a profile for your son on each website. It is free, and instructions on how to do it are on their website. Typically, you should do this during or right after his junior football season, but earlier if his varsity film and stats are impressive. It can make it easier for a college coach to find your son, although do not think that by creating such a profile alone will get your son discovered. Another feature of such profile is that they will post your son's, name, high school, stats, photo and his highlight film (*see* Chapter 5) as part of his profile. I just mailed them a DVD of our son's highlight film and they posted it on their sites.

These recruiting websites will also interview prospects and do short articles about them, but normally only after the kid has one or more scholarship offers.

I also had occasion to meet, and in some cases have meals with some of the sports writers from these sites. For example, I spent time with Jeff Baumhower (*notredame.scout.com*), David Lombardi *(stanford.scout.com)* and others. They are great guys. They love football and are very loyal to their site's team. However, they do not lose sight of the fact that they are dealing with 17 year old kids. They are circumspect, having seen the supposed "next big thing" super-studs roll through each year. If you have a chance to get their perspective on recruiting, it is worthwhile. However, be careful. You should assume that everything that you say to them will get back to the college coaches for that team. As journalist-entrepreneurs, they covet a good relationship with their team's coaches, and if they can help those coaches by giving them back channel information about your son, sometimes they will.

These websites also have fan "blogs". There is an astounding amount of interest and dialog about where high school seniors choose to go to play D-1 football. A good bit of it is useful. As with most of life, most of the participants in these blogs are very decent, reasonable people. However, there is a small percentage that needs to "get a life" and appear to be certifiable mental cases. Some others are simply rude. Moreover, speculation (very often wrong or incomplete) is the life blood of most of the blog chatter. I came to appreciate this after my son was playing college football and he would share inside information with me about the team (which I kept confidential). Yet, it was not uncommon to see blog posts on the sites for his team that claimed to be reporting "facts" or were drawing conclusions that were misleading or dead wrong.

These recruiting websites all have a system by which they rate and rank players at various positions. Along with the rankings, they all use a "star" system, such as where they classify a prospect as "NR" (not rated), 2-star, 3-star, 4-star, or 5-star, with more stars being better. *Rivals.com* and *ESPN* also use a numeric rating, whereas *Scout.com* does not. It is subjective and is their indicator of how highly they rate a prospect. For example, *Rivals.com* describes their ranking system as follows:

"Players are also ranked on their quality with a star ranking. A five-star prospect is considered to be one of the nation's top 25-30 players, four star is a top 250-300 or so player, three-stars is a top 750 level player, two stars means the player is a mid-major prospect and one star means the player is not ranked.

The ranking system ranks prospects on a numerical scale from 6.1-4.9:

6.1 **[5-Star]** Franchise Player; considered one of the elite prospects in the country, generally among the nation's top 25 players overall; deemed to have excellent pro potential; high-major prospect.

6.0-5.8 **[4-Star]** All-American Candidate; high-major prospect; considered one of the nation's top 300 prospects; deemed to have pro potential and ability to make an impact on college team.

5.7-5.5 **[3-Star]** All-Region Selection; considered among the region's top prospects and among the top 750 or so prospects in the country; high-to-mid-major prospect; deemed to have pro potential and ability to make an impact on college team.

5.4-5.0 **[2-Star]** Division I prospect; considered a mid-major prospect; deemed to have limited pro potential but definite Division I prospect; may be more of a role player.

4.9 **[NR]** Sleeper; no Rivals.com expert knew much, if anything, about this player; a prospect that only a college coach really knew about."

Many college coaches, when asked, will down play such website ratings or even declare them "irrelevant". Yet, most of those same coaches list those same rankings of recruits on their college's official team websites and/or tout to alumni groups their "top ranked" recruiting classes -- based on those very rating systems. If they are irrelevant, then why cite them? I do not know if it is true, but I have even read that some college coaches actually have bonus clauses in their employment contracts based on how high their recruiting classes are ranked.

Actually, in my opinion when looked at it in full context, the star system is statistically impressive *on average*. While far from perfect, the star system has been shown to be a very good indicator in terms of the overall *group.* Like all statistics, however, it is far less accurate in terms of predicting any one individual player. Internet bloggers love to hate the star system. Its merits and demerits are debated routinely.

E. **SPRING FOOTBALL AND OTHER SPORTS**

Some, but not all, states allow high school spring football. This tends to occur in the south with warmer weather. As the late Jones Ramsey said, "There are only two sports in Texas: football and spring football." If your son's school has this, then he will likely participate as part of his normal high school football program. If so, it may help his chances of being recruited, particularly if he attends a football powerhouse high school. This is because the NCAA allows D-1 college seven (7) assistant football coaches per team to visit high schools around the country and watch football practice during parts of April and May. This is known as an "Evaluation period". Note that by NCAA rule only assistant D-1 football coaches, not D-1 head coaches, may come out and evaluate your son during the spring. Coaches have limited time, so they cannot attend all schools. Thus, they tend to gravitate to high schools having a higher yield of D-1 prospects or schools where a prospect that they already have under consideration is practicing. If your son's school does not have spring football, this is a recruiting disadvantage over which you have no control.

This is another reason for your son to participate in a second sport and/or 7-on-7 football. D-1 football coaches can and do come to other sport's practices and observe athleticism.

I would strongly encourage your son to participate in camps, combines, 7-on-7 football, other sports, and spring football. However, time is limited so you must choose where to devote time and money. You can better balance those choices by understanding the benefits and limitations of each as discussed above.

CHAPTER 7

YOUR SON'S FIRST OFFER AND HIS DECISION

"A wise man makes his own decisions, an ignorant man follows public opinion."

- Chinese proverb

When your son gets his first offer, congratulations! It is quite an accomplishment. You should be proud; he is special. And he has beaten the odds. Treasure the moment and take him out to celebrate. It will be a huge relief off his and your minds and gives you affirmation that his dream to play college football is achievable.

A scholarship will certainly help the family finances. Also, if your son is a low-income student he may be eligible to apply for and receive a federal "Pell grant", in *addition* to the football scholarship. As of 2015 a Pell grant could be up to $5,730 and can help pay for travel and other various college expenses. Note that Pell grants are not limited just to football recruits.

The first thing to do upon receiving an offer is to be sure he does nothing to *lose* that offer. It happens. For example, if he gets arrested (guilty or not) or kicked off his high school team or suspended from school, the chances are very real that the scholarship offer will be withdrawn. He needs to keep his nose clean. Remind him that of the old saying, "nothing good happens after midnight". He also needs to keeps his grades up to be eligible. And, you and he should double check his *Facebook*, *Twitter* and other social networking pages, and scrub them clean. Coaches might withdraw a scholarships offers based on a student's foolhardy statements on social media. Those should also be monitored so "friends" do not post photos or comments that might cause concern or embarrassment to the football program that just offered him a scholarship.

If the offer is from his dream school, have him be certain. A list of some considerations is set forth in Appendix G. If it is what he wants and then have him accept it without artificial delay. If he delays too much, the offer may be withdrawn and given to someone else.

You and your son may think that what he is choosing where to play football. More than that, however, he is choosing who many of his best friends will be for the rest of his life. He should choose wisely. I cannot stress enough the importance of his evaluating the guys on the team, particularly in his recruiting class.

In any event, I suggest the following. First, earnestly thank the head coach and all other coaches that were involved in his recruitment. They put a lot of time and work to get to this point.

Second, politely ask the coach recruiting your son where your son is on their recruiting "board". Specifically, find out what position they are recruiting him for and how many other players that: (a) they have offered (or plan to offer) at his position; and, (b) how many they are willing to accept at his position in this recruiting class. This is important. No football team gets every recruit that they offer. As such, most every program offers more kids per position than they are willing to take. What this means is that if your son waits too long, other kids with offers at his position may make a verbal commitment, and your son's offer may then be withdrawn. The college coaches will normally talk to you about this. I even suggest that you ask them if they will keep you posted, in *advance*, if enough other kids commit that your son is in danger of losing his spot. This is one reason that I strongly suggest that you subscribe to a recruiting website like *Rivals, Scout* and/or *ESPN*. The respective website affiliate for each team tracks who commits to that team, almost on a daily basis. By following that, you can track how many other kids at your son's position have committed to that school. You can also track how many other such offerees to that school have committed to *other* schools, thereby reducing the chances that they will take that spot at the school that offered your son.

Third, find out the details of the offer. They may be stated in the offer letter. In particular, ask, "Coach, is the offer for a *guaranteed* four (4) year scholarship, or is it only a year-by-year scholarship?" Most are the latter, and thus could be pulled by the coach while your son is still in college (*e.g.* as a sophomore). However, perhaps this is negotiable, but only *before* signing a letter of intent. There obviously is a big difference in these types of scholarships, and not all offers are the same, even among the same recruiting class at the same college. If one school offers your son a guaranteed four year scholarship, whereas another school only offers a year-by-year scholarship, this may make his decision easy. Be sure that you ask. This is discussed more below in Chapter 10.

Fourth, stay in touch with the coaches. The last thing that you want is for the football coaches who offered your son to think that he has little interest. If so, he is effectively encouraging them to recruit other kids in his place. Do not be a pest, but return all calls and emails from them promptly, and reach out to them from time to time and visit them, particularly if they are close. Also, a key person in recruiting communications is often a non-coach member of the football staff with whom much of your contact. They usually have good people skills such as Stanford's Mike Eubanks, a true gentleman.

Fifth, have humility. There are a thousand other kids that they can still offer in place of your son. Even if your son has 50 offers, have humility to all. You son should never forget that one of them will eventually be his *coach*. Your son should treat them all the same way as he would if they were already his coach. They are grown, professional men at the very top of their business. They deserve the respect of a 17 year old kid. On our recruiting trips, I was dumb founded at the cockiness of a few (not most) of the recruits (and their parents) that enjoyed multiple offers. A few were arrogant and acted like they were God's gift to football and seemed to relish having the coaches who were recruiting them grovel. I kept thinking to myself, what is this coach going to do once this punk is his freshman piece of meat in a college football practice? Will the coach feed that kid, part by part, to the upperclassmen? Humility is not only morally correct, it is the smart thing to do.

If the school that offered is not your son's dream school, then having that first offer could help him with other schools. Admit it or not, coaches from one team are more likely to notice, and possibly to offer your son if another team has validated him with an offer. This seems particularly true amongst conference competitors. It can have a snowball effect. It is kind of like dating. If a boy is dating the popular girl, he may become more attractive to other girls. Do not rub your son's scholarship offer in the noses of other teams; but, do not ignore it either. If your son wants to get an offer from a particular school, quietly and respectfully make sure that they are aware that he has one or more other opportunities. Often, that will be easy. In recruiting, it is common for coaches to ask your son what other teams are recruiting him.

Your son has to strike a balance between his seeking other offers and risk losing the one or more offers that he already has received. This is largely determined by how highly sought after he is. The more he is sought after, the more he can afford to wait. Also, if he is genuinely conflicted then he should explore his options. Particularly, if you did not have the funds to pay for "unofficial" visits to schools of real interest, your son should probably take advantage of official (*i.e.* college paid) visit invites. He is allowed under NCAA rules to no more than five (5) official visits. However, taking five visits is very rare. Be advised, however, if your son is offered but not highly coveted by that team, they may withdraw the offer merely by his continuing to seek offers from other schools.

A typical agenda for an official visit is in Appendix F. By rule, they are limited to 48 hours, and the D-1 programs take full advantage of the available time. Official visits by your son are paid for by D-1 FBS teams. While D-1 programs may pay for a recruit's coach airfare, they may not pay for parent's airfare. They may, however, pay for family's driving mileage (if the recruit is with them) and certain food and lodging. If your son has been offered or is of interest to the program, an agenda for an unofficial visit (you pay) is usually about the same. Your son will meet with coaches, players, professors, academic advisors, strength coaches, and others. He will tour the campus, the stadium, the weight room, and the training and/or medical facilities. He will spend the evening with players already on the team. Some schools will require your son to sign an agreement to not engage in inappropriate conduct during such visit.

If your son has an offer he should not wait to verbally commit just for the sake of waiting or for the sake of taking official visits. It is rare for a recruit to have more than five schools that are *really* of interest. Usually, the real list is three schools or less. Your son owes it to the coaches recruiting him not to waste their time if he would not sign with them. Wanting to take, in effect, numerous paid vacations under the guise of official visits is, in my opinion, very bad form. Your son needs to be man enough to get past the ego stroking. For example, my son was recruited by several SEC schools, but he declined their early overtures because he had other offers and those SEC schools did not fit the academic profile that he wanted. Also, if you son is lucky enough to have multiple offers, remember life back before he had any offers. Somewhere out there is another kid, on the bubble, hoping to get an offer. The longer that your son delays, the more angst someone else will have to suffer. Plus, your son will get to take at least one official visit anyway to the school where he verbally commits.

Also, your son needs to consider the risk of injury, in high school football or otherwise. The tragic story of star football player James "Boobie" Miles losing his scholarship offers after injury is recounted in the book, and later movie, *Friday Night Lights*. Injuries happen, and if they do, scholarship offers may be withdrawn. They are, however, far less likely to be withdrawn after your son verbally commits to a school. If your son gets an offer, you should get a clear, express commitment from the head coach about his policy on that topic. All but one of our son's offering schools that we asked said that they would honor a scholarship, even after a career ending injury in high school (football, basketball or otherwise). But, this was true only *after* he verbally committed to them. I eventually figured out to ask head coaches directly about this issue, and

I suggest that you do the same once your son gets an offer. I do remember being very pleasantly surprised about this willingness of them to shift the risk of injury from the kid/family to the university, and I expressed that to one of the head coaches recruiting our son. In a refreshing moment of candor, that head coach told me that it was not that big of a deal because if they did not do that, other schools would use an unwillingness to do so against them in recruiting. Fortunately, we never had to see if that promise would be honored. In any event, the risk of injury is a big reason not to artificially delay committing.

Note that it may be possible, once your son has one or more offers, to get disability insurance for the value of a scholarship. Brent Williams, in his book *Recruit My Son*, reports that he negotiated such a policy in 2009 with Lloyds of London for $225,000 of coverage by paying a policy premium of $1,300.

After your son gets one or more offers, he will likely get called on the phone for interviews by the recruiting websites. The local newspaper may do the same. At first my wife and I had a few misgivings, but it actually was a very good learning experience for our son. Not many teenagers get the chance to deal with a media interview, and it was good for him. Your son should take those calls. They reporters and editors live their lives in the world of football recruiting and can positively influence future events in his recruiting. Also, those website reporters were always very nice and handle the recruits with kid gloves when interviewing and writing. However, your son should be positive and assume that everything he says will get back to the coaches of that team. It is a good idea to go over a few talking points in advance, and maybe even do a mock interview with him.

One factor that is frequently underestimated in deciding where to commit is the college team's depth chart. In the study, Drummond *et al., An Economic Model of the College Football Recruiting Process,* a team's depth chart was not a top factor in where elite recruits decided to go. If your son has multiple offers, however, in my opinion he should factor this in to his decision. He may feel like a football star now, but when he arrives on campus he will have an awaking about just how good the competition is to earn a starting spot. I talk about this more in Chapter 9. However, there is a great (free) tool to help your son see and understand the depth at each D-1 school. It is found on the *Scout.com* website for each individual team. It is a table, or grid, laying out position-by-position, who each of the older players is on the roster ahead of him. At that *Scout.com* team website, you will find the depth chart by clicking on the "Football Recruiting" menu, and under that then clicking on "Eligibility". The table will be displayed and is very helpful. I think that ego of high school recruits is one big reason that they may disregard the depth chart. They have always been the star player in their home town and it seems inconceivable to many that they would not be the star in college. Just remember that most every upperclassmen on the team ahead of him was also a star. The competition will be stiff and your son should consider the depth chart.

I believe that one of the most important factors in evaluating where to go play football is who are the other kids on the team and what is their character. This means primarily the kids in your son's recruiting class, but also the older players. Those guys will become your son's best friends throughout college and likely beyond. The young men at Stanford who are my son's teammates are simply exemplary. We also met some fantastic people on the recruiting trail that ended up at other schools.

When making the final decision, that is too personal for anyone to tell your son what to decide. However, one school that we visited for recruiting had us meet with a professor, Burke Robinson, whose specialty (in the field of business and management) was decision making. He taught classes on the subject and he had sage advice. He asked my son if most people were telling him to, "go with his gut". My son responded, "yes". The professor of decision making said that was the wrong approach. The decision was too important. He suggested that my son should carefully analyze and weigh all of the pros and cons of the decision.

"Go with your gut", is another piece of advice that you hear from a lot of recruiting coaches if your son has multiple offers. Another one is that he should choose a school that is the "right fit". Those sounds nice, but I am not sure what they really mean. They seem to be saying your son should not think; rather, he should decide based on feelings that he cannot or will not state out loud. I think that can be suspect. Your son has reasons in his "gut". If he won't state those reasons, there is a good chance that he is embarrassed to admit what are the *real* reasons. It might be that he understandably is embarrassed to admit that he likes school "X" over school "Y" because school "X" has a huge fan base that strokes his ego. If that is why he wants to go to school "X", so be it (he won't be the first). But he should be honest with himself why he is making that choice.

Another thing you hear repeated is your son "should choose a college based on the place he would want to be if he got injured and could no longer play football." This sounds lofty, but in my opinion is too simplistic. For your son to be in a position to get to choose between football schools, football must have been his *passion*. There are many great schools, and to try to ignore a major aspect of your son's life – college football – in making the decision seems absurd under the circumstances. However, the academics and college experience, apart from football, will hopefully be a major part of your son's decision. Coach Jim Harbaugh, a former *NFL* quarterback, had some better advice. He said do not think of playing in the *NFL* as "Plan A" while having a strong academic degree as a fallback "Plan B"; rather, he said that it should *all* be "Plan A". Namely, aspire to the *NFL* to then be followed by a successful life in the business world using the outstanding college degree. He pointed out that even the guys that make it to the *NFL* only are there for about 3-5 years on average and many *NFL* players do not make enough money in the league upon which to retire.

Regarding coaches that are recruiting your son, I sincerely believe that college football coaches on the whole are one of the best groups of people around. In my professional life as a patent and trademark attorney, I have had occasion to work with and against a wide range of professionals in almost any industry that you can imagine. There are honorable people, and there are scoundrels in each. And while there are a few bad apple coaches, as a percentage, the football coaches are a cut above most professions. They work incredibly hard, have a positive outlook on life, love their families, are wholesome, and want to help young people. So when you read about how some coach is horrible or incompetent (usually from some fan of another team) consider the source. That supposedly "horrible" coach is probably a person of higher character and ability than most people that you or I interact with daily.

Coaches, like all people, have strengths and weaknesses. I think that too often people oversimplify whether a coach is a "good" coach or a "bad" coach. All of them are better in some respects and weaker in others. In evaluating coaches consider the matrix in Table 5 (below). It separates out "football" skills and "people" skills, and it separates out

	Football	People
Games	• Winning. • Play calls. • Adjustments. • Risk management. • Clock management.	• Helping player's focus & state of mind. • Match-ups with opponent. • Substitutions. • Develop experience.
Preparation	• X's & O's knowledge. • Ability to teach. • Adjust playbook to fit player's abilities. • Game plan. • Fitness & strength training.	• Motivator. • Integrity / role model. • Surrounded by other good coaches. • Player talent evaluation. • Develop leaders. • Recruiting.

Table 5: Coaching Skills

skills during a "game" and skills in "preparation" for a game (and for life). Some coaches are great at teaching during practice the skills (X's & O's) of the game of football, but not so good at play calling. Other coaches may be great at recruiting, but not so good at making adjustments during a game. Also, the skill set to be a good head coach is not the same as those to be a good offensive or defensive coordinator. The same is true for position coaches. You need to consider which criteria are most important to your son and give priority to those.

College football coaching is also one of the most nomadic professions on the planet. They change jobs frequently, either because they were fired or because a better coaching job becomes available. As Vince Lombardi said, "If you aren't fired with enthusiasm, you will be fired with enthusiasm." It is ironic that the persons most involved in recruiting your son may be the ones least likely to be there throughout his college career. The true saints in all of college football are the *wives* of assistant coaches, constantly being uprooted due to their husband's career moves.

My son experienced quite a coaching carousel first hand. Charlie Weis, head coach at Notre Dame, recruited and offered my son, and my son eventually verbally committed to Notre Dame. Coach Weis' staff included one of the most accomplished and veteran defensive line coaches (the position where our son was being recruited) in the country, Randy Hart. Coach Hart represents what is good about football. Also, his resume includes being and NCAA D-1 national championship player and coach. Also, All-American and NFL All-Pro (and Super Bowl) star D-lineman Bryant Young was a graduate assistant at Notre Dame and a *great* person with whom I really looked forward to Blake having as a role model.

Coach Weis had gone to college at Notre Dame as an undergrad, and I met a guy that told me that he had lived in the same dorm as Coach Weis at Notre Dame. He said that Charlie Weis was regarded as a brilliant student and I met a classmate of his who told me that Charlie Weis had scored a perfect 1600 on his SAT. As we got to know Coach Weis as a person in recruiting, beyond his media image, he struck me as a guy who *really* cared about the kids on his team. For example, even after another kid broke his spine in high school he honored a prior scholarship offer to the kid since the kid had committed. Coach Weis' teams at Notre Dame as head coach overall had a winning record, but at 35-27 he was fired.

Charlie Weis replacement, Coach Brian Kelly, and his new D-line coach and defensive coordinator continued to recruit our son, including a gracious visit to our home. As is common, Coach Kelly had brought much of his staff with him from his prior school. Coach Kelly did not retain Coach Hart and Bryant Young (who later became the D-line coach at the University of Florida). Throughout the process, however, Coach Jim Harbaugh and his D-line Coach, D.J. Durkin at Stanford continued to recruit our son. But then Coach Durkin, (who was our son's primary recruiter and likely position coach), then went to the University of Florida to coach with Urban Meyer, and later to become UF's defensive coordinator. After coach Durkin's move, Coach Harbaugh hired (former Notre Dame) Coach Randy Hart to be Coach Durkin's replacement at Stanford. He and Coach Brian Polian (who later became a D-1 head coach at Nevada) continued to recruit our son to Stanford. Our son committed to Coach Harbaugh at Stanford. Then, a year later, Coach Harbaugh left to become the head coach of the NFL's San Francisco 49ers, leading them to the Super Bowl. He later became the head coach at the University of Michigan. Also, my son's college tenure saw four different defensive coordinators.

Yet it is not always that way; some coaches stay. Seasoned Coach Lance Anderson, our son's first position coach at Stanford, was the first coach that we met there and has remained throughout. He eventually rose to defensive coordinator at Stanford. He has coach a variety of positions and several of his players made NFL rosters. Coach Anderson was a great coach and also was named national recruiter of the year in 2012.

Likewise, David Shaw was there throughout, and he became Stanford's head coach after Coach Harbaugh. His team the following season (2011-2012) earned an 11-2 record and a Fiesta Bowl appearance, and the following years won two Pac-12 Championships and one of two Rose Bowls. Stanford was the only team that year to have played in four consecutive BCS bowls.

The coaching carousel came full circle our son's senior year. As he grew in size, he moved from linebacker to defensive line (DE) where Coach Hart again was the central coach in his daily college life.

The good news is that my wife raised our son to be wise, and he understood the inherent volatility of coaching jobs. Thus, he only placed limited weight on any one coach in deciding where to go. He can get along with most any personality and coaching style. As such, these comings and goings were not driving his decision. They are to be expected, and I would strongly suggest that your son try to discount his fondness for a particular coach in making a decision where to go. They often move on.

College coaches tend to leave in December and January, getting fired right after their losing season or getting hired by some other team right after their winning season. When a new head coach comes in, occasionally they will withdraw a kid's scholarship offer because in their assessment he does not fit into their system. This can be brutal to a kid in that it happens only a month or two before National Signing Day, in some cases leaving the kid with few options. Other times, the coach will honor the offer but also forewarn the recruit that he is not likely to play in games on his team. Still other times the new coach will want your son and continue to visit and recruit your son.

Regardless of turnover, in my opinion your son should not place as much importance on the *head* coach as you might think. Your son will spend *far* more time with his position coach. Yes, to the media, the fans, and the public, the head coach is the face of the program. However, your son will probably spend more one-on-one time with the head coach as a high school recruit than as a college player on the team. The head coach has literally hundreds of people that he is interacting with: coaches, staff, recruiting prospects, 105 players, administrators, alumni, and the media, just to name some. Thus, while the head coach is very important in terms of setting the tone and culture for a program, do not be swept up too much by his charms during recruiting.

An Indiana Basketball Hall of Fame high school head coach that I know told me he that had seen this several times over the years. He said in this regard, "Go with the coach that loves you." Of course, due to the fact that coaches come and go a lot (discussed above), this is hard to predict. Still, it is one factor to consider.

Speaking of likeable recruiters, Coach Jim Harbaugh is a great example. He is smart and funny. He also has this kid-like love of sports. However, he is a hard charger, particularly in football. He knows his stuff and was third in Heisman balloting for the 1986 season. In the *NFL*, he is one of the few players on the *Indianapolis Colts'* ring of fame in their stadium. He also was an example of the adage that it is a small world. In 1987 out of The University of Michigan, Jim Harbaugh was the first round draft pick by the *Chicago Bears*. My mother-in-law (Gloria McArdle) happened to be his realtor in Chicago back then. She had always raved about what a polite, respectful and humble young man he was to her, even as the new star quarterback of the *Bears*. Years later while he was recruiting her grandson, I was impressed that despite his fame and status in the *NFL*, he still remembered his realtor of more than 20 years earlier. When recruiting my son, he was selling a great product (Stanford University education and Stanford football), and he knew how to sell it. His "enthusiasm unknown to mankind" is hard to resist, and that made him a formidable recruiter. As a recruit and as parents, however, you need to both enjoy that but also try not to get too caught up in the charm either.

Another great coach and great recruiter that we got to know is Coach Pat Fitzgerald of Northwestern (my Alma mater). As a college player he was the first two-time winner in the history of college football (junior year and senior year) of both the Nagurski and the Bednarik national defensive awards. He is one *very* tough dude. In person he is even more remarkable. In my 50+ year old life I have had the opportunity to meet senators, governors, CEO's of major corporations, one rock star, sports celebrities and others – and none have exceeded Pat Fitzgerald in terms of presence and character. He is the most impressive individual that I have ever met. And yet, my son, who likewise *greatly* appreciated Coach Fitz and what he stood for, went elsewhere. The choice of where to go to college and play D-1 football should be based on weighing many factors, not just one person.

There were many other great coaches we encountered in recruiting, including for example class acts like Jim Grobe of Wake Forest, Al Groh of Virginia, Frank Beamer of Virginia Tech, Bill Lynch of Indiana, Frank Spaziani of Boston College, Bobby Johnson of Vanderbilt, Brian Polian, and many others. It makes you realize that despite an occasional unfortunate headline that gets much attention, the outlook for football overall is bright.

One item to understand is academic rankings. There are various "graduation rate" rankings (Federal, NCAA, and others), and various other general academic rankings of universities. You can bet that most programs recruiting your son will pick and choose among them and only show your son the most favorable rankings. Do you own homework to find the other rankings that the football program does not provide to you. Also, if academics are important to your son, beware of what I call the "bubble" football program. They are common at D-1 schools. Some football programs exist within very highly ranked universities; yet, a large percentage of the football players at some of those schools live in an academic "bubble" with an easy major of questionable value. In that situation, the overall ranking of the university means less. If that is what you son wants, that may be OK. But if the football program steers your son, against his desires and academic abilities, to a weak major, that may hurt his future.

Appendix G is a list of some of the questions that your son may want to consider in deciding where to go to college and play football.

Finally, once he commits, the football staff will help facilitate his transition to college. However, in the mean time when in doubt, ask them any question that might come up. All D-1 programs have a "compliance officer" on staff that is familiar with the complex NCAA rules. There are some very technical NCAA rules that may (or may not) apply, and your son does not want to risk his eligibility. For example, after our son had verbally accepted his offer from Notre Dame, to our surprise our son got unsolicited mail from fans wanting his autograph. Your son should first contact the university with such situations; they will be happy to help guide you as to what is permissible.

CHAPTER 8

YOUR SON SHOULD VISUALIZE LIFE AS A COLLEGE FRESHMAN

"Begin with the end in mind."

-Stephen Covey, author of "The 7 Habits of Highly Effective People".

While your son is a high school recruit, he should try to imagine life one year later as a freshman football player. He wants to play. He has always played. Heck, your son has always been a star player. He wants to be a starter and show his stuff. However, he should be realistic since the level of competition will be unlike he has ever faced. And he should keep that reality in mind when listening to a sales pitch by a coach who is trying to recruit him, particularly if they are filling his head with thoughts that he will be a starter his freshman year. A more honest sales pitch regarding playing time that your son may hear is, "You'll get a *chance to compete* for playing time." By realistically projecting into the future, he can make a better decision about where to end up.

Here is the reality. As a freshman, he will be low man on the totem pole, a youngster, under development, a kid, unproven and learning the playbook. Now he is a very strong boy. On campus, he will be going up against very strong *men.* The love that he felt as a high school recruit will be replaced with the same treatment given the other guys on the team. Most college coaches consider red-shirting a luxury and they *want* to red shirt him for the future. The legendary coach Paul "Bear" Bryant said, "You lose one game for each freshman you start." Red-shirting is by far the most common practice, and you will have many freshman teammate/friends sharing the same situation along with you. Many NFL stars red-shirted their freshman year in college. The list of red-shirted freshman is long and distinguished.

Remember this -- the coaches gave the same love and flattery that your son heard as a high school recruit to each class ahead of him. Those classes, like yours, have hot shots and super stars. They were all-state and all-world. If a coach tells your son that he *guarantees* that he will start as a true freshman, odds are that he is someone who is willing to stretch the truth. A D-3 head coach's advice for kids and parents was do not believe a coach's promise during recruiting about starting or playing time unless that coach assembles the whole team in a meeting with you present and makes the announcement there.

Few freshman at the D-1 FBS level even get to travel to away games, instead having to stay behind and watch them on TV. Most D-1 FBS conferences have rules limiting the size of the travel squad to about 70 players. Those rules help the universities contain costs while being equal with each other. Show me a football team that plays many freshman and I'll show you a team in trouble with a losing record. Indeed, I informally tracked players from the *Army All American* game, and it amazed me that even for players at that level how very few of them were starters as true freshman. Sure, there are a few exceptions. Also, by mid-season several had worked their way into "the two deep" – in other words they were second string.

And the lack of playing as a true freshman is directly related to the position that they play. As one college coach honestly told my son during recruiting, "the closer to the ball that you line up, the less likely you'll play as a true freshman." If your son plays offensive line, or in the defensive front seven (*i.e.* defensive line or linebacker), it is very rare for them to start as true freshman. This is because at those positions, size and strength are critical. Freshmen are boys among men. After several years in a college football weight lifting and nutrition program, your lineman or linebacker son will increase in both size and strength. And again, look at the general rule, not the exception to the rule. Yes, a few true freshmen started, but not many. Those who did were the outliers, and often were on teams with average or losing records and/or stepped in mid-season due to injuries to upper classmen.

By contrast, if your son's value is primarily pure speed, such as a wide receiver or cornerback or even running back, then his chances of seeing the field as a true freshman are somewhat better. Or if he is a great long snapper or field goal kicker, then age is less relevant. Those skills likely will not improve as much as a lineman will add size.

In addition to the physical barriers for true freshman, there are also mental barriers. All positions in college are more complex than high school football. College playbooks normally are far more complex than what your son experienced in high school. For example, my son's college team had about 350 offensive plays in their playbook. When they broke from the huddle, three plays had been called not including additional audibles. And that was just offense. Special teams and defense each have their own playbooks. And the playbook is critical. At higher level football, such as college (and even more so in the NFL) it is "assignment football". You must carry out your assignment or the team suffers. Reads must be made in the blink of an eye, with a 310 pound lineman bearing down on you. And if you do not know your assignment from the playbook, forget about it. You cannot get away with making up for mental mistakes with your athleticism. That may have worked in high school, but the players are too good in college football to allow that.

In fact, there are so few freshman starters that it is hard to even name a (true) freshman All-American team. To do it they include sophomores. In the Football Writers Association of America's Freshman All-American team typically, about one-third to one-half of them are really (academic) sophomores who were red shirted their freshman year, and thus had an extra year in the football program. As freshman, they were behind one or more upper classmen in the depth chart. So many Freshmen All-Americans did not even step onto the field their true freshman year.

In addition to the physical and mental barriers, there is also the disadvantage of a lack of collegiate experience. Experience, in football as in life, is important. And as a true freshman, you do not have much experience with the college game at college speed. It is much faster. The hits are harder. The schemes are more complex. You have less time to react. An error in where you throw the ball results in an interception. An error in your pursuit angle results in a missed tackle and a break away run.

The main time to gain experience, and to earn a starting spot on the team, is spring football. The NCAA allows each team fifteen (15) practices during the spring. Usually this is culminated by the team's "spring game", an inter-squad scrimmage. This spring practice is where much of the teaching of technique occurs and live experience is gained. This is also where much of the evaluation of who will play occurs. The college seniors from last season are now gone. The coaching staff is evaluating their new roster under live conditions for the first time. Unless your son enrolls early, namely begins college during December or January of his high school senior year (discussed more below), then he will miss this spring ball leading into his freshman season.

The other chance to gain experience is over the summer, and particularly at "camp" in August. This is where the team begins formal practice before the season. The team lives together, isolated, in a dorm. It is football 24-7 with no breaks. It is very much a grind. This is where starting positions are finalized. It is an extension of spring ball, but for the first time freshman get to try to earn a spot in the depth chart.

Many D-1 schools allow for early enrollment (second semester of the high school senior year), but some do not. Whether your son should *want* to do this is another matter. A friend and parent of a D-1 player that did this told me that kids that enroll early can get somewhat lost. They are half way between classes, not really being part of the sophomore class but not sharing the same bonding experience of the bulk of his freshman class arriving later. All of the new student orientation occurs at different times in the school calendar. Most of the other students on campus have registered for classes, taking the best ones, so your son may well be forced into a very limited choice of academic classes that remain. Your son will also miss spring of their high school year – prom, graduation, high school friends, and family. Whether this is right for your son and your family depends on his situation and temperament.

However, regarding early enrollment one should ask the question, why? What is the hurry? If he hates high school and is eager to get out, then early enrollment may be a good idea. But if he is enjoying himself in high school, he should not be too eager to leave that behind. Redshirt is not a dirty word. Your son will have only four (4) years of playing eligibility whether or not he enrolls early. Plus, those four (4) years may be more productive if he red-shirts. He will be a year older, bigger, and stronger. Patience is a virtue. The main downside of your son red-shirting, and it is a big one, is that he may (will) go crazy his freshman year. After many years of being the football star, he may not even step onto the field. That will be very hard. You need to help prepare him emotionally for that year in the semi-exile of red-shirting. But try to take the long view. As a high school senior looking forward, next season seems to be an eternity away. Yet as a college senior looking back, it will have gone by in a blink.

The time commitment to play college football is extraordinary. The so-called '20 hour rule' is very misleading because the way the NCAA rules count hours (called CARA, for "Countable Athletically Related Activities"). D-1 football entails more like 40-50 hours per week during the season, in addition to academics. Regardless of your views on player unionization, the federal National Labor Relations Board (NLRB) legal opinion, after a full trial regarding whether Northwestern football players where "employees", provides a detailed account of a D-1 football player's time commitment (footnotes omitted) throughout a year. It is very accurate. Quoting the Judge:

> The first week in August, the scholarship and walk-on players begin their football season with a month-long training camp, which is considered the most demanding part of the season. In training camp (and the remainder of the calendar year), the coaching staff prepares and provides the players with daily itineraries that detail which football-related activities they are required to attend and participate in. The itineraries likewise delineate when the players are to eat their meals and receive any necessary medical treatment.

For example, the daily itinerary for the first day of training camp in 2012 shows that the athletic training room was open from 6:30 a.m. to 8:00 a.m. so the players could receive medical treatment and rehabilitate any lingering injuries. Because of the physical nature of football, many players were in the training room during these hours. At the same time, the players had breakfast made available to them at the N Club. From 8:00 a.m. to 8:30 a.m., any players who missed a summer workout (discussed below) or who were otherwise deemed unfit by the coaches were required to complete a fitness test. The players were then separated by position and required to attend position meetings from 8:30 am. fundamentals. The players were also required to watch film of their prior practices at this time. Following these meetings, the players had a walk-thru from 11:00 a.m. to 12:00 p.m. at which time they scripted and ran football plays. The players then had a one-hour lunch during which time they could go to the athletic training room, if they needed medical treatment. From 1:00 p.m. to 4:00 p.m., the players had additional meetings that they were required to attend. Afterwards, at 4:00 p.m., they practiced until team dinner, which was held from 6:30 p.m. to 8:00 p.m. at the N Club. The team then had additional position and team meetings for a couple of more hours. At 10:30 p.m., the players were expected to be in bed ("lights out") since they had a full day of football activities and meetings throughout each day of training camp. After about a week of training camp on campus, the Employer's football team made their annual trek to Kenosha, Wisconsin for the remainder of their training camp where the players continued to devote 50 to 60 hours per week on football related activities.

After training camp, the Employer's football team starts its regular season which consists of 12 games played against other colleges, usually played on Saturdays, between the beginning of September and the end of November. During this time, the players devote 40 to 50 hours per week to football-related activities, including travel to and from their scheduled games. During each Monday of the practice week, injured players must report to the athletic training room to receive medical treatment starting at about 6:15 a.m. Afterwards, the football coaches require the players to attend mandatory meetings so that they can begin to install the game plan for their upcoming opponent. However, the only physical activity the coaches expect the players to engage in during this day is weightlifting since they are still recovering from their previous game. The next several days of the week (Tuesday through Thursday), injured players must report to the athletic training room before practice to continue to receive medical treatment. The coaches require all the players to attend mandatory practices and participate in various football related activities in pads and helmets from about 7:50 a.m. until 11:50 a.m. In addition, the players must attend various team and position meetings during this time period. Upon completion of these practices and meetings, the scholarship players attend a mandatory "training table" at the N Club where they receive food to assist them in their recovery. Attendance is taken at these meals and food is only provided to scholarship players and those walk-ons who choose to pay for it out of their own pocket.

Because NCAA rules limit the players' CARA hours to four per day, the coaches are not permitted to compel the players to practice again later in the day. The players, however, regularly hold 7-on-7 drills (which involve throwing the football without the participation of the team's offensive and defensive linemen) outside the presence of their coaches. To avoid violating the NCAA's CARA limitations, these drills are scheduled by the quarterback and held in the football team's indoor facility in the evening. A student athletic trainer is also present for these drills to provide medical assistance, if necessary. In the same way, around 8:00 p.m., the players will go to their coaches' offices to watch film on their own for up to a couple of hours.

During the regular competition season, the players' schedule is different on Friday than other days of the week because it is typically a travel day. For home games, the team will initially meet at 3:00 p.m. and have a series of meetings, walk-thrus and film sessions until about 6:00 p.m. The team will then take a bus to a local hotel where the players will be required to have a team dinner and stay overnight. In the evening, the players have the option of attending chapel and then watching a movie. At the conclusion of the movie, the players have a team breakdown meeting at 9:00 p.m. before going to bed.

About half of the games require the players to travel to another university, either by bus or airplane. In the case of an away game against the University of Michigan football team on November 9, 2012, the majority of players were required to report to the N Club by 8:20 a.m. for breakfast. At 8:45 a.m., the offensive and defensive coaches directed a walk-thru for their respective squads. The team then boarded their buses at 10:00 a.m. and traveled about five hours to Ann Arbor, Michigan. At 4:30 p.m. (EST), after arriving at Michigan's campus, the players did a stadium walk-thru and then had position meetings from 5:00 p.m. to 6:00 p.m. The coaches thereafter had the team follow a similar schedule as the home games with a team dinner, optional chapel, and a team movie. The players were once again expected to be in bed by 10:30 p.m.

On Saturday, the day of the Michigan game, the players received a wake-up call at 7:30 a.m. and were required to meet for breakfast in a coat and tie by no later than 8:05 a.m. The team then had 20 minutes of meetings before boarding a bus and departing for the stadium at 8:45 a.m. Upon arriving at the stadium, the players changed into their workout clothes and stretched for a period of time. They afterwards headed to the training room to get taped up, receive any medical treatment, and put on their football gear. About 65 minutes before kickoff, the players took the field and did additional stretches and otherwise warmed-up for the game. At noon, the game kicked off and Head Coach Fitzgerald, in consultation with his assistant coaches, was responsible for determining the starting lineup and which substitutions would be made during the course of the game. While most games normally last about three hours, this one lasted about four hours since it went into overtime. Following the game, the coaches met with the players, and some of those individuals were made available to the media for post-game interviews by the Employer's athletic department staff. Other players had to receive medical treatment and eventually everyone on the roster changed back into their travel clothes before getting on the bus for the five hour drive back to the

Evanston campus. At around 9:00 or 10:00 p.m., the players arrived at the campus.

Although no mandatory practices are scheduled on Sunday following that week's football game, the players are required to report to the team's athletic trainers for a mandatory injury check. Those players who sustained injuries in the game will receive medical treatment at the football facility.

In the years that the team qualifies for a Bowl game, the season will be extended another month such that the players are practicing during the month of December in preparation for their Bowl game – which is usually played in early January. The coaches expect the players to devote the same amount of hours on their football duties during the postseason (40 to 50 hours per week), with one key difference being that the players are no longer taking classes since the academic quarter ends in mid-December. While the players are allowed to leave campus for several days before Christmas, they must report back by Christmas morning. To ensure that the players abide by this schedule, they are required to give their flight itinerary to their position coaches before leaving campus.

Following the Bowl game, there is a two-week discretionary period where the players have the option to go into the weight room to workout. While the weight room is next to the football coaches' offices, NCAA rules prohibit coaches from conducting the players' workouts during this discretionary period. While the Employer's strength and conditioning coaches are allowed to monitor these workouts, various team leaders, including those players on the team leadership council, attempt to ensure that attendance is high at these optional workouts during this and the eight other discretionary weeks throughout the year.

In mid-January, the players begin a one-month period of winter workouts during, which they spend about one hour running and doing agility drills and another hour lifting weights four or five days per week. These mandatory workouts are conducted by the football team's strength and conditioning coaches as they critique each individual player's attitude and performance. During this time the players also receive medical treatment for any ailments or injuries. This treatment could take the form of something as simple as getting into a cold tub or having their ankles taped. As is done in the regular season, the scholarship players are required to attend mandatory "training table" after their workouts. In total, the players devote about 12 to 15 hours per week on these workouts.

In mid-February, the players have a one-week period referred to as "Winning Edge" which serves as a transition to Spring football. During this week, the football coaches separate the players into smaller groups and require them to compete with one another in various types of demanding competitions to test their levels of conditioning. The coaches also have the players lift weights in between these scheduled competitions. Overall, the players can expect to spend 15 to 20 hours on this week's mandatory activities.

From the conclusion of the "Winning Edge" until about mid-April, the players participate in Spring football which requires them to devote about 20 to 25 hours per week. In this period, the players wear their pads and helmets and resume practicing football skills. The football coaches also require the players to attend scheduled meetings so they can reinstall their offense and defense for the upcoming season. The players are similarly required to watch film of each day's practice to assist in their development while in these meetings. In addition, the coaches will designate times when the players must lift weights and improve their conditioning. This important two-month period serves as an opportunity for the players to impress their coaches and move up on the depth charts in the various positions they are competing for. At the conclusion of Spring football, the team holds its annual Spring game which is basically a scrimmage between the current eligible players.

Following the conclusion of Spring football, the players have a discretionary week in which there is no expectation that they remain on campus and train. The players then return to campus and begin Spring workouts, which are conducted by the strength and conditioning coaches. These mandatory workouts are similar to those performed in the winter and involve one hour of running and another hour of weightlifting. Besides one discretionary week in the first week in May, the workouts continue until about the beginning of June when the academic year ends.

At the end of the academic year, the players will return to their respective homes for a couple of weeks (which are discretionary weeks) before being required to report back to campus for Summer workouts, which are once again conducted by the strength and conditioning coaches. The team leaders will also use this time to teach the team's offense and defense to incoming freshmen. In fact, the players participate in 7-on-7 drills from 7:00 p.m. to 10:00 p.m., two times per week and watch film as part of their preparation for the upcoming season. In total, both the upperclassmen and incoming freshmen devote 20 to 25 hours per week on summer workouts before the start of training camp.

So part of choosing a college football program is trying to visualize the future. Have your son try to take an honest look ahead to the college freshman years and beyond. He should be realistic. That will help him make a better decision. It will also help emotionally prepare him for the competition, hard work and fun ahead. If he starts as a freshman, or at least plays some, you have even more reason to be proud of him.

CHAPTER 9

OVER-SIGNING, GRAYSHIRTING AND THE UGLY SIDE OF RECRUITING

"Have we got a college? Have we got a football team?
Well we can't afford both.
Tomorrow we start tearing down the college."

- Groucho Marx in the movie Horse Feathers

The majority of college football programs run a clean ship. They are competitive, but are fair, honest and ethical. Most of college football is *very* positive; but, at the same time do not be naïve either. One head coach warned us, "Recruiting is full of smoke and mirrors". Sadly in the unbridled zeal to win at football and make money, some college programs emotionally crush kids with sloppy or unscrupulous practices. Some others simply lie and cheat.

Over-signing is one such unethical, but legal, culprit. Over-signing means that a college program has more high school senior (or junior college) recruits sign National Letters of Intent than the program has spots on the team. When that happens, someone gets left out in the cold. Grayshirting (explained below) is one possible consequence of Over-signing. Dropping kids from the team is another. That someone left out in the cold is either one of the high school recruits or is one of the upperclassmen already on the roster. Note that if you sign onto a program and you dodge that bullet as a high school recruit, do not assume that you are safe. Remember, most NCAA scholarships are often only for one year and require renewal each year by the head coach (*compare*, guaranteed 4-year scholarship). The same coach that cut an upperclassman to make room for your son might later cut your son (and therefore take away his scholarship) if he does not pan out as the coach had hoped. And this is not limited to complete crash and burn football failures. I read a recent account of a high profile D-1 football program doing that, late in the recruiting calendar when a highly sought after high school senior decided to choose that college. But, they were full up. So the program cut a college junior from the team during the summer before his senior season. That junior in the past had been a starter in almost 20 games. Yet he was tossed overboard. According to the interview in the sports media, the kid was shocked. Yet, because the program's coach was willing to over-sign, he cut the upperclassman in the middle of his college career. Be wary of signing on with a program like that.

One thing that you can and should do, even after your son verbally commits to a team, is monitor the number of other verbal commits there are for that team. For FBS D-1 football, if the number of commits exceeds 25 then somebody will get left out. Also, monitor this as compared to the total number of older scholarship players on the roster that will return the season that your son is a freshman. If there are more than 60 upperclassmen scholarship players returning, then there is a good chance that the team will only have room for less than the 25 per year limit in your son's class.

The over-signing problem has improved over the years, and hopefully (in my parental opinion) will be fully outlawed by the NCAA at the insistence of university presidents who control the NCAA. So far, the problem varies from conference to conference and school to school. For example, on the positive side of this issue, the Big Ten Conference has rules that are far stricter than the current NCAA rules about Over-signing. As such, this practice is virtually non-existent in the Big Ten Conference. Many of the most aggressive over-signers are in the SEC. The NCAA stepped in and recently changed its rules to reduce, but not eliminate, this problem nationwide. This rule change followed after one

SEC school over-signed by having a whopping 38 recruits. The NCAA thereafter placed a limit of 28 signees per year, from which only 25 of those 28 signees can actually receive their scholarship that year. The SEC, in response to criticism, placed a limit of 25 (rather than 28) signees. On a sustained basis, however, even 25 scholarships leaves much room for abuse since there is an 85 total scholarship limit per team. Hence, depending on whether you look at college careers as lasting 4 years or 5 years (with redshirting), the math is somewhere between: 4 X 25 = 100 or 4 X 5 = 125. Thus, either result using the 25 man per year cap, 100 or 125, obviously exceeds the 85 scholarship total. It is more complicated due to kids flunking out, being kicked off the team for disciplinary issues, dropping out, being given a medical exemption due to injury (purported or real) or otherwise. One resource is a website devoted to this topic is: www.oversigning.com. It lists figures, by university, regarding their over-signing history. The SEC is not the only conference that has teams that over-sign, and not all SEC teams do this. At least one SEC coach has been outspoken against over-signing.

Fortunately, some leaders are speaking out even in view of the current 25 per year scholarship cap. Below is a February 2011 public letter from then President of the University of Florida, J. Bernard Machen:

"For most young people, the decision on where to attend college is one of life's most important events. It involves analysis and contemplation by the student and a contract of acceptance (and scholarship in the case of student-athletes) by the institution.

Once this contract is agreed to there is a great joy and it represents the beginning of a new journey for the student. It is a life-changing event.

Imagine the feeling if the student finds out, literally a few months before enrolling, that the institution is backing out of the contract. It is too late in the summer to go back to one's second choice. The student is told he will have to wait until next year. Sorry, but no acceptance, no scholarship. That's it.

In Division I college football this practice is known as "grayshirting" and, unfortunately, there are universities that sanction this activity. The universities, with full knowledge of what they are doing, extend more athletic scholarships than they have. These schools play roulette with the lives of talented young people. If they run out of scholarships, too bad. The letter-of-intent signed by the university the previous February is voided. Technically, it's legal to do this. Morally, it is reprehensible.

Associated with "grayshirting" -- and equally disgusting -- is the nefarious practice of prematurely ending student-athletes' scholarships. Some are just not renewed even though the student-athlete is doing what is asked of him.

Some students are mysteriously given a "medical exemption" which ends their athletic careers -- and makes another scholarship available for the football coach to hand out.

There are, to be sure, some legitimate circumstances that result in scholarship non-renewal but regardless of the situation it is the student athlete who is impacted and the university that benefits.

No university would allow this for the general student body. Imagine the uproar it would cause! What needs to happen in intercollegiate athletics is that universities must accept the moral responsibility to stop and prevent "grayshirting" and its associated actions. The football programs must be accountable and should honor institutional commitments to students. It is, after all, a moral contract."

Perhaps if his call is heeded, this problem will be outlawed someday. Some coaches, who get fired unless they win, will not self-regulate under a sense of ethics. Until the university presidents and their NCAA (who the presidents control) outlaw this, be advised and protect your son. Study the past and present number of scholarship signees per year at a school. If it consistently averages over about 20 kids per year, take an even closer look. You may be looking at a team who tosses kids off their roster.

Recent history confirms that some D-1 universities view your son more as a disposable employee than as a student. Whether or not a program "over-signs", some programs have been willing to dump your son from their roster if it helps their football program. For example, if he does not pan out to be as good a player as they thought, they may try to push him off the team to make room for younger recruits and/or make room for fifth-year players. Or, if the college hires a new coach to help them win more, the new coach may decide that your college son does not fit his style. If he/you cannot afford to pay tuition, depending on the school, he may have to drop out of college. The power to do this resided in the NCAA's *former* rule (Bylaw 15.3.3.1), that *mandated* that each NCAA school only offer athletic scholarships for one (1) year, renewable each year at the discretion of the coach. Thus, even if a college wanted to offer four (4) year athletic scholarships, it was prohibited from doing so by rule. This bizarre rule has since changed, but its history is relevant to help understand the outlook of some (and perhaps many) college football programs.

After an inquiry by the U.S. Justice Department, the NCAA board voted to allow (but not require) schools to offer full four (4) year scholarships. However, the NCAA has a voting procedure (called an "override") where its member schools may protest such a rules change. And protest some schools did. Eighty-two (82) of 355 D-1 schools, enough for an override, voted for the override. It seemed that most of these protests came from FCS and/or lower tier FBS schools that had athletic departments that were struggling financially. The written protests, posted on the NCAA website, included the following harsh rationale for keeping scholarships at one year. One FCS university wrote to the NCAA:

> "...the new coach may have a completely different style of offense/defense that the student athlete no longer fits into," ... "Yet, the institution is 'locked in' to a [four or five] year contract potentially with someone that is of no 'athletic' usefulness to the program."

Remember, your son – whom the new coach deemed no longer a "fit" – signed his National Letter of Intent with the school and not the old coach, will have to sit out a year if he wants to transfer. Yet, the old and new coaches are free to change schools at will. Their new "style" of offense/defense was more important to them than your son's education.

Another university was just as ruthless if your son got hurt playing for them. It stated to the NCAA:

> "Multiyear grants-in-aid become problematic when career-ending injuries occur," ... "The current award period is a year, and student-athlete already receives the benefit of a full year of aid if career-ending or season-ending injury occurs. Institutions can already assist

students in future years even though the amount of aid is decreased. But if all institutions begin awarding multiyear grants to remain competitive in the market place, the cost of a full grant for injured student-athlete will increase overall costs."

In other words, that school did not want to have to pay tuition for your son after he suffers a career-ending injuries while playing for them. But it is worse than that. They also wanted to *require* all the other schools to do the same, correctly fearing that they would be less attractive to a recruit who is being offered a four year scholarship by another school. They not only wanted to be ruthless; they wanted the NCAA to require every other school be just as ruthless. So much for some school's concern for the "student" in 'student-athlete'. Mind you, this is the schools, *not* the NCAA, advocating ruthlessness.

Fortunately this one ended well in 2012, but just barely. Due to the override, the NCAA Board of Directors submitted the question to a vote by the full membership. Sadly, while the majority those universities that voted (205 out of 330)(37 did not vote) cast their vote *against* four year scholarships, those opponents still fell short by two votes. To overrule the four year scholarship option previously approved by the NCAA Board required 207 votes. So now four (4) year scholarships are allowed (but not required) by the NCAA. If your son gets multiple scholarship offers, be sure that you know which schools are offering four year scholarships and which are offering less.

While education won one here, this bit of history is informative. It reveals how some universities view their scholarship athletes. And this was not limited to schools that were struggling with a financial deficit in their sports program. Apart from the many FCS schools, who generally have much less money, here are the major schools that voted against even *allowing* four (4) year scholarships, including some very wealthy programs: ***ACC:*** *Boston College, Clemson, Florida State, Georgia Tech, Virginia;* ***Big East:*** *Boise State, Cincinnati, Louisville, Navy, Rutgers, San Diego State;* ***Big 12:*** *Baylor, Iowa State, Kansas, Kansas State, Oklahoma, Oklahoma State, Texas Tech, TCU, Texas, West Virginia;* ***Big Ten:*** *Wisconsin;* ***Pac-12:*** *Arizona, Cal, Colorado, USC;* ***SEC:*** *Alabama, LSU, Tennessee, Texas A&M.* Most every school will say to you and your son that an education comes before football. Talk is cheap. Measure those words against how they actually voted.

Even now, however, which schools actually do offer 4-year guaranteed football scholarships seems to be a bit of a secret, and perhaps a big secret. In September of 2014, *CBSSports* published the results of an open records request for 43 universities on the topic. First, the fact they had to jump through those hoops is telling in and of itself. Why do universities seem to hide this? The results of their investigation there made it clear than still many schools did not offer multiyear scholarships. And even many that do only do so for a limited number of their athletes. Otherwise, as of the publishing of this book, I cannot readily find any list of which schools currently offer 4-year (or at least multi-year) football scholarships. It seems that some may offer 4-year guaranteed scholarships for highly coveted recruits, but not to other kids. It is simply not clear. Thus, if your son gets an offer, be sure to get clarification. However, in October 2014 the *Big-10* and the *Pac-12* now require their schools to provide 4-year scholarships so long as the player maintains good standing in school and follow the rules. It will be interesting to see which other conferences or schools follow.

A legal bill introduced in the U.S. Congress in 2013 to *require* 4-year guaranteed scholarships never made it to a vote.

Another problem with some teams can be the bad character of players on the team. Some programs do not seem to actually care much about character of the kid's on their team. Regarding this, *Sports Illustrated* and *CBS News* reported a study that they conducted of the top 25 pre-season ranked D-1 football programs of 2010. Of those top 25 teams, seven percent (7%) of their players had been charged with or cited for a crime, either in high school or college. Forty percent of those incidents were for robbery, violent crimes or sex offenses. At the extreme end, one of those top 25 ranked teams had 22 players that had been charged with crime. While that university took in over $35 million in football revenue that year, a criminal background check in one state (where a recruit lives) costs as little as $24. Yet, only two of these top 25 universities even did criminal background checks, and none of them checked juvenile records.

Some programs embarrass themselves with their justification to not check – they indicated that if they do criminal background checks, then their competing schools might use that against them in recruiting. Maybe more programs will figure out that they can sell to recruits (and their parents) that their team *does* conduct criminal background checks, and that they can be comfortable that their son is going to be surrounded by high-character friends on the team. As a parent during recruiting, you may want to ask about whether they do criminal background checks.

A few programs will take nearly anybody (ex-rapists, robbers, etc.) so long as they can play football well. Graduating, or for that matter even going to class, seems to some of these extreme programs to be largely a distraction from football. In fairness to the coaches in such programs, often they are behaving consistently with the outward rewards (money, glory) and punishments (getting fired) that their universities put in place for them. In short, football coaches (virtuous or sleazy) are a reflection of their university President and trustees. High level D-1 head coaches are paid millions of dollars to win football games. Many are not paid to be sure that their kids graduate. When nearly half of their players fail to graduate with a degree, that is not their problem, at least not if parents and recruits do not hold their programs accountable for their non-football record as well. They are off to the next recruiting class. Imagine if a coach's contract stated that he only got paid the same percentage of his base salary as the percentage of kids that stayed with his program four years and graduated. That would be a university putting its money where their mouth is.

Sometimes you see such a coach in a TV interview waxing philosophical and fondly recounting one of their former players who did succeed in the world after D-1 football. Yet, somehow they forget to mention the long list of their ex-players with no college degree. Those players are the forgotten ones. You never seem to hear that coach in those interviews say, "yeah, Jimmy was a heck of a nose tackle for us, but he didn't graduate so now he is stuck as the assistant toilet cleaner at the local BurgerDoodle." Parents, *you* need to be the one looking out for your 17 year old kid. Those programs will not. Some of those universities will not either – they are too fond of the big money that college football brings into their coffers. We have all read news accounts of corrupt booster money and other gifts that find its way to a prize recruit. Of course, these programs would, all things being equal, prefer kids of good character. But too often some of them just never seem to get around to actually acting on that.

A common justification used by such programs does not withstand scrutiny. They actually congratulate themselves for being *noble* and giving the convicted criminal a "second chance" by letting him play football for them (and their ticket gate). They would have you believe that they are doing *him* a favor. But what they know (but hope that you ignore) is that by so doing, they deprive *another* kid of the chance to go to college and to play D-1 football. The cap of 85 scholarships means that for each player added, another is left out. It is a zero sum game. Consider the following hypothetical, using a rating system of a football player's ability from zero to 100, with 100 being a perfect score. Player A is too poor to afford college, is a 92 rated football player, is a weak student, and has been in repeated trouble including a conviction for robbery. Player B is too poor to afford college, is an 88 rated football player, is a good student, has good character, and no criminal record. The win at all costs coach, and his fine university, welcome Player A (the convicted robber) with open arms. Meanwhile, Player B (good student, good character) gets no offer, and because he cannot afford college he does not get to go to college and does not get to play D-1 football. And for this these universities congratulate themselves? They are not being noble. They are simply awarding the opportunity based on football skills with little regard for academics or character. It's good for university cash flow but not so much for ethics. In deciding where to go to college your son should look at this with eyes wide open.

Of the 'bad character' programs, some having winning records and some have losing records. And when they win many of their fans adore them regardless. It is all very glamorous. I think that is even after the majority of coaches, who do care about good character, fill out their roster there are still enough skilled football players that are not of good character to fill out several other team rosters. Some programs go further and knowingly break the rules, or ignore rules being broken by others. My advice is to run from those environments. Guys on the team will become your son's best friends. On a roster filled with criminals, your son runs the risk of being exposed to some very bad culture and bad examples. There are plenty of good programs out there; avoid the bad ones.

Let me be clear – in my experience the bad football programs are the exception to the rule. Most football coaches are fine role models for your son. Also, assuming that there often is a correlation between money and corruption, it is reasonable to conclude that corruption is less likely and less severe at the D-2, D-3 and NAIA levels. The lesser amount of NCAA and NAIA recruiting restrictions present at those levels of football supports that conclusion.

Even the majority -- the honest programs -- when recruiting your son will put their best foot forward. They are in effect salesmen for their football program. And all salesmen emphasize the positive and deemphasize the negative. For example, some schools will not even pay for a scholarship player's summer school, food or dorm over the summer; or, they have numeric limits on how many players for whom they pay for that. During the recruiting process they may not lie about that, but they will not volunteer that problem either. Be sure that you ask because as a practical matter if he wants to play he will have to stay on campus over the summer. Likewise, the food during recruiting visits will be better, the locker room cleaner, and the people more cheerful. There is nothing wrong with putting their best foot forward, but you and your son should keep that in mind when evaluating programs.

Corruption can even occur with your son being a pawn without realizing it. One scenario is as follows. Some guy, maybe a trainer, a 7-on-7 coach, or other person who seems to have "connections" in college football, offers to help your son get recruited. Naturally, you and your son are grateful for the help. However, the closer he becomes to your son, the more influence he may have over your son, like a surrogate father figure. Or at least to college coaches, this guy may *appear* to have influence on your son. What you may not realize is that in exchange for money (from a corrupt university or a corrupt booster) paid to this guy he will try to influence your son's choice of where to play football.

In a publicized case, a high school head football coach pled guilty in federal court to accepting a $150,000 payment from an *SEC* university booster to steer the coach's star player to that booster's university's team. After starting several games, when the scandal came to light the player was released from the university team and had to transfer to a smaller school. His very real prospect of making an *NFL* roster was derailed.

Sometimes the payback to the manipulating adult is something other than cash. I spoke with a former college football staffer that told me of a high school head coach steering top players on his powerhouse high school team to one university, not for money, but rather to better position himself to get hired on as an assistant football coach at that university. The high school coach allegedly did not even notify his player-prospect of some interest expressed by other universities. While such practices are obviously very rare (and pathetic), keep a watchful eye out for your son. Do not abdicate the recruiting process to another person.

However, sometimes high school recruits are dishonest as well. For example, some lie about having a scholarship offer from a school when they do not. Presumably, this is for bragging rights or to try to pump up the perception of their value as a football player so as to trigger actual offers. Georgia Tech's head coach, Paul Johnson, was candid about this: "A lot of kids will say that they have offers, and we don't know who they are. It's easy for kids say they've got an offer from whomever and because of the NCAA rules, no one can refute what they say. I'm sure it happens a lot."

Also, corruption can occur after your son is at college. For example, an agent or the agent's runner may try to (illegally) provide a player with cash or other value. The motive often is to entice an NFL prospect to sign an agency contract so as to receive an agent's commission. In a football program, the team will hold multiple meetings with players reviewing compliance with the law and with NCAA rules.

The future of recruiting will continue to unfold. However, already there are some pretty scary indicators on the horizon. For-profit businesses are already starting to sell mail-in kits for genetic testing of kids for certain genes supposedly linked to athletic ability. These include testing for variants of a genes known as "ACE" and "ACTN3". This industry is in its early stage and certainly has critics, including statements from medical researchers that say that using these tests for sports purposes are based on gross assumptions and also raise ethical questions. Is our zeal to win football games without boundaries? May God help us.

But do not despair; just be wise in guiding your son in his choice.

CHAPTER 10

FROM ONE PARENT TO ANOTHER

"If you're mad at your kid, you can either raise him to be a nose tackle or send him out to play on the freeway. It's about the same."

- Bob Golic, NFL Pro-Bowl defensive lineman

A friend of mine quotes Stephen Covey: "The main thing is keeping the main thing the main thing." Your relationship with your son is more important than football. Football is a game. I love football intensely, and I do not mean to underestimate how important it could be in your son's life. It could fund a college education. It could open admissions doors to a university. It could lead to contacts later in a career. And, in very rare cases it could lead to playing a few years in the *NFL*. But, one goal that I set for myself in the recruiting process was for my son, in gaining a scholarship, to never lose his father. He did not. We had a lot of fun together in the process. However, he was one of the fortunate ones – he had many scholarship offers. I have to believe that it would have been far more stressful if he did not have any opportunities. Plan for that possibility of Ivy League, D-2, D-3, NAIA or JUCO football from the beginning as well. Do not put all of your son's eggs in the D-1 basket.

Your son has to actually *do* what he can do to get recruited. If you have to yell at your son, or get after him to lift weights, or to speed train in high school, or to go practice, then he probably does not have the inner drive and passion to play at the college level. Football is a disease. Either you have it or you do not. College football is a lot of work. It is so much work that I have known several ex-college football players that said playing in college killed, or came close to killing their love of the game. If your son, in the comparatively carefree world of high school football, is not self-motivated to want it and want it badly, then nothing else probably matters. That does not make him a bad person. If that is the case, accept it and love him for who he is.

Likewise, if you want him to play football badly, ask yourself this question: Why? Is it to save the cost of tuition? Is it an ego boost for you? Is he accomplishing what you could not? Do you want it because it is what he wants? I will tell you, if you are honest with yourself the answer to each of those probably is a little bit 'yes' to each. That's OK. I would be lying if I did not acknowledge some of those feelings myself. It is OK to be a proud parent. However, the first step is to admit that you have those 'issues'. Then you can deal with them and manage them. Then you can step back and focus on *his* feelings and on helping him.

Also, be considerate of siblings and other family members. Blake's sister, Grace, sacrificed a lot of weekends, spring break time, and otherwise to make time for his recruiting. She did so with a great attitude and later reflected positively on the experience by appreciating that she got a head start checking out some different college campuses. Our entire family is *very* appreciative of her unselfish support.

You also want to be wise in how you deal with college and high school coaches. Do not burn bridges. For example, if some college coach is not showing the proper level of interest in your son's talent, no amount of yelling at the coach or complaining will help. You would simply be dismissed as a 'problem' family, and the coach will be reassured in his initial impression that your son is not worth the trouble. And your son may be the one who pays the price later.

It is easier for a coach to say "no" than "yes" when deciding whether to give someone a scholarship. Do not give him a reason, such as lack of trust, to say "no" to your son. I think that many recruits (or their parents) exaggerate or outright lie about their son's speed, stats or other achievements just to get noticed. I do not know if that works initially, but I do know that coaches do their due diligence before giving him an offer. They do not just take dad's word for it that his son runs a 4.5 40-yard dash. Thus, if you or your son exaggerates or lies, you have just given the coach a good reason to ignore what you say in the future. No information is better than misleading information. And if the coach sizes you up as providing misleading information, your ability to talk with him is greatly diminished. This means that in the future when you want to give him honest, factual information that might help convince him that your son should receive an offer, he may simply tune it out. And that is true if you lie or exaggerate about just one or two things. Once a person learns that another is willing to lie, they rarely want to try to figure out when the other person is lying and when they are truthful. Life is too short, and it is rarely worth the trouble. Remember, there are 1,000 other kids that want that scholarship too.

College football coaches know more about football than you do. In fact, they have forgotten more about football than you know. So when dealing with college coaches, try to give them what they want – hard facts. Give the facts and avoid *characterizations*. Learn to appreciate the difference. Here are some examples to illustrate the difference:

(a) "His personal best pro-agility time is 4.2 seconds." (fact) vs. "He is the quickest player in the state." (characterization).

(b) "Note on film clip 3 how the quarterback saw my son coming and turned around and ran backwards." (fact) vs. "Quarterbacks are scared to death of my son." (characterization).

(c) "His 40 time at a combine last month was 4.75 seconds." (fact) vs. "My son is a fast as the wind." (characterization).

(d) "My son caught 13 touchdown passes his junior season." (fact) vs. "As a receiver, he has unbelievably good hands and breakaway speed." (characterization).

(e) "He weighs about 295 lbs., depending on the day." (fact) vs. "He blots out the sun." (characterization).

When you stick to the facts and they are later verified to be true the coach is more likely to actually listen to you in the future. That gives you the opportunity to credibly point out other positives facts about your son. Otherwise, you run the risk of being tuned out like the noise from so many other extremely proud fathers or mothers just bragging and exaggerating about their son.

Also, do not be a 'hover' mom or dad. Stand back, or better yet excuse yourself from the room and let the college coach have a man-to-man, eye-to-eye, one-on-one discussion with whom they are really interested in – your son. They are interested in evaluating him, not you.

Consider your recruiting efforts in terms of geography and distance from home. Normally, your son's chances of landing an offer are better if he targets a school in state or at least within 200 miles of home. Three Ph D. candidates at Florida State studied what factors recruits use in deciding which college football team to sign with. They (Drummond, Lynch and Plantania) published their results as, *An Economic Model of the College Football Recruiting Process, Journal of Sports Economics, February 2008, 9: 67-87.* They concluded that among heavily recruited players choosing from among only major-conference schools, distance from home was the most important factor in a recruit's choice.

What does this have to do with college *coaches,* and their offering your son or not? College coaches are smart and are well aware of this phenomenon - that a kid that they offer who lives nearby is more likely to commit to them than one who lives far away. The coach's recruiting time is limited. Thus, for many of them they tend to seek the highest return on their recruiting time investment by focusing mainly on kids in state or within about 200 miles. This is particularly true of colleges that are located in high population areas that are rich in good football prospects. Texas, Florida and California, all large population states, are prime examples.

There is another reason for your son to try to get the local, in-state universities to offer him a scholarship: it will improve his chances of *also* drawing interest from out-of-state football coaches. Those out-of-state coaches may reasonably assume that the in-state football coaches have a better idea of who are the high school football players within their own home state with college potential. If the home state universities do not offer your son, this could be viewed by the out-of-state coaches as a blemish on your son's football resume.

However, the recruiting focus on in-state kids is not always the case. The two main exceptions are: (1) schools located in low population states that cannot locally provide enough quality recruits to fill their roster (some examples: Oregon, Wisconsin, Iowa, Nebraska); and, (2) schools whose higher academic standards require them to cast a wider net (some examples: Stanford, Northwestern, Duke, Notre Dame, Ivy League schools). You can roughly gauge this by looking at a college team's roster on their website. It will show the hometown of each player.

What this means for you and your son is that in targeting schools, factor geography in to your strategy. The further away your son's preferred schools are, the more proactive he will need to be in letting them know that he is the exception, namely that he is interested in them and is willing to go to college further away from home. Otherwise, there is a good chance the coaches will never even learn that your son exists. This is particularly true if the school(s) that he is targeting are not within the two exceptions (low population state; high academics) mentioned above.

This focus on local kids is even more acute with D-2, D-3 and NAIA programs. They have neither the time, staff nor recruiting budget to cast a nationwide recruiting net. They tend to rely even more heavily on a network of local high school coaches and others.

Also, be aware that D-1 schools assign each of their position coaches a geographic recruiting territory. Thus, you should find out who that is for your territory when you call the football office and include him in all of your correspondence. Some teams post the coaches' territories on their website. If your son gets an offer, he (along with your son's future position coach) will be heavily involved in recruiting your son. D-2, D-3 and NAIA coaching staffs do this too, but often the regions do not collectively cover the entire nation, but rather are regions closer to campus.

It is important that your son shows a coach that he is truly interested in his college and its football program. Football coaches like enthusiasm. Also, they do not like giving offers and spending time recruiting a kid if they think that there is little chance of him going there. So show enthusiasm. Yet, I have also heard that at the same time you do not want to come across as being desperate. If you do, then the coaches may think that they could defer making a scholarship offer (and pursue more talented prospects) since your son will be available and would accept a football scholarship any time. Thus, balance the enthusiasm with subtly sharing with the coaches an honest list of other schools that also are viable school choices for your son.

So what do college coaches want? To review, here are the basics:

(a) Game highlight film (less than 7 minutes);

(b) Full game film (one or two games);

(c) See your son in person (the so-called 'eyeball' test);

(d) Talk with his head football coach about his ability, work ethic, and intangibles;

(e) Talk directly and privately with your son (without mom or dad steering the discussion) to assess him;

(f) See your son's running, agility and athleticism in person (such as at one of their football camps);

(g) Independently verifiable speed and other statistics (such as from combines);

(h) Accurate football statistics and honors (all-state; 128 tackles per season, etc.);

(i) Assurance that your son has interest in them and would be willing to come to their school, even if far away; and,

(j) Confirmation of his academic and amateur eligibility.

With those, hopefully your son will receive one or more offers.

Fig. 5: Spoils of War:
Player Rings and Souvenir Pins from Two Rose Bowls, Orange Bowl, Fiesta Bowl and U.S. Army All-American Bowl

Have fun and appreciate the journey. Football is a great game. Our son not only got his engineering degree, but college football made him a man. And I do not mean in a macho way, but rather he has made waking early, hard work, the concept of team, time management and learning from others part of who he is today. He also made lifelong friends on the team and made some remarkable business networking contacts with classmates, alums and other mentors. College football is one of the great treasures in American culture. The coaches, players and other people in football are some of the finest in the world. Football is part of the fabric that weaves Americans together across boundaries of race, religion, geography and socioeconomics. Help your son continue in the great world of football after high school. And enjoy yourself in the process. I treasured the one-on-one time with our son traveling together for campus visits. Start early, be proactive and best of luck with his recruitment.

APPENDICES

APPENDIX A: LETTER TO COACH - HIGHLIGHTS

[Date]

Re: [Son's Name] ([High school & State]) - Class of 2010

Dear Coach _____:

Enclosed is a DVD of **[Son's Name]** Junior Highlights. His jersey number is **#42**. He mainly plays MLB, but in some critical situations, they brought him in as fullback, normally in a wishbone formation. The DVD is about 7 minutes long, and is divided into four segments:

- RUSH DEFENSE
- PASS DEFENSE
- BLOCKING
- SPECIAL TEAMS

[Son's First Name] was named *All-State* (linebacker) by the [State] Football Coaches Association. He was also named first team *All-Conference* (conference is 80% class 5A schools). **[Son's First Name]** had one hundred and twenty-eight (128) total tackles for the season.

Also enclosed is a profile sheet with honors and stats [*see* Appendix C].

Good luck in your upcoming Bowl game.

Sincerely,

[name, home address, phone, e-mail]

APPENDIX B: LETTER TO COACH - FULL GAME FILM

[Date]

Re: [Son's Name] ([High school & State]) - Class of 2010

Dear Coach _____:

Enclosed is Junior Year (2008) full game film against XYZ High School. **[Son's Name]** is wearing white jersey #42. In this game, he plays exclusively middle linebacker.

[Son's Name]'s Stats for this game:

- Twelve (12) tackles (6 solo; 6 assist), of which two (2) were TFL's.
- Four (4) QB hurries.

Game Notes:

- XYZ High School won 7-6.
- After XYZ's opening drive, **[Son's First Name]**'s team made defensive adjustments and XYZ did not score any more points.
- One of XYZ's longer gains in the game occurred on a run up the middle early in the 2nd quarter on the one play that **[Son's First Name]** was out, having been required the play before to leave the game since he broke his helmet.

Opponent Information:

- XYZ High School, XYZ, [State]
- Enrollment: 2,100
- Class: 5A (largest class in [State])
- Pre-game Record: 4-2

Sincerely,

[name, home address, phone, e-mail]

APPENDIX C: FOOTBALL RESUME

Football Resume (Sample)

[SON'S NAME]:   Class of [year]

Height: [feet & inches]   Weight: [pounds]

[street address]

[city, state, zip code]

[home phone]

[email address]

H.S. Head Football Coach: [name of head coach]

[High School name]

Phone: [head coach's direct dial number(s)]

Email: [head coach's email address]

SPEED, SIZE, STRENGTH & AGILITY

[list all relevant data, such as 40-yard dash time, vertical jump, short shuttle time, standing broad jump, squat max, power-clean max, bench press max, arm length, arm span, hand size, etc.]

[also provide who, when and where each item of data came from, and if available a website link to allow the coach to verify the data from an independent source.]

[also mention other sports played]

FOOBALL HONORS (Jersey # [##])

[list all honors (individual and team) such as all-conference, all-state, team captain, team awards, etc.]

DEFENSIVE STATISTICS ([Position])

SENIOR SEASON
[list all applicable helpful stats, such as total tackles, TFL's, sacks, interceptions, forced fumbles, fumble recoveries, blocked kick's, blocked passes, pass break-ups, QB hurries.]

JUNIOR SEASON

SOPHOMORE SEASON

OFFENSIVE STATISTICS ([Position])

SENIOR SEASON
[list all applicable helpful stats, such as rushing yards, yards per game, yards per rush, yards after contact (YAC) passing yards, (zero) fumbles, pass completions and percentage completions, passer rating, pancake blocks, sacks allowed]

JUNIOR SEASON

SOPHOMORE SEASON

ACADEMICS

Core 16 GPA (on 4.0 scale): [core GPA]
Overall GPA (on 4.0 scale): [overall GPA]
Two-part SAT score: [SAT score]
Will graduate in [month, year]
NCAA Eligibility Center ID No.: [NCAA (or NAIA) ID #]

APPENDIX D: DVD LABEL ON HIGHLIGHT FILM

Fig. 6: DVD Label on Highlight Film

APPENDIX E: FILM CLIP NOTES WORKSHEET

Last update: [Date]

Better clip is <u>UNDERLINED</u>

GAME	Endzone CLIP #	Sideline CLIP #	In 2008 highlight	Rating (1-5) & Notes
Jefferson				
Fullback, 3rd and 4th quarter.	01 03 1	<u>22</u>	X	3-Tfl
	01 08 1	<u>27</u>	X	4-tfl. Threw FB into RB, knocking him down.
	01 11 1	<u>30</u>	X	3-T. short pass.
	<u>01 32 1</u>	52	X	2-T
	01 46 1	<u>67</u>	X	3-T

GAME	Endzone CLIP #	Sideline CLIP #	In 2008 highlight	Rating (1-5) & Notes
	01 47 1	68	X	3-T
	01 52 1	73		2-T
	01 53 1	74		2-fill hole, not tackle
	01 76 1	95		1-hurry QB
	01 80 1	99		3-B, pancake
	01 84 1	103	X	3-B, pancake
	01 85 1	104	X	5-B, pancake
	01 87 1	106	X	1-R, 3 yard gain.
	01 96 1	115	X	3-T
	01 100 1	119	X	3-T, 3rd and 1 stop.

GAME	Endzone CLIP #	Sideline CLIP #	In 2008 highlight	Rating (1-5) & Notes
	01 102 1	121	X	4-T, 4th and 1 stop, see clip 119 also.
	03 03	130	X	Int- on trick extra point.
	03 11	138		sustain block.
	03 13	140	X	3-B
Westside				
	01 04	26	X	2-T
	01 06	28	X	4-Sack
	01 09	31		1-T downfield after pass.

GAME	Endzone CLIP #	Sideline CLIP #	In 2008 highlight	Rating (1-5) & Notes
	<u>01 10</u>	32	X	3-T fill A gap
	<u>01 33</u>	55	X	4-blocked PAT
	01 42	63		2-T short pass flats
	01 49	70		1-T

Table 6: Film Clip Notes Worksheet

APPENDIX F: AGENDA FOR OFFICIAL VISIT

<u>Fri., September 16th</u>

6:30 PM	Arrive in Football Offices
7:15	Dinner with coaches and other recruits
8:30	Tour Strength and Conditioning Facilities
9:00	Released to freshman host

<u>Sat., September 17th</u>

7:45 AM	Arrive in Football Offices – Buffet breakfast
9:00	Meet with Recruiting Coordinator Coach Smith
9:30	Meet with Professor James – School of Business
10:30	Meet with Director of Academic Services
11:30	Walk with Team to the Stadium
12:00 PM	Pre-game Meet the Recruits (Head Coach Jones)
12:15	Pre-game on the sidelines
1:00	Kickoff vs. State (complimentary lunch in the stadium)
3:30	Post-game locker room
4:15	Meeting with Defensive Coordinator Jackson
5:00	Campus Tour (Graduate Asst. Thompson)
6:15	Dinner at *Big Steak House* with coaches and host
8:00	Hang out with host, other players and recruits

<u>Sun., September 18th</u>

10:00 AM	Arrive in Football Offices – Buffet breakfast
10:30	Meeting with strength coach Biggs
11:00	Tour Student Health and Trainer's Facilities
12:00 PM	Lunch with position coach James
1:00	Player Panel: Questions and Answers
1:30	Meeting with Athletic Director Larson
2:00	Meeting with Head Coach Jones
3:30	Depart Campus

APPENDIX G: CONSIDERATIONS IN PICKING A SCHOOL

Some key questions are in **bold**.

<u>GENERAL</u>

1. **How far away from home am I comfortable with?**

    a. two hour drive or less.

    b. six hour drive or less.

    c. half-day air travel.

    d. full-day air travel.

2. What do I want to do with my life after my football is over?

3. What are the *real* reasons that I want to play college football?

4. **Is the offer for a four (4) year scholarship or something less (*i.e.* one (1) year scholarships renewable each year only at the coaches option) ?**

5. [add more general factors important to your son here.]

<u>ACADEMIC</u>

1. **What are the school's graduation rates (Federal as well as NCAA) for football players?**

2. **Does the football program steer its players to weak majors?**

3. What is the academic reputation of the school?

4. Does the school offer a major in what I want to study?

5. What is the non-football job placement history of the football program?

6. If I suffered a career ending injury, would I still want to go to college here?

7. Am I guaranteed that my scholarship will also pay for summer school each summer if I want to do that?

8. Am I guaranteed that my scholarship will also pay for a dorm room and food each summer if I choose to attend summer school?

9. If I do not graduate with a degree, will the school pay for me to come back and complete my degree? For how long and under what conditions?

10. [add more academic related factors important to your son here.]

FOOTBALL

1. How much do I like and respect the guys in my recruiting class?

2. How much do I like and respect the upperclassmen?

3. How deep is the competition (depth chart) at my position, both within my recruiting class and with the upperclassmen?

4. How much do I like and respect my position coach and the coordinator over him?

5. How much do I like and respect the head coach and in particular the culture that he creates?

6. Is the team a winning, medium or losing program, and is it on the rise or declining?

7. What are the best estimates about the current coaches being around for most or my entire football career?

8. If I suffer a career ending injury while in high school, (even outside of football) will the school still provide admission and a scholarship?

9. If I suffer a career ending injury while in college, will the school still provide a scholarship?

10. How good are the facilities?

11. How good are the support services, including academic tutors, strength and conditioning coaches, medical support, training table, and otherwise?

12. What health insurance does the school provide, for what, and for how long? Is that paid for treatment/surgery after college, and if so for how long?

13. How much does the school over-sign and/or gray shirt recruits? *See* **Chapter 10.**

14. Excluding players drafted early by the NFL, what percentage of scholarship freshman football players remain on the team roster for all four (4) years?

15. What is the average game day attendance, and how important is football status and glory to me?

16. What is the NFL draft success of past players from those college program/coaches?

17. [Add more football related factors important to your son here.]

OTHER

1. How important is climate in my choice?

2. How important is the size and nature of the town, outside of campus, to my choice?

3. What type of summer internships or jobs do the players get, and how many openings are filled each summer?

4. How important are the girls on campus to my choice?

5. How important is the social scene on campus to my choice?

6. How good is the non-training table (dormitory) food on campus?

7. What is the rate of criminal (or juvenile) convicts or low character players on the team?

8. If my son needed surgery, how is that handled, with what doctors, and who pays?

9. [Add other miscellaneous factors important to your son here.]

APPENDIX H: NCAA D-1 RULES (PORTIONS)

NCAA D-1 MANUAL, Article 13 (Aug. 1, 2014)

(Select portions pertaining to non-football are deleted)

Article 13 - Recruiting

13.01 General Principles.

13.01.1 Eligibility Effects of Recruiting Violation. The recruitment of a student-athlete by a member institution or any representative of its athletics interests in violation of the Association's legislation, as acknowledged by the institution or established through the Association's infractions process, shall result in the student-athlete becoming ineligible to represent that institution in intercollegiate athletics. The Committee on Student-Athlete Reinstatement may restore the eligibility of a student involved in such a violation only when circumstances clearly warrant restoration. A student is responsible for his or her involvement in a violation of NCAA regulations during the student's recruitment, and involvement in a Level I or Level II violation (see Bylaws 19.1.1 and 19.1.2) may cause the student to become permanently ineligible for intercollegiate athletics competition at that institution. *(Revised: 7/31/14)*

13.01.2 Institutional Responsibility in Recruitment. A member of an institution's athletics staff or a representative of its athletics interests shall not recruit a prospective student-athlete except as permitted by this Association, the institution and the member conference, if any.

13.01.3 Additional Recruiting Restrictions. The Committee on Academic Performance shall have the authority to determine the circumstances that would require an institution or team that fails to satisfy the academic performance program to apply additional recruiting restrictions. The Committee on Academic Performance shall establish and annually publish to the membership such circumstances under which the additional restrictions apply (see Bylaw 14.8). *(Adopted: 4/29/04 effective 8/1/04)*

13.02 Definitions and Applications.

13.02.1 Business Day. A business day is any weekday that is not recognized as a national holiday, including any weekday during which an institution is closed for other reasons (e.g., holiday break). *(Adopted: 4/29/10 effective 8/1/10)*

13.02.2 Camps.

13.02.2.1 Diversified Sports Camp. A diversified sports camp is a camp that offers a balanced camping experience, including participation in seasonal summer sports and recreational activities, without emphasis on instruction, practice or competition in any particular sport.

13.02.2.2 Specialized Sports Camp. A specialized sports camp is a camp that places special emphasis on a particular sport or sports and provides specialized instruction.

13.02.3 Competition Site. The "competition site" is the facility in which athletics competition is actually conducted, including any dressing room or meeting facility used in conjunction with the competition.

13.02.4 Contact. A contact is any face-to-face encounter between a prospective student-athlete or the prospective student-athlete's parents, relatives or legal guardians and an institutional staff member or athletics representative during which any dialogue occurs in excess of an exchange of a greeting. Any such face-to-face encounter that is prearranged (e.g., staff member positions himself or herself in a location where contact is possible) or that takes place on the grounds of the prospective student-athlete's educational institution or at the site of organized competition or practice involving the prospective student-athlete or the prospective student-athlete's high school, preparatory school, two-year college or all-star team shall be considered a contact, regardless of whether any conversation occurs. However, an institutional staff member or athletics representative who is approached by a prospective student-athlete or the prospective student-athlete's parents, relatives or legal guardians at any location shall not use a contact, provided the encounter was not prearranged and the staff member or athletics representative does not engage in any dialogue in excess of a greeting and takes appropriate steps to immediately terminate the encounter. *(Revised: 1/11/94 effective 8/1/94)*

13.02.4.1 Evaluation Activities During Contact Period—Football. [FBS/FCS] In football, a visit to a prospective student-athlete's high school, preparatory school or two-year college, or an evaluation at any site that occurs during a contact period shall constitute a contact (for all prospective student-athletes in that sport at the educational institution) for that particular week even if no contact is made with a prospective student-athlete. *(Adopted: 1/11/94 effective 8/1/94, Revised: 1/10/95 effective 8/1/95)*

13.02.5 Periods of Recruiting Activities.

13.02.5.1 Contact Period. A contact period is a period of time when it is permissible for authorized athletics department staff members to make in-person, off-campus recruiting contacts and evaluations.

13.02.5.2 Evaluation Period. An evaluation period is a period of time when it is permissible for authorized athletics department staff members to be involved in off-campus activities designed to assess the academic qualifications and playing ability of prospective student-athletes. No in-person, off-campus recruiting contacts shall be made with the prospective student-athlete during an evaluation period.

13.02.5.3 Recruiting Period—Men's Basketball. In men's basketball, a recruiting period is a period of time when it is permissible for authorized athletics department staff members to make in-person, off-campus recruiting contacts and evaluations. *(Adopted: 10/27/11 effective 8/1/12)*

13.02.5.4 Quiet Period. A quiet period is a period of time when it is permissible to make in-person recruiting contacts only on the institution's campus. No in-person, off-campus recruiting contacts or evaluations may be made during the quiet period.

13.02.5.5 Dead Period. A dead period is a period of time when it is not permissible to make in-person recruiting contacts or evaluations on or off the institution's campus or to permit official or unofficial visits by prospective student-athletes to the institution's campus. It remains permissible, however, for an institutional staff member to write or telephone a prospective student-athlete during a dead period. *(Revised: 1/11/94, 12/6/13)*

13.02.5.5.1 Exception—Women's Volleyball. In women's volleyball, an institutional coaching staff member may have incidental contact with a two-year college prospective student-athlete who is attending and being honored at the annual American Volleyball Coaches Association (AVCA) awards banquet, provided no recruiting conversation occurs. *(Adopted: 10/30/03)*

13.02.5.5.2 Exception—After Commitment. A prospective student-athlete is no longer subject to the application of a dead period after one of the following events occurs: *(Adopted: 1/16/10 effective 8/1/10, Revised: 1/15/11 effective 8/1/11, 1/19/13 effective 8/1/13, 11/25/13)*

(a) The prospective student-athlete signs a National Letter of Intent (NLI) or the institution's written offer of admission and/or financial aid; or

(b) The institution receives a financial deposit in response to the institution's offer of admission.

13.02.6 Enrolled Student-Athlete. An enrolled student-athlete is an individual whose enrollment was solicited by a member of the athletics staff or other representative of athletics interests with a view toward the student's ultimate participation in the intercollegiate athletics program. Any other student becomes a student-athlete only when the student reports for an intercollegiate squad that is under the jurisdiction of the athletics department.

13.02.7 Evaluation. Evaluation is any off-campus activity designed to assess the academic qualifications or athletics ability of a prospective student-athlete, including any visit to a prospective student-athlete's educational institution (during which no contact occurs) or the observation of a prospective student-athlete participating in any practice or competition at any site. *(Revised: 1/10/91 effective 8/1/91, 1/11/94 effective 8/1/94)*

13.02.7.1 Exception—Football. In football, any evaluation that occurs during a contact period by a coaching staff member is a countable contact per Bylaw 13.02.4.1 rather than a countable evaluation. *(Adopted: 1/10/95 effective 8/1/95)*

13.02.7.2 Evaluation Days—Football, Softball, Women's Volleyball and Women's Sand Volleyball. An evaluation day is defined as one coach engaged in the evaluation of any prospective student-athlete on one day (12:01 a.m. to midnight). Two coaches making evaluations on the same day shall use two evaluation days. See Bylaws 13.1.7.9.3, 13.1.7.11, 13.1.7.12 and 13.1.7.13. *(Adopted: 1/9/96 effective 8/1/96, Revised: 1/12/99 effective 8/1/99, 4/27/00 effective 8/1/01, 4/25/02 effective 8/1/02, 4/28/05 effective 8/1/05, 1/14/08 effective 8/1/08, 4/14/08, 1/16/10 effective 8/1/10, 1/15/11 effective 8/1/11)*

13.02.8 Recruiting-Person Days—Men's Basketball. In men's basketball, a recruiting-person day is defined as one coach engaged in an off-campus recruiting activity of a men's basketball prospective student-athlete, including a prospective student-athlete who has signed a National Letter of Intent (or the institution's written offer of admission and/or financial aid), on one day (12:01 a.m. to midnight); two coaches engaged in recruiting activities on the same day shall use two recruiting-person days. Men's basketball staff members shall not exceed 130 recruiting-person days during the academic year. *(Adopted: 4/28/05 effective 8/1/05, Revised: 3/28/07, 5/9/08)*

13.02.8.1 Tournament Application. Each day of a tournament or tier of a tournament in which a coach engages in off-campus evaluation activity shall count as a separate recruiting-person day. *(Adopted: 12/12/06)*

13.02.9 Recruiting-Person Days—Women's Basketball. In women's basketball, a recruiting-person day is defined as one coach engaged in an off-campus recruiting activity of a women's basketball prospective student-athlete, including a prospective student-athlete who has signed a National Letter of Intent (or the institution's written offer of admission and/or financial aid), on one day (12:01 a.m. to midnight); two coaches engaged in recruiting activities on the same day shall use two recruiting-person days. Women's basketball staff members shall not exceed 112 recruiting-person days during the academic year. *(Adopted: 4/28/05 effective 8/1/05, Revised: 1/8/07 effective 8/1/07, 3/27/07, 5/9/08, 1/19/13 effective 8/1/13)*

13.02.9.1 Tournament Application. Each day of a tournament or tier of a tournament in which a coach engages in off-campus evaluation activity shall count as a separate recruiting person day. *(Adopted: 12/12/06)*

13.02.10 Home. In general, a prospective student-athlete's "home" is the prospective student-athlete's legal residence, or the community of the educational institution in which the prospective student-athlete is enrolled while residing there.

13.02.11 National Letter of Intent. The National Letter of Intent referred to in this bylaw is the official document administered by the Collegiate Commissioners Association and used by subscribing member institutions to establish the commitment of a prospective student-athlete to attend a particular institution.

13.02.12 Prospective Student-Athlete. A prospective student-athlete is a student who has started classes for the ninth grade. In addition, a student who has not started classes for the ninth grade becomes a prospective student-athlete if the institution provides such an individual (or the individual's relatives or friends) any financial assistance or other benefits that the institution does not provide to prospective students generally. An individual remains a prospective student-athlete until one of the following occurs (whichever is earlier): *(Revised: 1/11/89, 1/10/90, 4/28/05, 1/17/09, 1/19/13 effective 8/1/13)*

(a) The individual officially registers and enrolls in a minimum full-time program of studies and attends classes in any term of a four-year collegiate institution's regular academic year (excluding summer);

(b) The individual participates in a regular squad practice or competition at a four-year collegiate institution that occurs before the beginning of any term;

(c) The individual officially registers, enrolls and attends classes during the certifying institution's summer term prior to his or her initial full-time enrollment at the certifying institution; or

(d) The individual reports to an institutional orientation session that is open to all incoming students within 14 calendar days prior to the opening day of classes of a regular academic year term.

13.02.12.1 Exception—After Commitment. After an individual has signed a National Letter of Intent or the institution's written offer of admission and/or financial aid or after the institution has received his or her financial deposit in response to its offer of admission, the individual shall no longer be subject to the restrictions of Bylaw 13.1. The individual remains a prospective student-athlete for purposes of applying the remaining provisions of Bylaw 13 and other bylaws. *(Adopted: 4/28/05, Revised: 1/19/13 effective 8/1/13)*

13.02.13 Recruiting. Recruiting is any solicitation of a prospective student-athlete or a prospective student-athlete's relatives (or legal guardians) by an institutional staff member or by a representative of the institution's athletics interests for the purpose of securing the prospective student-athlete's enrollment and ultimate participation in the institution's intercollegiate athletics program.

13.02.13.1 Recruited Prospective Student-Athlete. Actions by staff members or athletics representatives that cause a prospective student-athlete to become a recruited prospective student-athlete at that institution are: *(Revised: 1/10/90, 1/11/94 effective 8/1/94, 1/10/05 effective 8/01/05, 12/13/05)*

(a) Providing the prospective student-athlete with an official visit;

(b) Having an arranged, in-person, off-campus encounter with the prospective student-athlete or the prospective student-athlete's parents, relatives or legal guardians;

(c) Initiating or arranging a telephone contact with the prospective student-athlete, the prospective student-athlete's relatives or legal guardians on more than one occasion for the purpose of recruitment; or

(d) Issuing a National Letter of Intent or the institution's written offer of athletically related financial aid to the prospective student-athlete. Issuing a written offer of athletically related financial aid to a prospective student-athlete to attend a summer session prior to full-time enrollment does not cause the prospective student-athlete to become recruited.

13.02.14 Representative of Athletics Interests. A "representative of the institution's athletics interests" is an individual, independent agency, corporate entity (e.g., apparel or equipment manufacturer) or other organization who is known (or who should have been known) by a member of the institution's executive or athletics administration to: *(Revised: 2/16/00)*

(a) Have participated in or to be a member of an agency or organization promoting the institution's intercollegiate athletics program;

(b) Have made financial contributions to the athletics department or to an athletics booster organization of that institution;

(c) Be assisting or to have been requested (by the athletics department staff) to assist in the recruitment of prospective student-athletes;

(d) Be assisting or to have assisted in providing benefits to enrolled student-athletes or their families; or

(e) Have been involved otherwise in promoting the institution's athletics program.

13.02.14.1 Duration of Status. Once an individual, independent agency, corporate entity or other organization is identified as such a representative, the person, independent agency, corporate entity or other organization retains that identity indefinitely. *(Revised: 2/16/00)*

13.02.15 Telephone Calls. All electronically transmitted human voice exchange (including videoconferencing and videophones) shall be considered telephone calls. *(Adopted: 1/10/95, Revised: 1/9/96 effective 8/1/96, 1/14/97, 4/27/00 effective 8/1/00, 9/6/00, 4/29/04 effective 8/1/04, 4/26/07 effective 8/1/07)*

13.02.16 Visits by Prospective Student-Athletes.

13.02.16.1 Official Visit. An official visit to a member institution by a prospective student-athlete is a visit financed in whole or in part by the member institution.

13.02.16.2 Unofficial Visit. An unofficial visit to a member institution by a prospective student-athlete is a visit made at the prospective student-athlete's own expense. The provision of any expenses or entertainment valued at more than $100 by the institution or representatives of its athletics interests shall require the visit to become an official visit, except as permitted in Bylaws 13.5 and 13.7. *(Revised: 2/22/07, 5/9/08)*

13.02.17 Individual Associated with a Prospective Student-Athlete—Men's Basketball. In men's basketball, an individual associated with a prospective student-athlete is any person who maintains (or directs others to maintain) contact with the prospective student-athlete, the prospective student-athlete's relatives or legal guardians, or coaches at any point during the prospective student-athlete's participation in basketball, and whose contact is directly or indirectly related to either the prospective student-athlete's athletic skills and abilities or the prospective student-athlete's recruitment by or enrollment in an NCAA institution. This definition includes, but is not limited to, parents, legal guardians, handlers, personal trainers and coaches. An individual who meets this definition retains such status during the enrollment of the prospective student-athlete at the institution. *(Adopted: 8/26/10)*

13.1 Contacts and Evaluations.

Recruiting contacts (per Bylaw 13.02.4) and telephone calls by institutional staff members or representatives of the institution's athletics interests are subject to the provisions set forth in this bylaw. *(Revised: 1/10/91 effective 7/1/91, 6/13/08)*

13.1.1 Contactable Individuals.

13.1.1.1 Time Period for Off-Campus Contacts—General Rule. Off-campus recruiting contacts shall not be made with an individual (or his or her relatives or legal guardians) before July 1 following the completion of his or her junior year in high school (July 7 after the junior year in high school in women's ice hockey and July 15 after the junior year in high school in women's gymnastics), or the opening day of classes of his or her senior year in high school (as designated by the high school), whichever is earlier. U.S. service academy exceptions to this provision are set forth in Bylaw 13.16.1. *(Revised: 1/10/91 effective 7/1/91, 1/11/94 effective 3/15/94, 1/10/95, 1/14/97 effective 5/1/97, 10/28/97, 4/26/01 effective 8/1/01, 4/29/04 effective 8/1/04, 4/28/05, 1/9/06, 2/26/07, 6/13/08, 4/30/09, 1/15/11)*

*****

13.1.1.2 Two-Year College Prospective Student-Athletes. A prospective student-athlete who was not a qualifier as defined in Bylaw 14.02.10.1 and who is enrolled in the first year of a two-year college may not be contacted in person on or off an institution's campus for recruiting purposes.

13.1.1.3 Four-Year College Prospective Student-Athletes. An athletics staff member or other representative of the institution's athletics interests shall not make contact with the student-athlete of another NCAA or NAIA four-year collegiate institution, directly or indirectly, without first obtaining the written permission of the first institution's athletics director (or an athletics administrator designated by the athletics director) to do so, regardless of who makes the initial contact. If permission is not granted, the second institution shall not encourage the transfer and the institution shall not provide athletically related financial assistance to the student-athlete until the student-athlete has attended the second institution for one academic year. If permission is granted to contact the student-athlete, all applicable NCAA recruiting rules apply. If an institution receives a written request from a student-athlete to permit another institution to contact the student-athlete about transferring, the institution shall grant or deny the request within seven business days (see Bylaw 13.02.1) of receipt of the request. If the institution fails to respond to the student-athlete's written request within seven business days, permission shall be granted by default and the institution shall provide written permission to the student-athlete. *(Revised: 1/10/91, 1/16/93, 1/11/94, 4/26/01, 4/29/04 effective 8/1/04, 4/29/10 effective 8/1/10)*

13.1.1.3.1 Hearing Opportunity. If the institution decides to deny a student-athlete's request to permit any other institution to contact the student-athlete about transferring, the institution shall inform the student-athlete in writing that he or she, upon request, shall be provided a hearing conducted by an institutional entity or committee outside the athletics department (e.g., the office of student affairs; office of the dean of students; or a committee composed of the faculty athletics representative, student-athletes and nonathletics faculty/staff members). The institution shall conduct the hearing and provide written results of the hearing to the student-athlete within 15 business days (see Bylaw 13.02.1) of receipt of the student-athlete's written request for a hearing. The student-athlete shall be provided the opportunity to actively participate (e.g., in person, via telephone) in the hearing. If the institution fails to conduct the hearing or provide the written results to the student-athlete within 15 business days, permission to contact the student-athlete shall be granted by default and the institution shall provide written permission to the student-athlete. *(Adopted: 1/11/94, Revised: 9/18/07, 4/29/10 effective 8/1/10)*

13.1.1.3.2 Student-Athlete Withdrawn From Four-Year College. A member institution may contact a student-athlete who has withdrawn officially from a four-year collegiate institution without obtaining permission from the first institution only if at least one academic year has elapsed since the withdrawal.

13.1.1.3.2.1 Exception—Official Religious Mission. An institution shall not contact a student-athlete who has begun service on an official religious mission without obtaining permission from the institution from which the student-athlete withdrew prior to beginning his or her mission if the student-athlete signed a National Letter of Intent (NLI) and attended the institution (with which he or she signed the NLI) as a full-time student. If such a student-athlete has completed his or her official religious mission and does not enroll full time in a collegiate institution within one calendar year of completion of the mission, an institution may contact the student-athlete without obtaining permission from the first institution. *(Adopted: 1/17/09 effective 8/1/09, Revised: 4/2/10)*

13.1.1.3.3 Transfer From Institution Placed on Probation by Committee on Infractions. It is not necessary for an institution to obtain permission in writing to recruit a student-athlete at an institution that has been placed on probation with sanctions that preclude it from competing in postseason competition during the remaining seasons of the student-athlete's eligibility. However, the student-athlete's institution must be notified of the recruitment and may establish reasonable restrictions related to the contact (e.g., no visits during class time), provided such restrictions do not preclude the opportunity for the student-athlete to discuss transfer possibilities with the other institution [see Bylaw 14.7.2-(c)]. *(Adopted: 1/10/92, Revised: 1/9/06 effective 8/1/06)*

13.1.1.3.4 Transfer From Institution Ineligible for Postseason Competition—Academic Performance Program. On approval by the Committee on Academic Performance, an institution may contact a student-athlete at another institution whose team is ineligible for postseason competition during the remaining seasons of the student-athlete's eligibility due to sanctions pursuant to the Academic Performance Program, without obtaining written permission from the other institution. The student-athlete's institution must be notified of the recruitment and may establish reasonable restrictions related to the contact (e.g., no visits during class time), provided such restrictions do not preclude the opportunity for the student-athlete to discuss transfer possibilities with the other institution [see Bylaw 14.7.2-(e)]. *(Adopted: 1/9/06 effective 8/1/06)*

13.1.1.3.5 Transfer While Ineligible Due to Positive Drug Test. If a student-athlete who is declared ineligible due to a positive drug test administered by the NCAA transfers to another NCAA institution, the institution from which the student-athlete transferred must notify the new institution of the student-athlete's ineligibility (see Bylaw 18.4.1.5.5). *(Adopted: 1/14/97 effective 8/1/97)*

13.1.2 Permissible Recruiters.

13.1.2.1 General Rule. All in-person, on- and off-campus recruiting contacts with a prospective student-athlete or the prospective student-athlete's relatives or legal guardians shall be made only by authorized institutional staff members. Such contact, as well as correspondence and telephone calls, by representatives of an institution's athletics interests is prohibited except as otherwise permitted in this section. Violations of this bylaw involving individuals other than a representative of an institution's athletics interests shall be considered institutional violations per Constitution 2.8.1; however, such violations shall not affect the prospective student-athlete's eligibility. *(Revised: 8/5/04)*

13.1.2.1.1 Off-Campus Recruiters. An institutional staff member is not permitted to recruit off campus until he or she has been certified on an annual basis as to knowledge of applicable recruiting rules per Bylaw 11.5.1.1. **[D]** *(Adopted: 1/10/91 effective 8/1/92, Revised: 4/27/00)*

13.1.2.2 General Exceptions. This regulation is not applicable to:

(a) **Admissions Program.** Off-campus recruiting contacts made by an institution's regular admissions program representative and directed at all prospective students including nonathletes.

(b) **Coach Who Is Prospective Student-Athlete's Parent or Legal Guardian.** Recruiting contact and evaluation limitations do not apply to a coaching staff member who is the parent (or legal guardian) of a participant in any activity being observed (e.g., practices, contests or camps), provided the attendance by the coaching staff member at such activity does not involve any personal contact with any other participating prospective student-athlete. *(Revised: 1/10/95, 1/14/97 effective 8/1/97)*

(c) **Spouse of Prospective Student-Athlete's Coach.** Recruiting contact and evaluation limitations do not apply to a coaching staff member observing a contest that involves prospective student-athletes coached by his or her spouse, provided the attendance by the coaching staff member at such a contest does not involve any personal contact with any prospective student-athlete participating in the contest. *(Adopted: 1/11/94)*

(d) **Established Family Friend/Neighbor.** Contacts made with a prospective student-athlete by an established family friend or neighbor, it being understood that such contacts are not made for recruiting purposes and are not initiated by a member of an institution's coaching staff.

(e) **Spouse of Staff Member.**

(1) **On Campus.** A spouse of an institutional staff member on campus.

(2) **Off Campus during Official Visit.** A spouse of an athletics department staff member during a prospective student-athlete's official visit and within a 30-mile radius of the institution's main campus during the prospective student-athlete's official visit.

(f) **Interpreter.** An interpreter present during an institution's in-person, off-campus contact with a prospective student-athlete or the prospective student-athlete's parents (or legal guardians), provided that if the institution is involved in making the arrangements for the use of the interpreter, the interpreter must be a faculty member or a professional interpreter. It is not permissible for the interpreter to be an enrolled student-athlete, a family member of an enrolled student-athlete or a representative of the institution's athletics interests. *(Adopted: 1/11/97)*

(g) **Unavoidable Incidental Contact.** An unavoidable incidental contact made with a prospective student-athlete by representatives of the institution's athletics interests, provided the contact is not prearranged by the representative or an athletics department staff member, does not take place on the grounds of the prospective student-athlete's educational institution or at the sites of organized competition and practice involving the prospective student-athlete or the prospective student-athlete's team (high school, preparatory school, two-year college or all-star team), is not made for the purpose of recruitment of the prospective student-athlete, and involves only normal civility.

(h) **Relatives (or Legal Guardians) of Enrolled Student-Athletes.** On-campus contacts between a prospective student-athlete or his or her relatives (traditional or nontraditional) or legal guardians accompanying the prospective student-athlete and the relatives (traditional and nontraditional) or legal guardians of an enrolled student-athlete. *(Adopted: 4/26/12)*

13.1.2.3 General Restrictions—Staff Members and Governing Board. The following are additional restrictions that apply to an institution's staff members and governing board: **[D]** *(Revised: 4/27/00, 7/31/13)*

(a) **Noncoaching Staff Members with Sport-Specific Responsibilities.** A noncoaching staff member with sport-specific responsibilities (except a staff member who only performs clerical duties) shall not attend an on- or off-campus athletics event in the staff member's sport that involves prospective student-athletes (e.g., high school contest, noninstitutional sports camp) unless the staff member is an immediate family member or legal guardian of a participant in the activity. A staff member who is an immediate family member or legal guardian of a participant may attend such an event, subject to the following conditions: *(Adopted: 1/16/10, Revised: 4/13/10, 4/29/10)*

    (i) Attendance shall not be for evaluation purposes (the staff member shall not provide information related to the performance of a prospective student-athlete back to the institution's coaching staff); and

    (ii) The staff member shall not have direct contact with a prospective student-athlete or a prospective student-athlete's parent (or legal guardian) or coach (other than the immediate family member, if applicable) participating in the activity.

(b) **Board of Governors/Regents.** Recruiting contacts on or off campus between a member of the institution's board of governors (or regents) and a prospective student-athlete are not permissible.

13.1.2.4 Other Restrictions, Athletics Representatives. The following are additional restrictions that apply to athletics representatives:

(a) **Telephone Conversation.** An athletics representative of a member institution may speak to a prospective student-athlete via the telephone only if the prospective student-athlete initiates the telephone conversation and the call is not for recruiting purposes. Under such circumstances, the representative must refer questions about the institution's athletics program to the athletics department staff;

(b) **Observing Prospective Student-Athlete's Contest.** An athletics representative may view a prospective student-athlete's athletics contest on his or her own initiative, subject to the understanding that the athletics representative may not contact the prospective student-athlete on such occasions;

(c) **Evaluation of Prospective Student-Athlete.** An athletics representative may not contact a prospective student-athlete's coach, principal or counselor in an attempt to evaluate the prospective student-athlete; and

(d) **Visiting Prospective Student-Athlete's Institution.** An athletics representative may not visit a prospective student-athlete's educational institution to pick up video or transcripts pertaining to the evaluation of the prospective student-athlete's academic eligibility or athletics ability.

13.1.2.5 Off-Campus Contacts or Evaluations. Only those coaches who are identified by the institution, in accordance with Bylaws 11.7.4.2, 11.7.5.2 and 11.7.6, may contact or evaluate prospective student-athletes off campus. Institutional staff members (e.g., faculty members) may contact prospective student-athletes for recruiting purposes in all sports, on campus, or within 30 miles of campus during the prospective student-athlete's official visit. **[D]** *(Revised: 1/10/91 effective 8/1/92, 8/5/04, 5/26/06, 7/31/13)*

13.1.2.5.1 Written Certification. A member institution shall certify in writing and have on file a list of those coaches who are permitted to contact or evaluate prospective student-athletes off campus. **[D]** *(Revised: 5/26/06)*

13.1.2.5.2 Department-Wide Responsibilities. An athletics department staff member who has department-wide responsibilities (e.g., recruiting coordinator) may not contact or evaluate prospective student-athletes off campus unless the staff member is counted as a countable coach in the applicable sport (see Bylaw 11.7.2 for restrictions related to recruiting coordination functions). **[D]** *(Revised: 5/26/06)*

13.1.2.6 Head Coach Restrictions—Bowl Subdivision Football. [FBS]

13.1.2.6.1 Assistant Coach Publicly Designated as Institution's Next Head Coach. [FBS] An institution's assistant coach who has been publicly designated by the institution to become its next head coach shall be subject to the recruiting restrictions applicable to the institution's head coach. *(Adopted: 1/16/10)*

13.1.2.6.2 Off-Campus Contact. [FBS] In bowl subdivision football, the head coach may make in-person, off-campus contact with a prospective student-athlete or the prospective student-athlete's relatives or legal guardians only during one calendar day. It is permissible for this contact to occur both at the site of the prospective student-athlete's educational institution and away from the institutional grounds. During such contact, the head coach may be accompanied by assistant coaches, who otherwise are required to observe the restrictions contained in the bylaws. **[D]** *(Revised: 1/10/92 effective 8/1/92, 8/5/04, 12/15/06)*

13.1.2.6.3 Spring Evaluation Period. [FBS] In bowl subdivision football, during the April 15 through May 31 evaluation period, the head coach shall not engage in off-campus recruiting activities, participate in an off-campus coaching clinic, visit a prospective student-athlete's educational institution for any reason or meet with a prospective student-athlete's coach at an off-campus location. *(Adopted: 1/14/08, Revised: 1/17/09)*

13.1.2.7 Student-Athlete. The following conditions apply to recruiting activities involving enrolled student-athletes: **[D]** *(Revised: 5/29/08)*

(a) **Off-Campus Contacts.** Off-campus in-person contact between an enrolled student-athlete and a prospective student-athlete is permissible, provided such contact does not occur at the direction of an institutional staff member. *(Revised: 5/29/08, 4/26/12)*

(b) **Transportation and Expenses.** An institution may not provide an enrolled student-athlete with transportation or expenses to recruit a prospective student-athlete except for those expenses specified in Bylaw 13.6.7.5 when the student-athlete serves as a student host. *(Revised: 8/5/04, 5/29/08)*

(c) **Written Correspondence.** It is permissible for an enrolled student-athlete to engage in written correspondence, provided it is not done at the direction or expense of the member institution. *(Revised: 5/29/08)*

13.1.2.8 Talent Scout. An institution may not pay any costs incurred by an athletics talent scout or a representative of its athletics interests in studying or recruiting prospective student-athletes. An institution may not provide any such person a fee or honorarium and thereby claim the person as a staff member entitled to expense money. **[D]** *(Revised: 8/5/04)*

13.1.2.8.1 Employment Prohibition. An institution may not employ an individual for the primary purpose of recruiting or evaluating prospective student-athletes and designate the individual as a coach if he or she does not reside in the institution's general locale. Such an individual would be considered an athletics talent scout rather than a regular institutional staff member.

13.1.2.8.2 Expense Prohibition. An institution may not pay expenses (other than meals provided in the institution's home community) for representatives of its athletics interests to visit its campus for the purpose of becoming familiar with the institution's academic and athletics programs and campus facilities in order to represent the institution better when recruiting prospective student-athletes. The provision of such expenses would be considered payment of costs incurred by athletics talent scouts.

13.1.3 Telephone Calls.

13.1.3.1 Time Period for Telephone Calls—General Rule. Telephone calls to an individual (or his or her relatives or legal guardians) may not be made before September 1 at the beginning of his or her junior year in high school (subject to the exceptions below). If an individual attends an educational institution that uses a nontraditional academic calendar (e.g., Southern Hemisphere), telephone calls to the individual (or his or her relatives or legal guardians) may not be made before the opening day of classes of his or her junior year in high school. Thereafter, an institution may make telephone calls to the prospective student-athlete at its discretion. *(Revised: 1/10/91 effective*

7/1/91, 1/16/93, 1/9/96 effective 8/1/96, 4/22/98, 4/26/01, 4/29/04 effective 8/1/04, 4/28/05 effective 8/1/05, 1/9/06, 6/13/08, 1/15/11, 1/18/14 effective 8/1/14)

*****

13.1.3.1.3 Exception—Football. [FBS/FCS] In football, one telephone call to an individual (or the individual's relatives or legal guardians) may be made from April 15 through May 31 of the individual's junior year in high school. Additional telephone calls to an individual (or the individual's relatives or legal guardians) may not be made before September 1 of the beginning of the individual's senior year in high school. Thereafter, such telephone contact is limited to once per week outside a contact period, but may be made at the institution's discretion during a contact period. *(Revised: 1/10/91 effective 7/1/91, 1/16/93, 1/11/94 effective 3/15/94, 1/10/95, 1/14/97 effective 5/1/97, 10/28/97, 1/8/07)*

*****

13.1.3.1.8 Application of Telephone Call Limitations. Once an institution reaches the applicable limit on telephone calls to a prospective student-athlete (or the prospective student-athlete's relatives or legal guardians) for a particular time period (e.g., one per month, one per week, two per week), the institution may not initiate an additional telephone call during the same time period, even if no direct conversation occurs during the additional call (e.g., voicemail message). *(Adopted: 12/13/05)*

13.1.3.1.9 Effect of Violations. Violations of Bylaw 13.1.3.1 and its subsections involving the first occasion when a staff member exceeds the permissible number of telephone calls during a given period (when it is otherwise permissible to call) shall be considered an institutional violation per Constitution 2.8.1 and shall not affect the prospective student-athlete's eligibility. *(Adopted: 8/5/04)*

13.1.3.2 Additional Restrictions.

13.1.3.2.1 During Conduct of Athletics Contest. Telephone calls to a prospective student-athlete (or the prospective student-athlete's relatives or legal guardians) may not be made during the conduct of any of the institution's intercollegiate athletics contests in that sport from the time the institution's team reports on call at the competition site at the direction of the coach until the competition has concluded and the team has been dismissed by the coach. *(Revised: 1/16/93, 1/9/96, 1/8/09)*

13.1.3.2.2 Telephone Calls Initiated by Prospective Student-Athlete at His or Her Expense. Institutional staff members may receive telephone calls placed by a prospective student-athlete at the prospective student-athlete's own expense at any time, including before July 1 following the prospective student-athlete's junior year in high school. *(Adopted: 1/10/92, Revised: 1/10/95, 8/14/02, 12/12/06, 4/26/12)*

13.1.3.3 Exceptions.

13.1.3.3.1 Official-Visit Exception. Institutional coaching staff members (see Bylaw 13.1.3.4.1) may make unlimited telephone calls to a prospective student-athlete during the five days immediately preceding the prospective student-athlete's official visit (per Bylaw 13.6) to that institution. If more than one call per week occurs under this exception and a scheduled official visit is canceled due to circumstances beyond the control of the prospective student-athlete or the institution (e.g., trip is canceled by the prospective student-athlete, inclement weather conditions), such calls shall not be considered institutional violations and shall not affect the prospective student-athlete's eligibility. However, the institution shall submit a report to the conference office noting the cancellation of the official visit and the reasons for such cancellation. *(Adopted: 1/10/92, Revised: 4/26/01, 12/12/06)*

13.1.3.3.1.1 Telephone Calls in Conjunction With Official Visit. Athletics department staff members may make unlimited telephone calls to a prospective student-athlete or those individuals accompanying the prospective student-athlete during the prospective student-athlete's official visit transportation and during his or her official visit. (See Bylaw 11.7.2.2.) *(Adopted: 1/16/10 effective 8/1/10)*

13.1.3.3.2 Letter-of-Intent Signing-Date Exception. Institutional coaching staff members (see Bylaw 13.1.3.4.1) may make unlimited telephone calls to a prospective student-athlete on the initial date for the signing of the National Letter of Intent and during the two days immediately following the initial signing date. *(Adopted: 1/10/92, Revised: 12/12/06)*

13.1.3.3.2.1 Football Exception. [FBS/FCS] In football, institutional coaching staff members may make unlimited telephone calls to prospective student-athletes during the period 48 hours before and 48 hours after 7 a.m. on the initial signing date for the National Letter of Intent. *(Adopted: 1/10/92, Revised: 12/12/06, 12/15/06)*

13.1.3.3.3 Off-Campus Contact Exception. Institutional coaching staff members (see Bylaw 13.1.3.4.1) may make unlimited telephone calls to a prospective student-athlete on the day a permissible, in-person, off-campus contact occurs with the prospective student-athlete. *(Adopted: 1/10/92, Revised: 1/16/93, 12/12/06)*

13.1.3.4 Permissible Callers.

13.1.3.4.1 Institutional Coaching Staff Members—General Rule. All telephone calls made to a prospective student-athlete (or the prospective student-athlete's parents, legal guardians or coaches) must be made by the head coach or one or more of the assistant coaches who count toward the numerical limitations in Bylaw 11.7.6 (see Bylaw 11.7.2). In bowl subdivision football and women's rowing, such telephone calls also may be made by a graduate assistant coach, provided the coach has successfully completed the coaches' certification examination per Bylaw 11.5.1.1. *(Revised: 1/10/95, 1/9/96 effective 8/1/96, 1/12/04 effective 8/1/04, 4/27/06 effective 8/1/06, 5/26/06, 12/12/06, 12/15/06, 4/26/12)*

13.1.3.4.1.1 Exceptions—Before Commitment. Before a prospective student-athlete signs a National Letter of Intent or the institution's written offer of admission and/or financial aid or before the institution receives a financial deposit in response to the institution's offer of admission, the following institutional staff members may make telephone calls to a prospective student-athlete (or the prospective student-athlete's parents or legal guardians) as specified: *(Adopted: 4/27/06 effective 8/1/06, Revised: 1/14/08 effective 8/1/08, 1/15/11 effective 8/1/11, 4/26/12)*

(a) **President or Chancellor/Faculty Athletics Representative/Director of Athletics/Senior Woman Administrator.** It is permissible for an institution's chancellor or president, faculty athletics representative, director of athletics and senior woman administrator to return (as opposed to initiate) telephone calls from a prospective student-athlete (or the prospective student-athlete's parents or legal guardians). Under such circumstances, there are no restrictions on the content of the conversation that may occur during the call; however, any return call is subject to any applicable limitations on the number of telephone calls that an institution may place to a prospective student-athlete. *(Adopted: 6/8/99, Revised: 3/8/06, 4/27/06 effective 8/1/06, 4/28/08)*

(b) **Academic Advisors.** It is permissible for academic advisors (including academic advisors within the athletics department) to make calls to a prospective student-athlete (or the prospective student-athlete's parents or legal guardians) related to admissions or academic issues, subject to any applicable limitation on the number of telephone calls an institution may place to a prospective student-athlete. *(Adopted: 1/10/95, Revised: 4/27/06 effective 8/1/06, 4/26/12)*

(c) **Compliance Administrators.** It is permissible for a compliance administrator to make telephone calls to a prospective student-athlete (or the prospective student-athlete's parents or legal guardians) with no limit on the timing or number of such telephone calls, provided the calls relate only to compliance issues. *(Adopted: 1/14/97, Revised: 1/9/06 effective 8/1/06, 4/27/06 effective 8/1/06, 1/14/08 effective 8/1/08, 4/26/12)*

(d) **Noncoaching Staff Members and Noncountable Coaches—Telephone Calls in Conjunction with Official Visit.** A noncoaching staff member or a coach who does not count toward the numerical limitations on head and assistant coaches in Bylaw 11.7.6 may initiate telephone calls to a prospective student-athlete or those individuals accompanying the prospective student-athlete during the prospective student-athlete's official visit transportation and during his or her official visit. *(Adopted: 1/16/10 ffective 8/1/10, Revised: 4/26/12)*

13.1.3.5 Nonpermissible Callers.

13.1.3.5.1 Representatives of Athletics Interests. Representatives of an institution's athletics interests (as defined in Bylaw 13.02.14) are prohibited from making telephonic communications with a prospective student-athlete or the prospective student-athlete's relatives or legal guardians.

13.1.3.5.1.1 Prospective Student-Athlete Initiates Call. An athletics representative of a member institution may speak to a prospective student-athlete via the telephone only if the prospective student-athlete initiates the telephone conversation and the call is not for recruiting purposes. Under such circumstances, the representative must refer questions about the institution's athletics program to the athletics department staff.

13.1.3.5.2 Enrolled Student-Athletes. Enrolled student-athletes or other enrolled students shall not make or participate in telephone calls to prospective student-athletes at the direction of a coaching staff member or financed by the institution or a representative of its athletics interests; however, they may receive telephone calls at the expense of the prospective student-athlete on or after the date on which an institution may begin placing telephone calls to a prospective student-athlete. An enrolled student-athlete may receive telephone calls made at the expense of a prospective student-athlete prior to the date on which an institution may begin placing telephone calls to a prospective student-athlete, provided there is no direct or indirect involvement by athletics department staff. *(Revised: 1/10/91 effective 7/1/91, 1/14/08 effective 8/1/08, 1/18/14 effective 8/1/14)*

> **13.1.3.5.2.1 Admissions Program Exception.** Telephone calls made by enrolled students (excluding student-athletes) pursuant to an institution's regular admissions program directed at all prospective students shall be permissible. *(Revised: 1/10/91 effective 7/1/91)*

13.1.3.6 Collect and Toll-Free Telephone Calls. Institutional coaching staff members (see Bylaw 13.1.3.4.1) may accept collect and toll-free (e.g., 1-800, 1-888) telephone calls placed by a prospective student-athlete and the prospective student-athlete's parents and legal guardians, provided the calls are placed not earlier than the date on which an institution may begin placing telephone calls to a prospective student-athlete. *(Adopted: 1/10/92, Revised: 1/11/94, 12/12/06, 1/18/14 effective 8/1/14)*

13.1.3.7 Telephone Calls Regarding Institutional Camp or Clinic Logistical Issues. Telephone calls to an individual (or his or her parents, legal guardians, relatives or coach) that relate solely to institutional camp or clinic logistical issues (e.g., missing registration information) are not subject to the restrictions on telephone calls, provided no recruiting conversation or solicitation of particular individuals to attend a camp or clinic occurs during such calls. *(Adopted: 9/24/09)*

13.1.4 Visit to Prospective Student-Athlete's Educational Institution. Visits to a prospective student-athlete's educational institution that will occur during that portion of the day when classes are being conducted for all students must receive the approval of the executive officer (or the executive officer's designated representative) of the prospective student-athlete's educational institution. *A coaching staff member may not visit a prospective student-athlete's educational institution during a dead period. (Revised: 10/27/11 effective 8/1/12, 12/6/13)*

*****

13.1.4.2 Football and Women's Basketball. In football and women's basketball, institutional staff members may visit a prospective student-athlete's educational institution on not more than one occasion during a particular week within a contact period, regardless of the number of prospective student-athletes enrolled in the institution or whether any prospective student-athlete is contacted on that occasion. *(Revised: 1/11/94 effective 8/1/94, 10/27/11 effective 8/1/12)*

> **13.1.4.2.1 Visits During Contact Period—Football.** [FBS/FCS] In football, one contact per prospective student-athlete is permitted during each week of the contact period as specified in Bylaw 13.17.4 either at the prospective student-athlete's educational institution or any other location (e.g., prospective student-athlete's home). A visit to the prospective student-athlete's educational institution and any other location (e.g., prospective student-athlete's home) during the same calendar day shall be considered one contact. *(Adopted: 1/10/92 effective 8/1/92, Revised: 1/11/94 effective 8/1/94, 12/15/06)*

> **13.1.4.2.2 Visits During Evaluation Period—Bowl Subdivision Football.** [FBS] In bowl subdivision football, not more than two coaches per institution may visit a prospective student-athlete's educational institution on any one calendar day during an evaluation period. *(Adopted: 4/29/10)*

*****

13.1.4.3 Multiple-Sport Athlete—Basketball or Football. If a prospective student-athlete is a multisport athlete being recruited by the same institution for more than one sport, one of which is football or basketball, all staff members from the same institution are permitted only one visit per week to the prospective student-athlete's educational institution, and all visits must take place on the same day of the week. *(Revised: 10/27/11 effective 8/1/12)*

13.1.4.4 Competition Not Involving Educational Institution Visited—Basketball and Football. An institution does not use its one visit per week to an educational institution if the coach observes competition between prospective student-athletes who do not attend that institution and the coach does not engage in recruitment activities with any prospective student-athlete who attends the institution where the competition is being conducted. *(Adopted: 1/16/93, Revised: 10/27/11 effective 8/1/12)*

13.1.5 Contacts.

*****

13.1.5.2 Football. [FBS/FCS] In football, each institution shall be limited to six in-person, off-campus recruiting contacts per prospective student-athlete at any site and shall include contacts made with the prospective student-athlete's relatives or legal guardians, but shall not include contacts made during an official visit per Bylaw 13.6. *(Adopted: 9/12/03, Revised: 12/15/06)*

*****

13.1.5.6 Counting Contacts and Evaluations. Evaluations that occur during the academic year count against the permissible number of recruiting opportunities, except for evaluations that occur on the same day as a permissible contact. Outside of the academic year, evaluations do not count against the annual number of recruiting opportunities. Contacts that occur with a prospective student-athlete count against the permissible number of total recruiting opportunities regardless of the time period (e.g., academic year or outside the academic year). All contacts and evaluations are subject to recruiting calendar restrictions. *(Revised: 10/30/12)*

13.1.5.7 On Same Day. Any number of contacts made during the same day (defined as 12:01 a.m. to midnight) shall count as one contact. *(Revised: 1/10/91 effective 8/1/91)*

13.1.5.8 Letter-of-Intent Signing. Any in-person, off-campus contact made with a prospective student-athlete for the purpose of signing a letter of intent or other commitment to attend the institution or attendance at activities related to the signing of a letter of intent or other commitment to attend the institution shall be prohibited. *(Revised: 1/10/95 effective 8/1/95)*

13.1.5.8.1 Delivery of Letter of Intent. In-person, off-campus delivery of a letter of intent by an institutional staff member shall be prohibited. The letter may be delivered by express mail, courier service, regular mail, electronic mail or facsimile machine. *(Adopted: 1/10/92, Revised: 1/10/95 effective 8/1/95, 11/22/04)*

13.1.5.9 Post-High School Contacts. In sports other than men's basketball, the contact limitations apply to the period in which the prospective student-athlete is enrolled in high school and the period beginning October 15 following the prospective student-athlete's completion of high school. In men's basketball, an institution shall be limited to three contacts with a prospective student-athlete beginning October 15 following the prospective student-athlete's completion of high school. *(Revised: 1/10/90, 10/27/11 effective 8/1/12)*

13.1.6 Contact Restrictions at Specified Sites.

13.1.6.1 Prospective Student-Athlete's Educational Institution. Any staff member desiring to contact a prospective student-athlete at the prospective student-athlete's high school, preparatory school or two-year college first shall obtain permission for such contact from that institution's executive officer (or the executive officer's authorized representative). Contact may be made only when such permission is granted and, in basketball, may not be made during the time of the day when classes are in session. Institutions also are bound by this provision when recruiting international prospective student-athletes. **[D]** *(Revised: 8/5/04, 10/27/11 effective 8/1/12, 1/19/13 effective 8/1/13)*

13.1.6.2 Practice or Competition Site. Recruiting contact may not be made with a prospective student-athlete prior to any athletics competition (including a noninstitutional, private camp or clinic, but not an institutional camp or clinic) in which the prospective student-athlete is a participant during the day or days of competition, even if the prospective student-athlete is on an official or unofficial visit. Contact includes the passing of notes or verbally relaying information to a prospective student-athlete by a third party on behalf of an institutional staff member and telephone calls. Such contact shall be governed by the following: **[D]** *(Revised: 1/11/89, 1/10/91, 1/11/94, 1/9/96 effective 7/1/96, 4/3/02, 4/24/03, 3/23/06, 12/12/06, 9/18/07, 1/15/14)*

(a) Contact shall not be made with the prospective student-athlete at any site prior to the contest on the day or days of competition;

(b) Contact shall not be made with the prospective student-athlete from the time he or she reports on call (at the direction of his or her coach or comparable authority) and becomes involved in competition-related activity (e.g., traveling to an away-from-home game) to the end of the competition even if such competition-related activities are initiated prior to the day or days of competition;

(c) Contact shall not be made after the competition until the prospective student-athlete is released by the appropriate institutional authority and departs the dressing and meeting facility;

(d) Contact shall not be made with the prospective student-athlete involved in competition that requires participation on consecutive days (e.g., a tournament) until after his or her final contest is completed and he or she is released by the appropriate institutional authority and leaves the dressing and meeting facility. Contact shall not be made with a prospective student-athlete involved in a tournament that is not conducted on consecutive days until after his or her final contest is completed on a day before a break in the days of the tournament and he or she is released by the appropriate institutional authority and leaves the dressing and meeting facility;

(e) Contact with a prospective student-athlete who is on an extended road trip (e.g., traveling with a team from one contest or event to another), is permitted at the conclusion of a competition and prior to the commencement of travel to the next competition, provided he or she has been released by the appropriate institutional authority and departs the dressing and meeting facility; and

(f) Coaching staff members may not send electronic correspondence to a prospective student-athlete while he or she is on call for competition at the competition site (e.g., arena, stadium). Coaching staff members may send general correspondence (including electronic correspondence) to a prospective student-athlete while he or she is on call and not at the competition site or while the prospective student-athlete is at any location once he or she has been released by the appropriate authority, provided the general correspondence is sent directly to a prospective student-athlete (e.g., the front desk of the hotel, the prospective student-athlete's personal fax machine) and there is no additional party (e.g., camp employee, coach) involved in disseminating the correspondence (see Bylaw 13.4). For additional restrictions in basketball, see Bylaw 13.1.6.2.1.

*****

13.1.6.2.2 Approved Events. It is permissible for athletics staff members who are responsible for conducting an approved athletics event (see Bylaw 13.11.3) involving prospective student-athletes to come in normal contact with participants; however, under no circumstances may recruitment take place.

13.1.6.2.3 Athletics Events Outside Contact Period—Football and Basketball. In-person contact with a prospective student-athlete shall not be made on or off the institution's campus at the site of practice or competition for any athletics event in which the prospective student-athlete participates outside the permissible contact periods in football and basketball. When a prospective student-athlete in football or basketball participates in an athletics contest or event (including a noninstitutional, private camp or clinic, but not an institutional camp or clinic) on an institution's campus outside of a contact period, it is not permissible for an authorized institutional staff member to have contact with the prospective student-athlete until the calendar day following his or her release from the contest or event. Further, if a prospective student-athlete is visiting an institution's campus immediately before or after participating in an athletics contest or event on the institution's campus, the prospective student-athlete must depart the locale of the institution the calendar day before or after the contest or event. *(Revised: 1/11/89, 4/3/02, 6/1/07)*

13.1.6.2.4 Bowl Games. During a dead period, a prospective student-athlete may attend an institution's bowl game practice session at the bowl site, provided the practice is open to the general public and the prospective student-athlete observes the practice only from an area reserved for that purpose for the general public. No contact between the prospective student-athlete and institutional staff members or representatives of the institution's athletics interests may occur. *(Adopted: 1/10/92, Revised: 5/27/11)*

13.1.6.3 All-Star Contests—Football. [FBS/FCS] In football, in-person contact with a prospective student-athlete who is participating in an all-star contest shall not be made from the time the prospective student-athlete arrives in the locale of the contest until he returns to his home or to his educational institution. *(Adopted: 10/30/13)*

13.1.7 Limitations on Number of Evaluations.

13.1.7.1 Visit (Without Contact) to Prospective Student-Athlete's Educational Institution. A visit (without contact) by a coaching staff member to a prospective student-athlete's educational institution counts as an evaluation for all prospective student-athletes in that sport at that educational institution. *(Adopted: 1/10/92)*

13.1.7.1.1 Competition Not Involving Educational Institution Visited. A member institution does not use an evaluation for prospective student-athletes at an educational institution if the coach observes competition at that institution between prospective student-athletes who do not attend that institution. *(Adopted: 1/11/94)*

13.1.7.2 Evaluations Are Sport Specific. The limitations on the number of evaluations in Bylaw 13.1.7 are sport specific; therefore, a prospective student-athlete being earnestly recruited [see Bylaw 15.5.9.7.1-(d)] by an institution in more than one sport may be evaluated on the permissible number of occasions in each of those sports during the academic year. Evaluations are counted against the sport of the coach making the evaluation. *(Adopted: 1/10/92)*

13.1.7.2.1 Recruiting Opportunities in Cross Country and Track and Field. An institution is limited to a total of seven recruiting opportunities (contacts and evaluations combined) during the academic year during which the prospective student-athlete competes in any or all of the sports of cross country and indoor and outdoor track and field, provided not more than three of the opportunities are contacts. **[D]** *(Adopted: 1/16/93)*

*****

13.1.7.4 Limitations on Number of Evaluations—Football. [FBS/FCS] In football, institutional staff members shall be limited to three evaluations during the academic year during which the prospective student-athlete competes or practices on any team. Not more than one evaluation may be used during the fall evaluation period and not more than two evaluations may be used during the April 15 through May 31 evaluation period. An authorized off-campus recruiter may use one evaluation to assess the prospective student-athlete's athletics ability and one evaluation to assess the prospective student-athlete's academic qualifications during the April 15 through May 31 evaluation period. If an institution's coaching staff member conducts both an athletics and an academic evaluation of a prospective student-athlete on the same day during the April 15 through May 31 evaluation period, the institution shall be charged with the use of an academic evaluation only and shall be permitted to conduct a second athletics evaluation of the prospective student-athlete on a separate day during the evaluation period. **[D]** *(Adopted: 9/12/03)*

13.1.7.4.1 Head Coach Restriction—Spring Evaluation Period. [FBS] In bowl subdivision football, during the April 15 through May 31 evaluation period, the head coach [and any assistant coach who has been publicly designated by the institution to become the next head coach (see Bylaw 13.1.2.6.1)] shall not engage in off-campus recruiting activities, participate in an off-campus coaching clinic, visit a prospective student-athlete's educational institution for any reason or meet with a prospective student-athlete's coach at an off-campus location. *(Adopted: 1/14/08, Revised: 1/17/09, 1/16/10)*

*****

13.1.7.7 On Same Day. Any number of evaluations or observations made during the same calendar day (defined as 12:01 a.m. to midnight) shall count as one evaluation. *(Adopted: 1/16/93)*

*****

13.1.7.9 Football Evaluations.

13.1.7.9.1 Time Period for Counting Football Evaluations. [FBS/FCS] In football, the time period during which the three permissible evaluations may take place shall be from April 15 through April 14 of the following academic year. *(Adopted: 1/10/92 effective 5/1/92, Revised: 1/16/93, 4/27/00 effective 8/1/00)*

13.1.7.9.2 Limitations on the Number of Spring Evaluations. [FBS/FCS] In football, institutional staff members shall not visit a prospective student-athlete's educational institution on more than two calendar days during the spring evaluation period. A visit to a prospective student-athlete's educational institution that only includes contact with a signed prospective student-athlete during the spring evaluation period shall be considered one of the institution's two permissible days at that institution. **[D]** *(Adopted: 1/10/91 effective 8/1/91, Revised: 4/27/00 effective 8/1/00, 1/14/08 effective 8/1/08, 4/24/08 effective 8/1/08)*

13.1.7.9.3 Evaluation Days. [FBS/FCS] In football, each institution is limited to 42 (54 for U.S. service academies) evaluation days (see Bylaw 13.02.7.2) during the fall evaluation period and 168 (216 for U.S. service academies) evaluation days during the spring evaluation period. **[D]** *(Adopted: 4/25/02 effective 8/1/02, Revised: 8/14/02, 2/21/05, 5/1/05, 12/15/06, 2/22/08 effective 8/1/08, 4/14/08, 1/16/10 effective 8/1/10)*

13.1.7.9.4 Scholastic and Nonscholastic Activities—Bowl Subdivision Football. [FBS] In bowl subdivision football, all live athletics evaluations shall be limited to: **[D]** *(Adopted: 1/9/06 effective 8/1/06, Revised: 1/14/08, 4/30/09 effective 8/1/09, 1/16/10 effective 8/1/10, 10/30/13)*

(a) Regularly scheduled high school, preparatory school and two-year college contests and practices;

(b) Regular scholastic activities involving prospective student-athletes enrolled only at the institution at which the regular scholastic activities occur; and

(c) Events, other than all-star contests and associated activities (e.g., practice, banquets, coaches clinics, etc.), that are organized and conducted solely by the applicable state high school athletics association, state preparatory school association or state or national junior college athletics association.

13.1.7.9.4.1 Other Evaluation Events—Bowl Subdivision Football. [FBS] In bowl subdivision football, an institutional staff member shall not attend a recruiting event (other than those permitted pursuant to

Bylaw 13.1.7.9.4) in which information (e.g., athletics or academic credentials, highlight or combine video) related to prospective student-athletes is presented or otherwise made available. **[D]** *(Adopted: 4/30/09 effective 8/1/09, Revised: 1/16/10 effective 8/1/10)*

13.1.7.9.5 Scholastic and Nonscholastic Activities—Championship Subdivision Football. [FCS] In championship subdivision football, live athletics evaluations may be conducted at scholastic or nonscholastic athletics activities, other than all-star contests and associated activities (e.g., practice, banquets, coaches clinics, etc.), provided there is no institutional involvement in arranging or directing such activities. An institutional staff member may attend a recruiting event (other than a permissible live athletics event) in which information (e.g., athletics or academic credentials, highlight video) related to prospective student-athletes is presented or otherwise made available. **[D]** *(Adopted: 1/16/10 effective 8/1/10, Revised: 1/15/11, 10/30/13)*

13.1.7.9.6 All-Star Contests. [FBS/FCS] In football, an institutional staff member shall not attend an all-star contest or other activities associated with such a contest (e.g., practice, banquets, coaches clinics, etc.). *(Adopted: 10/30/13)*

13.1.7.10 Evaluations in Team Sports. In team sports, an institution shall use an evaluation for each prospective student-athlete participating in a practice or contest observed by the institution's coach, except an evaluation that occurs on the same day as a permissible contact (see Bylaw 13.1.5.6). An institution's coach who is attending an event in which prospective student-athletes from multiple educational institutions participate in drills (e.g., combine) shall use an evaluation only for each prospective student-athlete participating in the event that the coach observes engaging in the drills. In football, an observation that occurs during a permissible contact period shall count only as a contact per Bylaw 13.02.4.1. *(Revised: 6/28/04, 5/14/05, 10/30/12)*

*****

13.1.7.15 Tournament Evaluations. Evaluation during each day of a tournament held during the academic year shall count as a separate evaluation except as follows (see Bylaws 13.1.4.1 and 13.1.4.2.3.1): *(Revised: 1/14/97, 3/22/06)*

(a) Evaluation of multiple contests in a tournament that occurs on consecutive days (and normally at the same site) shall count as a single evaluation.

(b) Evaluation of multiple contests in a single tier of a tournament (e.g., sectional, district, regional) shall count as a single observation. If a particular tier of a tournament is subdivided into identifiable segments (e.g., conducted on different weekends), evaluation of contests in each identifiable segment counts as a single observation.

  13.1.7.15.1 Other Multiple-Day Events. Evaluations at a multiple-day event (e.g., jamboree, round robin, showcase) constitute separate evaluations for each day of the event unless the event is conducted in a tournament format in which a winner of the event is determined. *(Adopted: 12/13/05)*

13.1.7.16 Open Events in Which College Teams Compete. An institution does not use an evaluation if the institution's team competes in an open event (e.g., track and field meet) in which prospective student-athletes also compete. *(Adopted: 1/10/92)*

13.1.7.17 Coaches' Attendance at Elite International Events. Coaching staff members may attend Olympic, Pan American, World Championships, World Cup, World University Games or World University Championships competition that occurs outside the permissible contact and evaluation periods. However, attendance at qualifying competition for such events, including tryouts, and attendance at junior-level competition (e.g., Youth Olympic Games, Junior World Championships, U19 World University Games) that may be associated with the specified elite international events, remains subject to the applicable recruiting calendars. *(Adopted: 1/9/06 effective 8/1/06, Revised: 8/11/11, 1/14/12)*

13.1.7.18 Evaluation of Individuals Before They Become Prospective Student-Athletes. In sports other than men's basketball, a coaching staff member may observe an individual who has not entered the ninth grade participating in an athletically related activity, provided such observation occurs during a contact or evaluation period when it is permissible to evaluate prospective student-athletes. In men's basketball, a coaching staff member may observe an individual who has not entered the seventh grade participating in an athletically related activity, provided such observation occurs during a period when it is permissible to evaluate prospective student-athletes. **[D]** *(Adopted: 12/12/06, Revised: 6/9/10, 10/27/11 effective 8/1/12)*

13.1.7.19 Off-Campus Observation of Recruiting or Scouting Service Video. Off-campus observation of a prospective student-athlete via video made available by a recruiting or scouting service is considered an evaluation activity and is subject to applicable evaluation regulations. *(Adopted: 1/16/10)*

13.1.7.20 Coaches' Involvement in Local Sports Clubs—No Requirement to Count Evaluations. A coaching staff member is not required to count evaluations for any observations of prospective student-athletes that occur while he or she is participating in permissible activities and acting on behalf of a local sports club (e.g., coaching or instructional activities, scouting future opponents). *(Adopted: 1/10/13)*

13.1.8 Banquets, Meetings and NCAA Promotional Activities.

13.1.8.1 Banquets or Meetings at a Prospective Student-Athlete's Educational Institution. *(Revised: 4/15/09)*

*****

(d) **Football. [FBS/FCS]**

(1) **During a Contact Period.** In football, a coach who speaks at a meeting or banquet at a prospective student-athlete's educational institution during a contact period, uses one of the institution's six in-person, off-campus recruiting contacts per prospective student-athlete and also uses the institution's once-per-week visit to a prospective student-athlete's educational institution.

(2) **Outside a Contact Period.** In football, a coach may speak at a meeting or banquet at a prospective student-athlete's educational institution outside a contact period without such attendance being considered an evaluation or a visit to a prospective student-athlete's educational institution (except for dead periods per Bylaw 13.02.5.5), provided: *(Revised: 9/9/98, 2/22/01, 5/18/05)*

(i) The meeting or banquet is initiated and conducted by the educational institution;

(ii) The coach does not make a recruiting presentation in conjunction with the appearance;

(iii) The coach does not have direct contact with any prospective student-athlete (or a prospective student-athlete's parents or legal guardians) in attendance; and

(iv) The coach does not engage in any evaluation activities.

13.1.8.2 Banquets or Meetings at Locations Other Than a Prospective Student-Athlete's Educational Institution. A coach may speak at a meeting or banquet at which prospective student-athletes are in attendance at a location other than a prospective student-athlete's educational institution (except during a dead period per Bylaw 13.02.5.5) outside of a contact period (recruiting period in men's basketball) or may speak at such a meeting or banquet during a contact period (recruiting period in men's basketball) without using one of the institution's permissible contacts or evaluations, provided: *(Revised: 4/15/09, 10/27/11 effective 8/1/12)*

(a) The meeting or banquet is initiated and conducted by an entity other than the coach's institution;

(b) The coach does not make a recruiting presentation in conjunction with the appearance;

(c) The coach does not have any direct contact with any prospective student-athlete (or a prospective student-athlete's parents or legal guardians) in attendance; and

(d) The coach does not engage in any evaluation activities.

13.1.8.3 Attendance Outside a Contact or Evaluation Period. In sports with recruiting calendars (see Bylaw 13.17), a coach is not permitted to attend a banquet or meeting that is designed to recognize prospective student-athletes and that occurs outside a contact or evaluation period (or in men's basketball, a recruiting period), unless the coach will speak at the function. In all sports, during a dead period, a coaching staff member may not attend a meeting or banquet at which prospective student-athletes are in attendance, except as provided in Bylaw 13.1.8.4. *(Adopted: 6/8/99, Revised: 8/14/02, 1/19/13 effective 8/1/13, 12/6/13)*

13.1.8.4 Postseason Game Exception—Football. [FBS/FCS] In football, a coach may speak at or attend a meeting or banquet (at which prospective student-athletes are in attendance) in conjunction with the institution's appearance in a postseason contest that occurs during a dead period only if the meeting or banquet is open to the general public, it is a scheduled activity associated with the contest, and the coach does not make a recruiting presentation or have any direct contact with any prospective student-athlete (or a prospective student-athlete's parents or legal guardians) in attendance. *(Adopted: 9/15/97)*

13.1.8.5 NCAA Promotional Activities Exception. An institution's coach may participate in NCAA promotional activities (e.g., autograph sessions, fan festivals and opening ceremonies) at NCAA championship events, provided contacts with prospective student-athletes are not prearranged and recruiting activities do not occur. *(Adopted: 4/28/05)*

13.1.9 Funeral/Memorial Services. An institutional staff member may attend the funeral or memorial services of a student-athlete, a prospective student-athlete or a member of the student-athlete's or a prospective student-athlete's immediate family, at which prospective student-athletes also may be in attendance, provided no recruiting contact occurs. The involved prospective student-athlete must have signed a National Letter of Intent, or a written offer of admission and/or financial aid with the institution, or the institution must have received a financial deposit in response to the institution's offer of admission. *(Adopted: 4/28/05, Revised: 1/15/11 effective 8/1/11)*

13.1.10 Conference-Sponsored Sportsmanship Initiatives. A conference office may coordinate sportsmanship initiatives that may involve prospective student-athletes and their educational institutions subject to the following conditions (see Bylaws 13.4.3.4, 13.10.2.3 and 13.15.1.8): *(Adopted: 4/26/07 effective 8/1/07)*

(a) Any participating prospective student-athlete must attend a high school within a 30-mile radius of a conference member institution's campus;

(b) Any initiative that requires the actual presence of a prospective student-athlete shall not take place on an institution's campus; and

(c) An institution's student-athletes may participate, subject to the conditions of Bylaw 12.5.1.1.

13.2 Offers and Inducements.

13.2.1 General Regulation. An institution's staff member or any representative of its athletics interests shall not be involved, directly or indirectly, in making arrangements for or giving or offering to give any financial aid or other benefits to a prospective student-athlete or his or her relatives or friends, other than expressly permitted by NCAA regulations. Receipt of a benefit by a prospective student-athlete or his or her relatives or friends is not a violation of NCAA legislation if it is determined that the same benefit is generally available to the institution's prospective students or their relatives or friends or to a particular segment of the student body (e.g., international students, minority students) determined on a basis unrelated to athletics ability. **[R]** *(Revised: 10/28/97, 11/1/00, 3/24/05)*

> **13.2.1.1 Specific Prohibitions.** Specifically prohibited financial aid, benefits and arrangements include, but are not limited to, the following: *(Adopted: 4/23/08)*
>
> (a) An employment arrangement for a prospective student-athlete's relatives;
>
> (b) Gift of clothing or equipment;
>
> (c) Co-signing of loans;
>
> (d) Providing loans to a prospective student-athlete's relatives or friends;
>
> (e) Cash or like items;
>
> (f) Any tangible items, including merchandise;
>
> (g) Free or reduced-cost services, rentals or purchases of any type;
>
> (h) Free or reduced-cost housing;
>
> (i) Use of an institution's athletics equipment (e.g., for a high school all-star game);
>
> (j) Sponsorship of or arrangement for an awards banquet for high school, preparatory school or two-year-college athletes by an institution, representatives of its athletics interests or its alumni groups or booster clubs; and
>
> (k) Expenses for academic services (e.g., tutoring, test preparation) to assist in the completion of initial-eligibility or transfer-eligibility requirements or improvement of the prospective student-athlete's academic profile in conjunction with a waiver request.
>
> *****

13.2.2 Awards to Prospective Student-Athletes. A member institution is limited to providing the following awards to prospective student-athletes: *(Adopted: 1/10/91)*

(a) Awards to prospective student-athletes for outstanding athletics accomplishments are prohibited, except as provided in (c) below;

(b) Awards to high school, preparatory school or two-year-college athletics teams in the name of an NCAA member institution are prohibited, regardless of the institution's involvement (or lack thereof) in the administration of the award; and

(c) Any award presented at regularly scheduled high school, preparatory school and two-year-college athletics contests or matches under the provisions of Bylaw 13.11.3.4 must be limited in value to $50 but may bear the institution's name and logo.

13.2.3 Employment of Prospective Student-Athletes.

13.2.3.1 Prior to Completion of Senior Year—Nonathletics Award Winners. An institution's athletics department may employ a prospective student-athlete who is not an athletics award winner and not recruited by the institution, provided the employment is arranged through normal institutional employment procedures (e.g., local newspaper, bulletin board listings). Any compensation received by the prospective student-athlete must be for work actually performed and commensurate with the going rate for such services in the locale. (See Bylaw 13.12.1.7.1.1.) *(Adopted: 4/29/04, Revised: 6/10/04, 1/19/13 effective 8/1/13)*

13.2.3.2 Prior to Completion of Senior Year—Athletics Award Winners. An institution may employ a prospective student-athlete who is an athletics award winner in any department outside intercollegiate athletics, provided the employment is arranged through normal institutional employment procedures (e.g., local newspaper, bulletin board listings) and without the intervention of any member of the institution's coaching staff. Any compensation received by the prospective student-athlete must be for work actually performed and commensurate with the going rate for such services in the locale. For purposes of this bylaw, institutional recreation programs, even if reporting to the athletics director, may be considered outside the intercollegiate athletics department. An institution may hire a prospective student-athlete, who is an athletics award winner, in its recreation programs, only if recreation and facility managers and no intercollegiate coaches are involved with the hiring and supervision of these employees. (See Bylaws 13.12.1.7.1 and 13.12.1.7.1.1.) *(Adopted: 4/29/04 effective 8/1/04, Revised: 1/19/13 effective 8/1/13)*

13.2.3.3 After Completion of Senior Year. An institution may arrange for employment or employ any prospective student-athlete (regardless of athletics award winner status), provided the employment does not begin prior to the completion of the prospective student-athlete's senior year in high school. (See Bylaws 13.12.1.7.1 and 13.12.1.7.1.1.) *(Revised: 1/19/13 effective 8/1/13)*

13.2.3.3.1 Two-Year College Prospective Student-Athletes. Once a prospective student-athlete has enrolled as a full-time student in a two-year college, the arrangement of employment by an institution for such a prospective student-athlete shall be permitted, provided the employment does not begin prior to the time period in which the prospective student-athlete has officially withdrawn from or has completed requirements for graduation at the two-year college. (See Bylaws 13.12.1.7.1 and 13.12.1.7.1.1.) *(Adopted: 1/12/99, Revised: 1/19/13 effective 8/1/13)*

13.2.3.4 Transportation to Summer Job. An institution or its representatives shall not provide a prospective student-athlete free transportation to and from a summer job unless it is the employer's established policy to transport all employees to and from the job site.

13.2.4 Loans to Prospective Student-Athletes. Arrangement of educational loans by an institution for a prospective student-athlete shall be permitted, provided the loan is not made prior to the completion of the prospective student-athlete's senior year in high school. Such loans must be from a regular lending agency and based on a regular repayment schedule.

13.2.5 Summer Housing for Prospective Student-Athletes. An institution may rent dormitory space to a prospective student-athlete during the summer months at the regular institutional rate, provided it is the institution's policy to make such dormitory space available on the same basis to all prospective students. *(Revised: 4/28/05 effective 8/1/05, 1/19/13 effective 8/1/13)*

13.2.6 Medical Expenses—Basketball. In basketball, an institution may finance medical expenses (including rehabilitation and physical therapy expenses) for a prospective student-athlete who sustains an injury while participating in: *(Adopted: 1/14/12, Revised: 1/19/13)*

(a) An on-campus evaluation (see Bylaw 13.11.2.1);

(b) A voluntary summer workout conducted by an institution's strength and conditioning coach with department-wide duties (see Bylaw 13.11.3.8); or

(c) Required summer athletic activities (see Bylaw 13.11.3.9).

13.2.7 Medical Expenses—Football.

13.2.7.1 Medical Expenses—Bowl Subdivision Football. [FBS] In bowl subdivision football, an institution may finance medical expenses (including rehabilitation and physical therapy expenses) for a prospective student-athlete who sustains an injury while participating in voluntary summer conditioning activities that are conducted by an institution's strength and conditioning coach with department-wide duties (see Bylaw 13.11.3.7.1) or while participating in required summer athletic activities (see Bylaw 13.11.3.10). *(Adopted: 4/24/03 effective 5/1/03, Revised: 12/15/06, 10/30/13)*

13.2.7.2 Medical Expenses—Championship Subdivision Football. [FCS] In championship subdivision football, an institution may finance medical expenses (including rehabilitation and physical therapy expenses) for a prospective student-athlete who sustains an injury while participating in voluntary summer conditioning activities that are conducted by an institution's strength and conditioning coach with department-wide duties or a countable coach who is a certified strength and conditioning coach (see Bylaw 13.11.3.7.2) or while participating in required summer athletic activities (see Bylaw 13.11.3.10). *(Adopted: 4/24/03 effective 5/1/03, Revised: 4/29/04, 12/15/06, 5/4/09, 10/30/13)*

13.2.8 Life-Threatening Injury or Illness. An institution may provide a donation (up to $100) to a charity on behalf of a prospective student-athlete or may provide other reasonable tokens of support (e.g., flowers) in the event of the death of the prospective student-athlete or the death or life-threatening injury or illness of a member of the prospective student-athlete's immediate family, provided the prospective student-athlete has signed a National Letter of Intent, or a written offer of admission and/or financial aid with the institution, or the institution must have received a financial deposit in response to the institution's offer of admission. *(Adopted: 1/12/04, Revised: 4/28/05, 5/26/06, 1/15/11 effective 8/1/11)*

13.2.9 Benefits for Prospective Student-Athlete's Family Members. An institutional staff member may provide a benefit to a member of the prospective student-athlete's family, provided: *(Revised: 5/11/05)*

(a) The family member has a pre-existing established relationship with the institutional staff member; and

(b) The benefit provided is consistent with the nature and level of benefits that the institutional staff member has provided to the family member prior to the prospective student-athlete starting classes for the ninth grade.

13.4 Recruiting Materials.
13.4.1 Recruiting Materials and Electronic Correspondence—General Rule. An institution shall not provide recruiting materials, including general correspondence related to athletics, or send electronic correspondence to an individual (or his or her parents or legal guardians) until September 1 at the beginning of his or her junior year in high school. If an individual attends an educational institution that uses a nontraditional academic calendar (e.g., Southern Hemisphere), an institution shall not provide recruiting materials, including general correspondence related to athletics, or send electronic correspondence to the individual (or his or her parents or legal guardians) until the opening day of classes of his or her junior year in high school. **[D]** *(Revised: 1/10/91 effective 8/1/91, 1/10/92, 1/11/94 effective 8/1/94, 1/10/95 effective 8/1/95, 1/9/96 effective 7/1/96, 11/1/01 effective 4/1/02, 4/29/04 effective 8/1/04, 1/10/05, 4/28/05 effective 8/1/05, 4/26/07, 4/15/08, 6/13/08, 3/29/10, 10/27/11 effective 6/15/12, 1/18/14, 1/18/14 effective 8/1/14)*

*****

13.4.1.3 Printed Recruiting Materials. As specified below, an institution may provide only the following printed materials to a prospective student-athlete, his or her parents or legal guardians, coaches or any other individual responsible for teaching or directing an activity in which a prospective student-athlete is involved: **[D]** *(Adopted: 4/28/05 effective 8/1/05, Revised: 4/15/08, 4/29/10 effective 8/1/10, 5/27/11, 1/18/14 effective 8/1/14)*

(a) **General Correspondence.** There are no restrictions on the design or content of general correspondence and attachments, except that the size of the printed material may not exceed 8 ½ by 11 inches when opened in full. There are no restrictions on the design or content of an envelope used to send general correspondence and attachments, except that the size of the envelope may not exceed 9 by 12 inches. *(Revised: 3/8/06, 5/25/06, 12/12/06, 1/8/07 effective 8/1/07, 4/15/08, 4/24/08 effective 8/1/08, 4/29/10 effective 8/1/10, 1/18/14 effective 8/1/14)*

(b) **Camp or Clinic Information.** Camp or clinic information may be provided at any time. (See Bylaw 12.5.1.6.) *(Revised: 4/15/08, 9/24/09, 1/18/14 effective 8/1/14)*

(c) **Questionnaires.** An institution may provide questionnaires at any time. *(Revised: 4/14/08)*

(d) **Nonathletics Institutional Publications.** An institution may provide nonathletics institutional publications available to all students at any time (e.g., official academic, admissions and student-services publications published by the institution and available to all students).

(e) **Educational Material Published by the NCAA.** Educational material published by the NCAA (e.g., NCAA Guide for the College-Bound Student-Athlete) may be provided at any time. *(Revised: 4/15/08)*

> **13.4.1.3.1 Express Mail Services.** An institution is not permitted to use express mail delivery services and may only use first-class mail or a lesser rate of service (e.g., parcel post) with no extra services (e.g., certified mail, delivery confirmation) to provide permissible printed recruiting materials to prospective student-athletes, their parents or legal guardians, their coaches or any other individual responsible for teaching or directing an activity in which a prospective student-athlete is involved, who resides within the 50 United States, other than the National Letter of Intent or other written admissions and/or financial aid commitment to attend the institution. **[D]** *(Adopted: 4/28/05 effective 8/1/05, Revised: 5/12/05, 1/14/08, 4/15/08, 1/18/14 effective 8/1/14)*

13.4.1.4 Electronic Correspondence—General Rule. Electronic correspondence (e.g., electronic mail, Instant Messenger, facsimiles, text messages) may be sent to a prospective student-athlete (or the prospective student-athlete's parents or legal guardians). Before a prospective student-athlete has signed a National Letter of Intent or the institution's written offer of admission and/or financial aid, or the institution has received his or her financial deposit in response to its offer of admission, the correspondence must be sent directly to the prospective student-athlete (or his or her parents or legal guardians) and must be private between only the sender and recipient (e.g., no use of chat rooms, message boards or posts to "walls"). (See Bylaws 13.1.6.2 and 13.10.2.) There are no content restrictions on attachments to electronic correspondence, except that video and audio materials must conform to the requirements of Bylaw 13.4.1.7, may not be created for recruiting purposes and may not be personalized to include a prospective student-athlete's name, picture or likeness. **[D]** *(Adopted: 4/28/05 effective 8/1/05, Revised: 12/12/06, 4/26/07 effective 8/1/07, 4/15/08, 4/29/10 effective 8/1/10, 1/15/11 effective 8/1/11, 1/18/14 effective 8/1/14)*

> **13.4.1.4.1 Exception—Cross Country/Track and Field, Football and Swimming and Diving.** In cross country/track and field, football and swimming and diving, electronically transmitted correspondence that may be sent to a prospective student-athlete (or the prospective student-athlete's parents or legal guardians) is limited to electronic mail and facsimiles. All other forms of electronically transmitted correspondence (e.g., Instant Messenger, text messaging) are prohibited. **[D]** *(Adopted: 4/28/05 effective 8/1/05, Revised: 12/12/06, 4/26/07 effective 8/1/07, 4/15/08, 4/29/10 effective 8/1/10, 1/15/11 effective 8/1/11, 1/18/14 effective 8/1/14)*

>> **13.4.1.4.1.1 Exception—Electronic Transmissions After Commitment—Cross Country/Track and Field, Football and Swimming and Diving.** In cross country/track and field, football and swimming and diving, there shall be no limit on the forms of electronically transmitted correspondence sent to a prospective student-athlete (or the prospective student-athlete's relatives or legal guardians) after one of the following events occurs: *(Adopted: 1/15/11 effective 8/1/11, Revised: 7/31/13, 1/18/14 effective 8/1/14)*

>> (a) The prospective student-athlete signs a National Letter of Intent (NLI) or the institution's written offer of admission and/or financial aid; or

>> (b) The institution receives a financial deposit in response to the institution's offer of admission.

> *****

>> **13.4.1.4.3 Exception—Electronic Mail and Facsimiles Regarding Institutional Camp or Clinic Logistical Issues—Cross Country/Track and Field, Football and Swimming and Diving.** In cross country/track and field, football and swimming and diving, electronic mail and facsimiles to an individual (or his or her parents, legal guardians, relatives or coach) that relate solely to institutional camp or clinic logistical issues (e.g., missing registration information) are not subject to the restrictions on recruiting materials, provided the correspondence does not contain recruiting language and no solicitation of particular individuals to attend a camp or clinic occurs. **[D]** *(Adopted: 9/24/09, Revised: 10/27/11 effective 6/15/12, 1/19/13 effective 8/1/13, 1/18/14, 1/18/14 effective 8/1/14)*

13.4.1.5 Other Recruiting Materials. An institution may post recruiting materials not listed in Bylaw 13.4.1.3 on its website. General information (e.g., information not created for recruiting purposes) posted to an institution's website (e.g., press release, competition schedule) may be sent to a prospective student-athlete via permissible electronic correspondence or such information may be printed and provided to a prospective student-athlete as an attachment to general correspondence or during any permissible on- or off-campus contact. **[D]** *(Adopted: 4/28/05 effective 8/1/05, Revised: 1/17/09, 1/18/14 effective 8/1/14)*

13.4.1.6 Responding to Prospective Student-Athlete's Request. Institutional staff members (including athletics staff members) may respond to a prospective student-athlete's letter or electronic correspondence requesting information from an institution's athletics department prior to the permissible date on which an institution may begin to provide recruiting materials to a prospective student-athlete, provided the written response does not include information that would initiate the recruitment of the prospective student-athlete or information related to the institution's athletics program (e.g., the reply contains an explanation of current NCAA legislation or a referral to the admissions department). An electronic reply must be a permissible form of electronic correspondence. **[D]** *(Revised: 5/26/06, 4/20/11, 1/18/14 effective 8/1/14)*

13.4.1.7 Video/Audio Materials. An institution may not produce video or audio materials to show to, play for or provide to a prospective student-athlete except as specified in this section. Permissible video or audio material may only be provided to a prospective student-athlete via permissible electronic correspondence, except as provided in Bylaw 13.4.1.7.4. **[D]** *(Adopted: 1/11/94 effective 8/1/94, Revised: 1/9/96 effective 8/1/96, 12/12/06, 1/8/07, 1/16/10, 3/29/10, 4/28/11 effective 8/1/11, 6/13/11, 1/18/14 effective 8/1/14)*

13.4.1.7.1 Media Available to All Students. Official academic admissions and student-services media produced by the institution and available to all students may be provided to prospective student-athletes. **[D]** *(Revised: 1/16/10, 3/29/10)*

13.4.1.7.2 Material Not Created for Recruiting Purposes. An institution may produce video or audio material to show to, play for or provide to a prospective student-athlete, provided such material includes only general information related to an institution or its athletics programs and is not created for recruiting purposes. **[D]** *(Adopted: 1/16/10, Revised: 3/29/10)*

13.4.1.7.3 Computer-Generated Recruiting Presentations. An institution may produce a computer-generated recruiting presentation (e.g., using presentation software) to show to, play for or provide to a prospective student-athlete, subject to the following provisions: **[D]** *(Adopted: 1/8/07, Revised: 1/14/08, 1/16/10, 3/29/10)*

(a) The presentation may be posted to the institution's website;

(b) The presentation may include general informational video/audio material that relates to an institution or its athletics programs and is not created for recruiting purposes;

(c) The presentation may not be personalized to include a prospective student-athlete's name, picture or likeness; and

(d) The presentation may not be created by an entity outside the institution.

13.4.1.7.4 Pre-enrollment Information. An institution may provide any necessary pre-enrollment information (that is not otherwise considered to be general information related to an institution or its athletics programs) regarding orientation, conditioning, academics and practice activities in a video format (e.g., video playbook, games clips) to a prospective student-athlete, provided he or she has signed a National Letter of Intent or institutional financial aid agreement, or has been officially accepted for enrollment. Such information may be provided via a digital media storage device (e.g., DVD, flash drive). **[D]** *(Adopted: 12/26/06, Revised: 1/16/10, 3/29/10, 6/13/11)*

13.4.2 Conference Restrictions. A member conference is precluded from providing recruiting materials to prospective student-athletes. **[D]** *(Revised: 1/11/94 effective 8/1/94, 4/24/03 effective 8/1/03, 3/26/04)*

13.4.3 Advertisements and Promotions.

13.4.3.1 Recruiting Advertisements. The publication of advertising or promotional material, by or on behalf of a member institution, designed to solicit the enrollment of a prospective student-athlete is not permitted, except as provided in Bylaw 13.4.3.1.1. Accordingly, a member institution may not buy or arrange to have space in game programs or other printed materials published to provide information concerning the athletics participation or evaluation of prospective student-athletes (e.g., recruiting publications) for any purpose whatsoever, including advertisements, a listing of prospective or enrolled student-athletes who will attend the institution and informative materials related to the institution. **[D]** *(Revised: 4/28/05 effective 8/1/05)*

13.4.3.1.1 Nonathletics Institutional Advertisements. An institution (or a third party acting on behalf of the institution) may publish nonathletics institutional advertisements or promotional material (e.g., use of signage, booths, kiosks and distribution of printed materials) at high school or two-year college athletics events provided: **[D]** *(Adopted: 4/28/05 effective 8/1/05)*

(a) The funds generated by the advertisements or promotional materials are not used for the high school or two-year college's athletics program;

(b) The institution's athletics department is not involved in the advertisement or promotional activities;

(c) The advertisements or promotional materials do not contain athletics information [unless as noted in Bylaw 13.4.1.3-(d)]; and

(d) The institution documents the cost of the advertising and promotional activities.

13.4.3.2 Camp or Clinic Advertisements or Promotions. An institutional camp or clinic advertisement or promotion (e.g., camp brochure, website, newspaper or magazine advertisement) must indicate that the camp or clinic is open to any and all entrants (limited only by number, age, grade level and/or gender). *(Revised: 4/22/14)*

13.4.3.2.1 Camp or Clinic Advertisements in Recruiting Publications. Advertisements for an institution's camp or clinic may be placed in a recruiting publication (other than a high school, two-year college or nonscholastic game program), provided the publication includes a camp directory that meets the following requirements: **[D]** *(Revised: 1/11/94, 9/12/03, 9/24/09, 4/22/14)*

(a) The size (not to exceed one-half page) and format of such advertisements must be identical; and

(b) The camp directory must include multiple listings of summer camps on each page (at least two summer-camp advertisements of the same size must appear on each page).

13.4.3.2.2 Advertisements Directed Toward a Particular Audience. An institution may advertise or promote an institutional camp or clinic toward a particular audience (e.g., elite camp), provided the advertisement or promotion indicates that the camp or clinic is open to any and all entrants (limited only by number, age, grade level and/or gender). **[D]** *(Adopted: 9/24/09)*

13.4.3.3 NCAA or Conference Championship Posters. An institution hosting an NCAA or conference championship may produce a poster promoting the championship and send it to a high school coach and/or his or her educational institution. It is not permissible to send such a poster to a prospective student-athlete. **[D]** *(Adopted: 10/28/99, Revised: 4/6/00, 1/10/05 effective 8/1/05)*

13.4.3.3.1 NCAA or Conference Championship Promotional Materials. The NCAA or member conference [or a third party acting on behalf of the NCAA or member conference (e.g., host institution, host conference, or local organizing committee)] may produce and provide championship-promotional materials to any individual or group, provided the materials: **[D]** *(Adopted: 1/10/05)*

(a) Are solely for the purpose of promoting the championship event rather than the host institution, and use factual information (e.g., date, time, location, identification of host school/conference, ticket information, photos of previous championships);

(b) Are not sent exclusively to prospective student-athletes;

(c) Are available to the general public; and

(d) Do not promote the institution's athletics program.

13.4.3.4 Conference-Sponsored Sportsmanship Initiatives. A conference office may buy or arrange to have space in game programs or other printed materials published to provide information concerning the athletics participation of prospective student-athletes, provided the content of the printed materials is limited exclusively to promoting sportsmanship, and the materials are not designed to solicit the enrollment of prospective student-athletes. In addition, a conference office may produce posters, limited exclusively to promoting sportsmanship, which may be sent to any educational institution. It shall not be permissible to send any printed materials related to a sportsmanship initiative (e.g., poster) to a prospective student-athlete. *(Adopted: 4/26/07 effective 8/1/07)*

13.4.3.5 Miscellaneous Promotions. Member institutions and their representatives of athletics interests are prohibited from financing, arranging or using recruiting aids (e.g., newspaper advertisements, bumper stickers, message buttons) designed to publicize the institution's interest in a particular prospective student-athlete. **[D]** *(Revised: 10/28/97)*

13.5 Transportation.

13.5.1 General Restrictions. An institution may not provide transportation to a prospective student-athlete other than on an official paid visit or, on an unofficial visit, to view a practice or competition site in the prospective student-athlete's sport and other institutional facilities and to attend a home athletics contest at any local facility when accompanied by an institutional staff member. During the official paid visit, transportation may be provided to view a practice or competition site and other institutional facilities located outside a 30-mile radius of the institution's campus. **[R]** *(Revised: 1/11/89, 10/28/97, 11/1/00, 1/9/06 effective 8/1/06, 4/27/06)*

13.5.1.1 Nonpermissible Transportation. If nonpermissible transportation is provided, the institution may not avoid a violation of this rule by receiving reimbursement for mileage from the prospective student-athlete.

13.5.2 Transportation on Official Paid Visit.

13.5.2.1 General Restrictions. A member institution may pay the prospective student-athlete's actual round-trip transportation costs for his or her official visit to its campus from any location, provided the prospective student-athlete returns to the original point of departure, or if return transportation is provided to the prospective student-athlete's home, educational institution or site of competition, the cost does not exceed round-trip expenses from the prospective student-athlete's original point of departure. Use of a limousine or helicopter for such transportation is prohibited. **[R]** *(Revised: 1/9/06, 5/26/06)*

13.5.2.2 Automobile Transportation. If a prospective student-athlete travels by automobile on an official paid visit, the institution may pay round-trip expenses to the individual incurring the expense (except the prospective student-athlete's coach as set forth in Bylaw 13.8.1.2) at the same mileage rate it allows its own personnel. Any automobile may be used by the prospective student-athlete, provided the automobile is not owned or operated or its use arranged by the institution or any representative of its athletics interests. **[R]** *(Revised: 1/11/94)*

13.5.2.2.1 Use of Automobile. The institution or representatives of its athletics interests shall not provide an automobile for use during the official visit by the prospective student-athlete or by a student host. **[R]**

13.5.2.2.2 Coach Accompanying Prospective Student-Athlete and Parents and Legal Guardians. Except as permitted in Bylaw 13.5.2.4, coaching staff members shall not accompany a prospective student-athlete in the coach's sport to or from an official visit unless the prospective student-athlete travels only by automobile. If such transportation is used, the 48-hour period of the official visit shall begin when the coach begins transporting the prospective student-athlete and his or her parents or legal guardians, if applicable, to campus. A coach who makes an in-person, off-campus contact (any dialogue in excess of an exchange of a greeting) with that prospective student-athlete (or the prospective student-athlete's parents or legal guardians) during a permissible contact period prior to transporting the prospective student-athlete and his or her parents or legal guardians, if applicable, to campus for an official visit is charged with a countable contact. On completion of the 48-hour period, the coach shall terminate contact with the prospective student-athlete and his or her parents or legal guardians, if applicable, immediately. **[R]** *(Adopted: 1/10/95 effective 8/1/95, Revised: 1/14/97 effective 8/1/97, 11/12/97, 1/14/08 effective 8/1/08)*

13.5.2.2.2.1 Football Championship Subdivision Exception. **[FCS]** In championship subdivision football, any member of an institution's athletics department (except a volunteer coach per Bylaw 11.01.5) who has been certified pursuant to a conference certification program may provide such transportation for a prospective student-athlete between the prospective student-athlete's home or educational institution and the member institution. *(Adopted: 1/10/91 effective 8/1/91, Revised: 12/15/06)*

13.5.2.2.3 On-Campus Transportation. An institution transporting a prospective student-athlete (and those accompanying a prospective student-athlete) around campus during the official visit must use institutional vehicles normally used to transport prospective students while visiting the campus. In addition, coaching staff members or student hosts may use personal vehicles to transport a prospective student-athlete (and those accompanying the prospective student-athlete) around campus during an official visit. **[R]** *(Adopted: 8/5/04)*

13.5.2.3 Air Transportation. An institution providing air transportation to a prospective student-athlete to and from an official campus visit must use commercial transportation at coach-class airfare. Coaching staff members shall not accompany a prospective student-athlete to or from an official visit when air travel is used, except as permitted in Bylaw 13.5.2.4. **[R]** *(Revised: 1/10/95 effective 8/1/95, 8/5/04)*

13.5.2.3.1 Ticket Discounts. An institution may not arrange payment of the airline ticket to allow a prospective student-athlete (or the prospective student-athlete's relatives, friends or legal guardians) to take advantage of ticket bonuses, rebates, refunds, upgrades or other benefits connected with the purchase of the ticket. **[R]** *(Revised: 8/5/04)*

13.5.2.4 From Airport or Bus or Train Station. During the official visit, any member of an institution's athletics department staff may provide ground transportation for a prospective student-athlete and the prospective student-athlete's parents, relatives or legal guardians between the campus and any bus or train station or airport. If a prospective student-athlete is transported by a member of the institution's athletics department from an airport or bus or train station other than the major airport or bus or train station nearest the institution, the 48-hour official visit period begins with the initiation of the ground transportation by the member of the institution's athletics department staff. *(Revised: 4/28/05, 7/27/07)*

13.5.2.5 Visiting Two or More Institutions. Two or more institutions to which a prospective student-athlete is making official visits on the same trip may provide travel expenses, provided there is no duplication of expenses, only actual and necessary expenses are provided, and the 48-hour visit limitation is observed at each institution. **[R]**

13.5.2.6 Transportation of Prospective Student-Athlete's Relatives, Friends or Legal Guardians. An institution shall not permit its athletics department staff members or representatives of its athletics interests to pay, provide or arrange for the payment of transportation costs incurred by relatives, friends or legal guardians of a prospective student-athlete to visit the campus or elsewhere; however, an institution may: **[R]**

(a) Provide automobile-mileage reimbursement to a prospective student-athlete on an official visit, even if relatives or friends accompany the prospective student-athlete; *(Revised: 1/11/94, 5/12/05)*

(b) Permit the parents or legal guardians of a prospective student-athlete to ride in an automobile driven by a coaching staff member for the purpose of providing ground transportation to a prospective student-athlete as part of an official visit; and*(Adopted: 1/14/08 effective 8/1/08)*

(c) Provide transportation between its campus and any bus or train station or airport for the parents, relatives or legal guardians of a prospective student-athlete making an official visit. *(Revised: 7/27/07)*

> **13.5.2.6.1 Exception—Transportation Expenses for a Prospective Student-Athlete's Parents or Legal Guardians—Basketball.** In basketball, an institution may pay the actual round-trip costs for a prospective student-athlete's parents or legal guardians (expenses for up to two people) to accompany the prospective student-athlete on his or her official visit. *(Adopted: 10/27/11 effective 8/1/12, Revised: 1/19/13 effective 8/1/13)*

13.5.3 Transportation on Unofficial Visit. During any unofficial recruiting visit, the institution may provide the prospective student-athlete with transportation to view practice and competition sites in the prospective student-athlete's sport and other institutional facilities and to attend a home athletics contest at any local facility. An institutional staff member must accompany the prospective student-athlete during such a trip. Payment of any other transportation expenses, shall be considered a violation.**[R]** *(Revised: 1/11/89, 4/27/00, 3/10/04, 4/28/05, 1/9/06 effective 8/1/06, 4/27/06)*

13.5.4 Transportation Prior to Initial Enrollment. An institution or its representatives shall not furnish a prospective student-athlete, directly or indirectly, with transportation to the campus for enrollment. However, it is permissible for any member of the institution's staff to provide: *(Revised: 4/26/01 effective 8/1/01, 1/9/06, 10/17/13)*

(a) Transportation from the nearest bus or train station or major airport to the campus on the occasion of the prospective student-athlete's initial arrival at the institution to attend classes for a regular term or to participate in preseason practice, or for initial enrollment for the institution's summer term for a prospective student-athlete who has been awarded athletically related financial aid for his or her initial summer term; and

(b) Transportation from and to the nearest bus or train station or major airport on the occasion of the prospective student-athlete's arrival and departure from the institution to attend the institution's required new-student orientation, provided the prospective student-athlete has been accepted for admission to the institution.

13.6 Official (Paid) Visit.

13.6.1 Institutional Policies. An institution must have written departmental policies related to official visits that apply to prospective student-athletes, student hosts, coaches and other athletics administrators that are approved by the institution's president or chancellor and kept on file at the institution and conference office. The institution is responsible for the development and enforcement of appropriate policies and penalties regarding specified areas, as identified by the NCAA Division I Board of Directors. The institution shall have an outside entity (e.g., conference office) evaluate its policies related to official visits once every four years. The institution may be held accountable through the NCAA infractions process for activities that clearly demonstrate a disregard for its stated policies. *(Adopted: 8/5/04, Revised: 3/8/06, 7/31/14)*

13.6.2 Limitations on Official Visits.

> **13.6.2.1 One-Visit Limitation.** A member institution may finance only one visit to its campus for a prospective student-athlete.

13.6.2.2 Number of Official Visits—Prospective Student-Athlete Limitation. A prospective student-athlete may take a maximum of five expense-paid visits to Division I institutions, with not more than one permitted to any single institution. This restriction applies regardless of the number of sports in which the prospective student-athlete is involved. *(Revised: 1/12/04, 10/28/11)*

13.6.2.2.1 First Opportunity to Visit. In sports other than basketball, a prospective student-athlete may not be provided an expense-paid visit earlier than the opening day of classes of the prospective student-athlete's senior year in high school. In men's basketball, a prospective student-athlete may not be provided an expense-paid visit earlier than January 1 of his junior year in high school. In women's basketball, a prospective student-athlete may not be provided an expense-paid visit earlier than the Thursday following the NCAA Division I Women's Basketball Championship game of the prospective student-athlete's junior year in high school. **[D]** *(Revised: 11/1/01 effective 4/1/02, 4/3/02, 8/5/04, 4/28/05, 5/12/05, 10/27/11 effective 8/1/12, 1/19/13 effective 8/1/13)*

*****

13.6.2.3 Post-High School Visits. The one-visit limitation and the limitations on total official visits apply separately to the period in which the prospective student-athlete is in high school and to the period beginning October 15 following the prospective student-athlete's completion of high school. Thus, a prospective student-athlete may be provided a maximum of 10 official visits—five while in high school and five beginning with the October 15 following the prospective student-athlete's completion of high school. A prospective student-athlete is not required to graduate from high school in order to receive a permissible post-high school visit. **[D]** *(Revised: 1/11/89, 1/10/90, 6/21/01, 1/12/04, 8/5/04)*

13.6.2.3.1 Nonqualifier in First Year. A person who is not a qualifier and who is enrolled at a two-year college may not be provided an expense-paid visit to a member institution until he or she has completed an academic year at a two-year college.

13.6.2.3.2 Transfer Student. If a student-athlete attending a four-year institution desires to transfer and that institution provides the permission required (per Bylaw 13.1.1.3), it is permissible for a second institution to provide the student-athlete one official visit to that institution's campus.

13.6.2.4 Visit to Off-Campus Contest. An institution may not provide a prospective student-athlete with transportation to attend an off-campus contest outside a 30-mile radius of the member institution's main campus. **[D]** *(Revised: 4/24/03, 8/5/04, 1/9/06 effective 8/1/06, 11/1/07 effective 8/1/08, 8/21/12)*

13.6.2.5 Visit While Competing in Open Event. A host institution may pay the expenses of a recruited prospective student-athlete to participate in an established "open" event, provided the expenses of all other competitors in that event are paid; the expenses are not paid from athletics department (nonmeet) funds; and the expenses of the prospective student-athlete are limited to actual transportation, room and board. This trip shall be considered the one paid visit to the institution's campus with the prospective student-athlete remaining not more than 48 hours.

13.6.2.6 Number of Official Visits—Institutional Limitation. The total number of official visits a member institution may provide prospective student-athletes in the following sports on an annual basis (August 1 through July 31) shall be limited to: **[D]** *(Revised: 1/11/89, 1/10/91 effective 8/1/91, 1/11/94 effective 8/1/94, 11/12/97, 1/12/99 effective 8/1/99, 10/29/09)*

(a) Football—56.

(b) Basketball—12.

(c) Baseball—25.

13.6.2.6.1 Exception—National Service Academies—Football, Basketball and Baseball. The national service academies may provide 70 official visits in football, 56 of which may be provided prior to the initial National Letter of Intent signing date, 15 official visits in basketball, 12 of which may be provided prior to the initial National Letter of Intent signing date, and 31 official visits in baseball, 25 of which may be provided prior to the National Letter of Intent signing date. **[D]** *(Adopted: 1/10/95, Revised: 1/14/97 effective 8/1/97, 4/25/02 effective 8/1/02, 10/29/09)*

13.6.2.6.2 Unused Visits—Football. [FBS/FCS] In football, an institution may retain a maximum of six unused visits from the previous academic year. Such visits may be used only during the following academic year. **[D]** *(Adopted: 1/14/97 effective 8/1/97, Revised: 11/1/01 effective 8/1/02, 12/15/06, 10/29/09)*

13.6.2.6.3 Exception—Institution That Does Not Subscribe to the National Letter of Intent. A member institution that does not subscribe to the National Letter of Intent may provide 70 official visits in football, 56 of which may be provided prior to the initial National Letter of Intent signing date. **[D]** *(Adopted: 1/11/94 effective 8/1/94, Revised: 10/20/09)*

13.6.2.6.4 Written Record Required. The institution must maintain a written record of the paid visits of its football, basketball and baseball prospective student-athletes. **[D]** *(Revised: 1/12/99 effective 8/1/99, 10/29/09)*

13.6.2.6.5 Multiple-Sport Prospective Student-Athletes. A prospective student-athlete in football and one or more other sports (including basketball or baseball) shall be counted against the visit limitation in football. A prospective student-athlete in basketball and one or more other sports (other than football) shall be counted against the visit limitation in basketball. A prospective student-athlete in baseball and one or more other sports (other than football or basketball) shall be counted against the visit limitation in baseball. **[D]** *(Revised: 1/12/99 effective 8/1/99, 10/29/09)*

13.6.2.6.6 Exception—Head Coaching Change. In baseball, basketball and football, an institution may provide additional official visits (up to 25 percent of the limitation for the particular sport) after a new head coach is hired, provided the previous head coach used 75 percent or more of the official visits permitted for that academic year. **[D]** *(Adopted: 1/11/94 effective 8/1/94, Revised: 1/12/99 effective 8/1/99, 4/29/04, 11/1/07 effective 8/1/08, 10/29/09, 8/21/12)*

13.6.3 Requirements for Official Visit. The following requirements must be met before an institution may provide an official visit to a prospective student-athlete: **[D]** *(Adopted: 4/26/07 effective 8/1/07, Revised: 5/9/07, 11/1/97 effective 8/1/08)*

(a) A high school or preparatory school prospective student-athlete must present the institution with a score from a PSAT, SAT, PLAN or ACT taken on a national testing date under national testing conditions, except that a state-administered ACT may be used to meet the requirement. The score must be presented through a testing agency document, on a high school or preparatory school academic transcript (official or unofficial) or through the use of the applicable testing agency's automated-voice system. An international prospective student-athlete who requires a special administration of the PSAT, SAT, PLAN or ACT may present such a score upon the approval of the Academic Cabinet or the Initial-Eligibility Waivers Committee; *(Revised: 11/1/07 effective 8/1/08)*

(b) A prospective student-athlete must present the institution with a high school (or college) academic transcript;

(c) A high school or preparatory school prospective student-athlete must register with the NCAA Eligibility Center; and *(Revised: 5/9/07)*

(d) A high school or preparatory school prospective student-athlete must be placed on the institution's institutional request list (IRL) with the NCAA Eligibility Center. *(Revised: 5/9/07)*

13.6.3.1 NCAA Eligibility Center. A prospective student-athlete's fulfillment of these academic requirements may be certified by the NCAA Eligibility Center approved by the Executive Committee. *(Adopted: 4/26/07 effective 8/1/07)*

13.6.4 Length of Official Visit. An official visit to an institution shall not exceed 48 hours. A prospective student-athlete may remain in the locale in which the institution is located after the permissible 48-hour period for reasons unrelated to the official visit, provided that at the completion of the 48-hour visit, the individual departs the institution's campus, and the institution does not pay any expenses thereafter, including the cost of return transportation to the prospective student-athlete's home. Additionally, if the prospective student-athlete does not return home prior to attending the institution, the one-way transportation to the campus would be considered a violation of Bylaw 13.5.4, which prohibits transportation to enroll. **[D]** *(Revised: 1/9/96 effective 8/1/96, 8/5/04)*

13.6.4.1 48-Hour Period Defined. The 48-hour period of the official visit begins at the time the prospective student-athlete arrives on the institution's campus, rather than with the initiation of the prospective student-athlete's transportation by a coach or the time of the prospective student-athlete's arrival at the airport or elsewhere in the community (see Bylaws 13.5.2.4, 13.6.4.1.1 and 13.6.4.1.2). The prospective student-athlete's transportation to and from the campus must be without delay for personal reasons or entertainment purposes. The institution may not pay any expenses for entertainment (other than the actual and reasonable cost of meals) in conjunction with the prospective student-athlete's transportation. At the completion of the 48-hour visit, the prospective student-athlete must depart the institution's campus immediately; otherwise, the institution may not pay any expenses incurred by the prospective student-athlete upon departure from the institution's campus, including the cost of the prospective student-athlete's transportation home. *(Revised: 9/24/09)*

13.6.4.1.1 Coach Accompanying Prospective Student-Athlete. If a coach accompanies a prospective student-athlete on an official visit by automobile, per Bylaw 13.5.2.2.2, the 48-hour period shall begin when the coach begins transporting the prospective student-athlete to campus. A coach who makes an in-person, off-campus contact (any dialogue in excess of an exchange of a greeting) with the prospective student-athlete or the prospective student-athlete's parents during a permissible contact period prior to transporting the prospective student-athlete to campus for an official visit is charged with a countable contact. Upon completion of the 48-hour period, the coach shall terminate contact with the prospective student-athlete and his or her parents or legal guardians immediately. *(Adopted: 1/14/97 effective 8/1/97)*

13.6.4.1.2 Lodging in the Locale of the Institution Before Visit. A prospective student-athlete may receive lodging in the locale of the institution without beginning the 48-hour period if the prospective student-athlete arrives in the locale too late to begin the official visit that day. In sports other than basketball, such expenses may not be provided for any other individual who is accompanying the prospective student-athlete on the official visit (e.g., parents, spouse) before the start of the 48-hour period, including the cost of additional occupants in the same room, if applicable. In basketball, an institution may provide such expenses for a prospective student-athlete's parents or legal guardians (expenses for up to two people) without beginning the 48-hour period. *(Adopted: 9/24/09, Revised: 10/27/11 effective 8/1/12, 1/19/13 effective 8/1/13)*

13.6.4.2 Exception to 48-Hour Period for Extenuating Circumstances. An official visit may extend beyond 48 hours for reasons beyond the control of the prospective student-athlete and the institution (e.g., inclement weather conditions, natural disaster, flight delays or cancellations, airport security activity). In such instances, the institution shall submit a report to the conference office noting the details of the circumstances. *(Adopted: 4/26/07 effective 8/1/07)*

13.6.5 Transportation on Official Visit. For regulations relating to transportation on the official visit, see Bylaw 13.5.2.

13.6.6 Accommodations on Official Visit. A prospective student-athlete on an official visit shall be provided lodging and take meals as regular students normally do. Local commercial facilities may be used but at a scale comparable to that of normal student life and only within a 30-mile radius of the institution's campus. Lodging may not include special accessories (e.g., jacuzzis, suites) that are not available generally to all guests residing at the establishment. (See Bylaw 13.6.7.7 for restrictions on meals provided to prospective student-athletes on official visits.) *(Revised: 8/5/04)*

13.6.7 Entertainment/Tickets on Official Visit.

13.6.7.1 General Restrictions. An institution may provide entertainment, pursuant to Bylaw 13.6.7.5, on the official visit only for a prospective student-athlete and the prospective student-athlete's parents (or legal guardians) or spouse and only within a 30-mile radius of the institution's main campus. Entertainment and contact by representatives of the institution's athletics interests during the official visit are prohibited. It is not permissible to entertain other relatives or friends (including dates) of a prospective student-athlete at any time at any site. **[R]** *(Revised: 10/28/97, 11/1/00, 4/23/14)*

13.6.7.1.1 Meals and Lodging While in Transit. It is permissible for an institution to pay a prospective student-athlete's actual costs for reasonable expenses (e.g., meals, lodging) incurred while traveling to and from campus on the official visit. In basketball, an institution may pay the actual costs for meals and lodging for a prospective student-athlete's parents or legal guardians (expenses for up to two people) that are incurred while traveling to and from campus to accompany the prospective student-athlete on his or her official visit. *(Revised: 10/27/11 effective 8/1/12, 1/19/13 effective 8/1/13)*

13.6.7.2 Complimentary Admissions. During the official visit, a maximum of three complimentary admissions to a home athletics event at any facility within a 30-mile radius of the institution's main campus in which the institution's intercollegiate team practices or competes may be provided to a prospective student-athlete. Such complimentary admissions are for the exclusive use of the prospective student-athlete and those persons accompanying the prospective student-athlete on the visit and must be issued only through a pass list on an individual-game basis. Such admissions may provide seating only in the general seating area of the facility used for conducting the event. Providing seating during the conduct of the event (including intermission) for the prospective student-athlete or those persons accompanying the prospective student-athlete in the facility's press box, special seating box(es) or bench area is specifically prohibited. **[R]** *(Revised: 1/10/90 effective 8/1/90, 1/11/94, 10/28/97, 11/1/00, 4/26/01 effective 8/1/01, 4/24/03, 1/9/06, 4/24/08 effective 8/1/08)*

13.6.7.2.1 Exception—Nontraditional Family. If a prospective student-athlete is a member of a nontraditional family (e.g., divorce, separation), the institution may provide up to two additional complimentary admissions to the prospective student-athlete in order to accommodate the parents accompanying the prospective student-athlete (e.g., stepparents) to attend a home athletics event. **[R]** *(Adopted: 4/24/08 effective 8/1/08)*

13.6.7.2.2 Exception—Football. In football, an institution may provide up to two additional complimentary admissions to the prospective student-athlete in order to accommodate family members accompanying the prospective student-athlete to attend a home athletics event. A family member is an individual with any of the following relationships to the prospective student-athlete: spouse, parent or legal guardian, child, sibling, grandparent, domestic partner or any individual whose close association with the prospective student-athlete is the practical equivalent of a family relationship. **[R]** *(Adopted: 4/24/14)*

13.6.7.2.3 Conference Tournaments. A member institution may not provide complimentary admissions to a prospective student-athlete for a postseason conference tournament. The prospective student-athlete may purchase tickets only in the same manner as any other member of the general public. **[R]** *(Revised: 1/10/91 effective 8/1/91, 1/10/92, 4/28/08 effective 8/1/08)*

13.6.7.2.4 NCAA Championships or Other Postseason Contests. The provision of complimentary or reduced-cost admissions to prospective student-athletes for an NCAA championship (all rounds) or other postseason contests (e.g., bowl game, NAIA or NIT championship) constitutes excessive entertainment and is prohibited. The prospective student-athlete may purchase these tickets only in the same manner as any other member of the general public. **[R]** *(Revised: 1/10/92, 4/28/08 effective 8/1/08)*

13.6.7.2.5 Purchase of Game Tickets in Same Locale. An institution may reserve tickets, only for the use of immediate family members accompanying a prospective student-athlete during an official visit and for seat locations adjacent to the complimentary seats being provided to the prospective student-athlete. These tickets must be purchased at face value. **[R]** *(Adopted: 1/10/92, Revised: 4/28/08 effective 8/1/08)*

13.6.7.2.6 Exception. A member institution may provide complimentary admissions to a prospective student-athlete for a home athletics event that has been relocated outside a 30-mile radius of the institution's main campus due to the home facility's inoperable conditions (e.g., construction or facility repairs), which result in the facility being unavailable for safe use. *(Adopted: 4/28/05)*

13.6.7.3 Parking. An institution may arrange special on-campus parking for prospective student-athletes during an official visit. *(Adopted: 1/10/92)*

13.6.7.4 Cash to Prospective Student-Athlete. The institution or representatives of its athletics interests shall not provide cash to a prospective student-athlete for entertainment purposes.

13.6.7.5 Student Host. The student host must be either a current student-athlete or a student designated in a manner consistent with the institution's policy for providing campus visits or tours to prospective students in general. The institution may provide the following to a student host entertaining a prospective student-athlete: **[R]** *(Revised: 1/10/90 effective 8/1/90, 1/10/92, 1/9/96 effective 8/1/96, 10/28/97, 11/1/00, 8/5/04, 5/12/05, 4/27/06, 10/28/07, 2/23/09, 4/26/12 effective 8/1/12)*

(a) A maximum of $40 for each day of the visit to cover all actual costs of entertaining the student host(s) and the prospective student-athlete (and the prospective student-athlete's parents, legal guardians or spouse), excluding the cost of meals and admission to campus athletics events. The cost of entertainment of the institution's athletics department staff members who accompany the prospective student-athlete is also excluded. If an athletics department staff member serves as the prospective student-athlete's host, his or her entertainment costs must be included in the entertainment allowance. The entertainment allowance may not be used for the purchase of souvenirs, such as T-shirts or other institutional mementos. It is permissible to provide the student host with an additional $20 per day for each additional prospective student-athlete the host entertains;

(b) Complimentary meals, provided the student host is accompanying the prospective student-athlete during the prospective student-athlete's official visit; and *(Adopted: 1/10/92, Revised: 2/23/09)*

(c) Complimentary admissions to campus athletics events, provided the student host is accompanying the prospective student-athlete to the events during the prospective student-athlete's official visit. *(Revised: 2/23/09)*

13.6.7.5.1 Multiple Hosts. If several students host a prospective student-athlete, the $40-per-day entertainment money may be used to cover the actual and necessary expenses incurred by the prospective student-athlete and all hosts. Only one student host per prospective student-athlete may be provided a free meal if restaurant facilities are used. **[D]** *(Revised: 1/10/92, 1/16/93, 1/9/96 effective 8/1/96, 4/24/03 effective 8/1/03, 3/26/04, 4/26/12 effective 8/1/12)*

13.6.7.5.2 Nonqualifier Prohibition. The student host must be enrolled in the member institution being visited by a prospective student-athlete. A nonqualifier (see Bylaw 14.02.10.2) may not serve as a student host during his or her first academic year in residence. **[D]** *(Revised: 3/19/97, 4/24/03 effective 8/1/03, 3/26/04)*

Delayed effective date. See specific date below.

13.6.7.5.2 Nonqualifier and Academic Redshirt Prohibition. The student host must be enrolled in the member institution being visited by a prospective student-athlete. A nonqualifier (see Bylaw 14.02.10.3) or an academic redshirt (see Bylaw 14.02.10.2) may not serve as a student host during his or her first academic year in residence. **[D]** *(Revised: 3/19/97, 4/24/03 effective 8/1/03, 3/26/04, 8/2/12 effective 8/1/16, for students initially enrolling full time in a collegiate institution on or after 8/1/16)*

13.6.7.5.3 Use of Automobile. The institution or representatives of its athletics interests shall not provide an automobile for use by the prospective student-athlete or the student host. **[R]** *(Revised: 4/24/03 effective 8/1/03)*

13.6.7.6 Student Support Group Assisting in Recruiting. An institution may not provide a free meal or entertainment to a member of an institutional student support group that assists in the recruitment of a prospective student-athlete during an official visit unless the student is designated as the one student host for that prospective student-athlete. Any additional arrangement between the institution and members of such a support group (e.g., compensation, providing a uniform) is left to the discretion of the institution. *(Adopted: 1/16/93)*

13.6.7.7 Meals on Official Visit. The cost of actual meals, not to exceed three per day, on the official visit for a prospective student-athlete and the prospective student-athlete's parents, legal guardians, spouse or children need not be included in the $40-per-day entertainment expense. Meals must be comparable to those provided to student-athletes during the academic year. A reasonable snack (e.g., pizza, hamburger) may be provided in addition to the three meals. **[R]** *(Adopted: 1/10/92, Revised: 1/11/94 effective 8/1/94, 1/10/95 effective 8/1/95, 8/5/04, 1/9/06, 4/26/12 effective 8/1/12)*

13.6.7.7.1 Entertainment at Staff Member's Home. A luncheon, dinner or brunch at the home of an institutional staff member (e.g., the athletics director, a coach, a faculty member or the institution's president) may be held for a prospective student-athlete on an official visit, provided the entertainment is on a scale comparable to that of normal student life, is not excessive in nature and occurs on only one occasion. **[R]** *(Revised: 1/9/96)*

13.6.7.7.2 Exception—Meals—Football. [FBS/FCS] In football, an institution may provide meals for up to four family members accompanying a prospective student-athlete on an official visit. A family member is an individual with any of the following relationships to the prospective student-athlete: spouse, parent or legal guardian, child, sibling, grandparent, domestic partner or any individual whose close association with the prospective student-athlete is the practical equivalent of a family relationship. **[R]** *(Adopted: 10/30/13)*

13.6.7.8 Normal Retail Cost. If a boat, snowmobile, recreational vehicle or similar recreational equipment (including those provided by an institutional staff member or a representative of the institution's athletics interests) is used to entertain a prospective student-athlete or the prospective student-athlete's parents (or legal guardians) and spouse, the normal retail cost of the use of such equipment shall be assessed against the $40-per-day entertainment figure; further, if such normal retail costs exceeds the $40-per-day entertainment allowance, such entertainment may not be provided. **[R]** *(Adopted: 1/10/92, Revised: 1/9/96 effective 8/1/96, 4/24/03 effective 8/1/03, 4/17/12 effective 8/1/12)*

13.6.7.9 Activities During Official Visit. An institution may not arrange miscellaneous, personalized recruiting aids (e.g., personalized jerseys, personalized audio/video scoreboard presentations) and may not permit a prospective student-athlete to engage in any game-day simulations (e.g., running onto the field with the team during pregame introductions) during an official visit. Personalized recruiting aids include any decorative items and special additions to any location the prospective student-athlete will visit (e.g., hotel room, locker room, coach's office, conference room, arena) regardless of whether the items include the prospective student-athlete's name or picture. *(Adopted: 8/5/04, Revised: 5/14/05)*

13.6.7.10 Professional Tryout or Workout Activities. During an official visit, a prospective student-athlete may not attend events in which professional tryout or workout activities occur. (See Bylaw 13.7.2.7.) *(Adopted: 1/8/07)*

13.6.8 Entertainment on Official Visit for Spouse, Parent or Legal Guardian of Prospective Student-Athlete. A member institution shall limit entertainment and lodging on the prospective student-athlete's official visit to a prospective student-athlete, the prospective student-athlete's parents (or legal guardians) and spouse. An institution shall limit meals on the prospective student-athlete's official visit to a prospective student-athlete, the prospective student-athlete's parents (or legal guardians), spouse and children. **[R]** *(Revised: 4/25/02 effective 8/1/02, 1/9/06)*

13.6.8.1 Exception—Meals—Football. [FBS/FCS] In football, an institution may provide meals for up to four family members accompanying a prospective student-athlete on an official visit. A family member is an individual with any of the following relationships to the prospective student-athlete: spouse, parent or legal guardian, child, sibling, grandparent, domestic partner or any individual whose close association with the prospective student-athlete is the practical equivalent of a family relationship. **[R]** *(Adopted: 10/30/13)*

13.6.9 Lodging for Additional Persons. Additional persons (e.g., prospective student-athlete's brother, sister, friend) may stay in the same room as the prospective student-athlete or parents, spouse or legal guardians of the prospective student-athlete, but the institution shall not pay the costs resulting from the additional occupants. The additional occupants shall not be prospective student-athletes being recruited by the institution. **[R]** *(Adopted: 1/10/92, Revised: 4/24/03 effective 8/1/03)*

13.7 Unofficial (Nonpaid) Visit.
13.7.1 Number Permitted. A prospective student-athlete may visit a member institution's campus at his or her own expense an unlimited number of times. A prospective student-athlete may make unofficial visits before his or her senior year in high school.

*****

13.7.2 Entertainment/Tickets.

13.7.2.1 General Restrictions. During an unofficial visit, the institution may not pay any expenses or provide any entertainment except a maximum of three complimentary admissions (issued only through a pass list) to a home athletics event at any facility within a 30-mile radius of a member institution's main campus in which the institution's intercollegiate team practices or competes. Such complimentary admissions are for the exclusive use of the prospective student-athlete and those persons accompanying the prospective student-athlete on the visit and must be issued on an individual-game basis. Such admissions may provide seating only in the general seating area of the facility used for conducting the event. Providing seating during the conduct of the event (including intermission) for the prospective student-athlete or the prospective student-athlete's parents (or legal guardians) or spouse in the facility's press box, special seating box(es) or bench area is specifically prohibited. Complimentary admissions may not be provided during a dead period, except as provided in Bylaw 13.7.2.5. **[R]** *(Revised: 1/10/90 effective 8/1/90, 1/11/94, 4/24/03, 12/6/13)*

13.7.2.1.1 Exception—Nontraditional Family. If a prospective student-athlete is a member of a nontraditional family (e.g., divorce, separation), the institution may provide up to two additional complimentary admissions to the prospective student-athlete in order to accommodate the parents accompanying the prospective student-athlete (e.g., stepparents) to attend a home athletics event. *(Adopted: 1/15/11 effective 8/1/11)*

13.7.2.1.2 Meals. A prospective student-athlete on an unofficial visit to an institution may pay the actual cost of meals (or the regular cost of training-table meals) and eat with other prospective student-athletes who are on their official visits or with enrolled student-athletes. **[R]**

13.7.2.1.2.1 Exception—Championship Subdivision Football. [FCS] A championship subdivision football program that restricts its total number of official visits to 25 may provide one meal to a football prospective student-athlete in the institution's on-campus student dining facilities without the visit counting as an official visit. The institution also may provide one meal to the prospective student-athlete's parents or legal guardians in the institution's on-campus student dining facilities without the visit counting as an official visit, provided it is the institution's normal policy to provide such a meal under similar circumstances to all prospective students' parents or legal guardians visiting the campus. A prospective student-athlete who is given such a meal may not also be provided by the institution with an official visit in any sport. **[R]** *(Adopted: 1/11/94, Revised: 12/15/06)*

*****

13.7.2.1.3 Housing—Lodging in Dormitories. A prospective student-athlete on an unofficial visit may stay in an enrolled student-athlete's dormitory room only if the prospective student-athlete pays the regular institutional rate for such lodging. **[R]**

13.7.2.1.4 Transportation During Unofficial Visit. For regulations relating to transportation on an unofficial visit, see Bylaw 13.5.3.

13.7.2.1.5 Reserving Game Tickets. An institution may not reserve tickets (in addition to the permissible complimentary admissions) to be purchased by a prospective student-athlete (or individuals accompanying the prospective student-athlete) on an unofficial visit. Tickets may be purchased only in the same manner as any other member of the general public. **[R]** *(Adopted: 1/10/92)*

13.7.2.1.6 Parking. An institution may not arrange special parking for prospective student-athletes to use while attending a member institution's campus athletics event during an unofficial visit. **[R]** *(Adopted: 1/10/92)*

13.7.2.1.7 Academic Interviews. An athletics department staff member may arrange academic interviews for a prospective student-athlete on an unofficial visit.

13.7.2.1.8 Student Host. A student host used during an unofficial visit must either be a current student-athlete or a student who is designated in a manner consistent with the institution's policies for providing campus visits or tours to prospective students in general. *(Revised: 8/5/04)*

13.7.2.2 Home Games at Site Other Than Regular Home Facility. If an institution schedules any regular-season home games at a site not designated as its regular home facility, the host institution may provide a maximum of three complimentary admissions to any such game for the exclusive use of a prospective student-athlete and those persons accompanying the prospective student-athlete. Tournament and postseason games are excluded. The institution shall not arrange or permit any other entertainment or payment of expenses, including transportation, except as permitted in Bylaw 13.5.3. **[R]** *(Revised: 4/24/03)*

13.7.2.3 Conference Tournaments. A member institution may not provide complimentary admissions to a prospective student-athlete for a postseason conference tournament. The prospective student-athlete may purchase tickets only in the same manner as any other member of the general public. **[R]** *(Revised: 1/10/91 effective 8/1/91)*

13.7.2.4 NCAA Championships or Other Postseason Contests. The provision of complimentary or reduced-cost admissions to prospective student-athletes for an NCAA championship (all rounds) or other postseason contests (e.g., bowl game, NAIA or NIT championship) constitutes excessive entertainment and is prohibited. The prospective student-athlete may purchase tickets to such events only in the same manner as any other member of the general public. **[R]** *(Revised: 1/10/92)*

13.7.2.5 Visit Unrelated to Recruitment. The limitations on providing entertainment to a prospective student-athlete shall not extend to a visit to the institution's campus for a purpose having nothing whatsoever to do with the prospective student-athlete's athletics recruitment by the institution (e.g., band trip, fraternity weekend, athletics team's attendance at a sporting event with the high school coach). The institution's athletics department or representatives of its athletics interests may not be involved in any way with the arrangements for the visit, other than the institution providing (in accordance with established policy) free admissions to an athletics event on a group basis, rather than personally to the prospective student-athlete. Such admissions may be provided during a dead period. **[R]** *(Revised: 12/6/13)*

13.7.2.6 Visit Related to National Student-Athlete Day or National Girls and Women in Sports Day. The limitations on providing entertainment to a prospective student-athlete shall not extend to a visit to the institution's campus for activities related to National Student-Athlete Day and National Girls and Women in Sports Day. **[R]** *(Adopted: 1/14/97, Revised: 4/22/98 effective 8/1/98)*

13.7.2.7 Professional Tryout or Workout Activities. During an unofficial visit, a prospective student-athlete may not attend events in which professional tryout or workout activities occur. (See Bylaw 13.6.7.10.) **[R]** *(Adopted: 1/8/07)*

13.7.3 Activities During Unofficial Visit. An institution may not arrange miscellaneous, personalized recruiting aids (e.g., personalized jerseys, personalized audio/visual scoreboard presentations) and may not permit a prospective student-athlete to engage in any game-day simulations (e.g., running onto the field with the team during pregame introductions) during an unofficial visit. Personalized recruiting aids include any decorative items and special additions to any location the prospective student-athlete will visit (e.g., hotel room, locker room, coach's office, conference room, arena) regardless of whether the items include the prospective student-athlete's name or picture. *(Adopted: 8/5/04, Revised: 5/14/05, 4/27/06)*

13.8 Entertainment, Reimbursement and Employment of High School/College-Preparatory School/Two-Year College Coaches and Other Individuals Associated With Prospective Student-Athletes.
13.8.1 Entertainment Restrictions. Entertainment of a high school, preparatory school or two-year college coach or any other individual responsible for teaching or directing an activity in which a prospective student-athlete is involved shall be limited to providing a maximum of two complimentary admissions (issued only through a pass list) to home intercollegiate athletics events at any facility within a 30-mile radius of the institution's main campus, which must be issued on an

individual-game basis. Such entertainment shall not include food and refreshments, room expenses, or the cost of transportation to and from the campus or the athletics event. It is not permissible to provide complimentary admissions to any postseason competition (e.g., NCAA championship, conference tournament, bowl game). An institutional coaching staff member is expressly prohibited from spending funds to entertain the prospective student-athlete's coach on or off the member institution's campus. **[R]** *(Revised: 4/3/02, 8/5/04, 4/28/05 effective 8/1/05)*

13.8.1.1 Exception—Nonathletics Personnel. An institutional department outside the athletics department (e.g., president's office, admissions) may host nonathletics high school, preparatory school or two-year college personnel (e.g., guidance counselors, principals) in conjunction with a home intercollegiate athletics event and may provide such individuals reasonable expenses (e.g., food, refreshments, parking, room) and a nominal gift, provided the visit is not related to athletics recruiting and there is no involvement by the institution's athletics recruiting and there is no involvement by the institution's athletics department in the arrangements for the visit, other than providing (in accordance with established policy) free admissions to an athletics event.**[R]** *(Adopted: 3/8/12)*

13.8.1.2 Transportation Reimbursement. An institution shall not reimburse a high school, preparatory school or two-year college coach for expenses incurred in transporting a prospective student-athlete to visit the campus. **[R]**

13.8.1.3 Transportation to Off-Campus Contest. If a high school, preparatory school or two-year college coach transports members of his or her athletics squad to an off-campus site to watch NCAA member institutions compete, an institution may not reimburse the coach for the transportation costs or provide complimentary tickets for the coach or any of the team members. **[R]**

13.8.1.4 Purchase of Game Tickets. An institution may not reserve tickets (in addition to the permissible complimentary admissions) to be purchased by high school, preparatory or two-year college coaches (or individuals accompanying them) to attend an institution's athletics contest. Tickets may be purchased only in the same manner as any other member of the general public. **[R]** *(Adopted: 1/10/92)*

13.8.1.5 Noncoaching-Related Organization. If a high school, preparatory school or two-year college coach is a member of a noncoaching-related organization (e.g., state high school principals association, college fraternity alumni organization, institution's alumni association), an institution may entertain the group, provided there is no direct involvement by the institution's athletics department. **[R]**

13.8.2 Material Benefits. Arrangements by an institution that involve a material benefit for a high school, preparatory school or two-year college coach, or for any other individual responsible for teaching or directing an activity in which a prospective student-athlete is involved, (e.g., the provision of a gift such as a tangible item bearing the institution's insignia, the offer to pay a portion of the coach's or other individual's personal expenses, compensation based on the number of campers sent to an institution's camp, or an arrangement to provide transportation for the coach or other individual) are prohibited. **[R]** *(Revised: 8/5/04)*

13.8.2.1 Gifts at Coaches' Clinic. An institution may not provide gifts to high school, preparatory school or two-year college coaches in conjunction with its coaches' clinic or other events. This specifically prohibits the provision of a door prize to the coach, even if the cost of the prize is included in the cumulative admission fee (the admission fee charged to each person, when combined, would cover the cost of the prize). Materials (e.g., clipboards, file folders) may be provided to each person attending the clinic, provided the items are included in the registration or admission fee. **[R]** *(Revised: 1/16/93, 1/11/94)*

13.8.3 Employment Conditions.

13.8.3.1 Employment in Athletically Related Institutional Activities—Basketball. An institution shall not employ (either on a salaried or a volunteer basis) an individual as a speaker or presenter at any athletically related institutional event or activity (e.g., booster club function, outside consultant) if that individual is involved in coaching prospective student-athletes or is associated with a prospective student-athlete as a result of the prospective student-athlete's participation in basketball. *(Adopted: 1/17/09)*

13.8.3.2 Individual Associated with a Prospective Student-Athlete—Men's Basketball. In men's basketball, during a two-year period before a prospective student-athlete's anticipated enrollment and a two-year period after the prospective student-athlete's actual enrollment, an institution shall not employ (or enter into a contract for future employment with) an individual associated with the prospective student-athlete in any athletics department noncoaching staff position or in a strength and conditioning staff position. *(Adopted: 1/16/10; a contract signed before 10/29/09 may be honored, Revised: 6/13/11)*

13.8.3.2.1 Application. A violation of Bylaw 13.8.3.2 occurs if an individual associated with a prospective student-athlete (see Bylaw 13.02.17) is employed by the institution and, at the time of employment, a student-athlete who enrolled at the institution in the previous two years (and remains enrolled at the institution) was a prospective student-athlete by which the individual meets the definition of an individual associated with a prospective student-athlete. A violation of Bylaw 13.8.3.2 also occurs if an individual associated with a prospective student-athlete is employed and, within two years after such employment, a prospective student-athlete by which the individual meets the definition of an individual associated with a prospective student-athlete enrolls as a full-time student in a regular academic term at the institution. In either case, the student-athlete becomes ineligible for intercollegiate competition unless eligibility is restored by the Committee on Student-Athlete Reinstatement.*(Adopted: 6/20/13)*

13.8.3.3 Graduate Teaching Assistants. A high school, preparatory school or two-year college coach who is enrolled in a bona fide postgraduate program at a member institution is permitted to receive legitimate compensation as a graduate teaching assistant.

13.8.3.4 Employment in Different Sport. A high school, preparatory school or two-year college coach who remains associated with the high school, preparatory school or two-year college in a coaching capacity in a different sport may be employed as a member of an institution's coaching staff. *(Revised: 3/16/07)*

13.8.3.5 Employment in Same Sport. A high school, preparatory school or two-year college coach who remains associated with the high school, preparatory school or two-year college in a coaching capacity in the same sport shall not be employed as a member of an institution's coaching staff.

13.8.3.5.1 Contract for Future Employment. A member institution is permitted to enter into a contractual agreement with a high school, preparatory school or two-year college coach for an employment opportunity that begins with the next academic year, provided the employment contract with the member institution is not contingent upon the enrollment of a prospective student-athlete and the coach does not begin any coaching duties (e.g., recruiting, selection of coaching staff) for the member institution while remaining associated with the high school, preparatory school or two-year college.

13.9 Letter-of-Intent Programs, Financial Aid Agreements.

13.9.1 Requirements for Offer of Athletically Related Financial Aid. The following requirements must be met before an institution may provide a written offer of athletically related financial aid (per Bylaw 15.3.2.2) to a prospective student-athlete: **[D]***(Adopted: 4/26/07 effective 8/1/07, Revised: 4/30/09 effective 8/1/10)*

(a) A high school or preparatory school prospective student-athlete must register with the NCAA Eligibility Center;

(b) A high school or preparatory school prospective student-athlete must be placed on the institution's institutional request list (IRL) with the NCAA Eligibility Center; and

(c) A high school, preparatory school or transfer (if applicable) prospective student-athlete must complete the amateurism certification questionnaire administered by the NCAA Eligibility Center.

13.9.2 Letter of Intent Restriction. A member institution may not participate in an institutional or conference athletics letter-of-intent program or issue an institutional or conference financial aid agreement that involves a signing date that precedes the initial regular (as opposed to early) signing date for the National Letter of Intent program in the same sport. However, an institution may permit a prospective student-athlete to sign an institutional or conference letter of intent during the National Letter of Intent early signing period in the applicable sport. **[D]** *(Revised: 8/5/04, 12/12/06, 4/26/07 effective 8/1/07)*

13.9.2.1 Mailing of Financial Aid Offer. An institutional or conference financial aid form may be included in the normal mailing of the National Letter of Intent, but none of the forms enclosed in the mailing may be signed by the prospective student-athlete prior to the initial signing date in that sport in the National Letter of Intent program. **[D]** *(Revised: 8/5/04)*

13.9.2.2 Written Offer of Aid Before Signing Date. Before August 1 of a prospective student-athlete's senior year in high school, an institution shall not, directly or indirectly, provide a written offer of athletically related financial aid or indicate in writing to the prospective student-athlete that an athletically related grant-in-aid will be offered by the institution. On or after August 1 of a prospective student-athlete's senior year in high school, an institution may indicate in writing to a prospective student-athlete that an athletically related grant-in-aid will be offered by the institution; however, the institution may not permit the prospective student-athlete to sign a form indicating his or her acceptance of such an award before the initial signing date in that sport in the National Letter of Intent program. **[D]** *(Revised: 8/5/04, 4/29/10 effective 8/1/10, 3/3/11)*

13.9.2.3 Limitation on Number of National Letter of Intent/Offer of Financial Aid Signings—Bowl Subdivision Football. [FBS] In bowl subdivision football, there shall be an annual limit of 25 on the number of prospective student-athletes who may sign a National Letter of Intent or an institutional offer of financial aid from December 1 through May 31. **[D]** *(Adopted: 1/16/10 effective 8/1/10, Revised: 1/14/12 effective 8/1/12)*

> **13.9.2.3.1 Exception—Counter During Same Academic Year. [FBS]** A prospective student-athlete who signs a National Letter of Intent or an institutional offer of financial aid and becomes an initial counter for the same academic year in which the signing occurred (e.g., midyear enrollee) shall not count toward the annual limit on signings. *(Adopted: 1/14/12 effective 8/1/12)*

13.10 Publicity.

13.10.1 Presence of Media During Recruiting Contact. A member institution shall not permit a media entity to be present during any recruiting contact made by an institution's coaching staff member. **[D]** *(Adopted: 1/9/96, Revised: 1/14/97)*

13.10.2 Publicity Before Commitment.

> **13.10.2.1 Comments Before Commitment.** Before the signing of a prospective student-athlete to a National Letter of Intent or an institution's written offer of admission and/or financial aid or before the institution receives his or her financial deposit in response to its offer of admission, a member institution may comment publicly only to the extent of confirming its recruitment of the prospective student-athlete. The institution may not comment generally about the prospective student-athlete's ability or the contribution that the prospective student-athlete might make to the institution's team; further, the institution is precluded from commenting in any manner as to the likelihood of the prospective student-athlete committing to or signing with that institution. **[D]** *(Revised: 1/14/97, 1/19/13 effective 8/1/13)*

>> **13.10.2.1.1 Evaluations for Media, Recruiting Services.** Athletics department staff members shall not evaluate or rate a prospective student-athlete for news media, scouting services or recruiting services. **[D]** *(Revised: 1/19/13 effective 8/1/13)*

> **13.10.2.2 Radio/TV Show.** A member institution shall not permit a prospective student-athlete or a high school, college preparatory school or two-year college coach to appear, be interviewed or otherwise be involved (in person or via film, audio tape or videotape) on: **[D]** *(Revised: 8/5/04)*

(a) A radio or television program conducted by the institution's coach;

(b) A program in which the institution's coach is participating; or

(c) A program for which a member of the institution's athletics staff has been instrumental in arranging for the appearance of the prospective student-athlete or coach or related program material.

>> **13.10.2.2.1 Announcer for Broadcast of Prospective Student-Athlete's Athletics Contest.** A member of the athletics staff of a member institution may not serve as an announcer or commentator for any athletics contest in which a prospective student-athlete is participating, or appear (in person or by means of film, audio tape or videotape) on a radio or television broadcast of such contest. This restriction does not apply to contests involving national teams in which prospective student-athletes may be participants, including the Olympic Games. **[D]** *(Revised: 1/10/95, 1/12/99, 8/5/04)*

>> **13.10.2.2.2 Game Broadcast/Telecast.** A prospective student-athlete may not be interviewed during the broadcast or telecast of an institution's intercollegiate contest. A member institution may not permit a station telecasting a game to show a videotape of competition involving high school, preparatory school or two-year college prospective student-athletes. **[D]** *(Revised: 8/5/04)*

13.10.2.3 Conference-Sponsored Sportsmanship Initiatives. It is permissible for a conference to broadcast at any time, and through any medium, a public service announcement that may include prospective student-athletes, provided the following criteria are met (see Bylaw 13.1.10): *(Adopted: 4/26/07 effective 8/1/07)*

(a) A conference office is responsible for development of the public service announcement;

(b) The scope of the public service announcement is limited exclusively to promoting sportsmanship; and

(c) The public service announcement is not designed to solicit the enrollment of prospective student-athletes.

13.10.2.4 Prospective Student-Athlete's Visit. A member institution shall not publicize (or arrange for publicity of) a prospective student-athlete's visit to the institution's campus. Further, a prospective student-athlete may not participate in team activities that would make the public or media aware of the prospective student-athlete's visit to the institution (e.g., running out of the tunnel with team, celebratory walks to or around the stadium/arena, on-field pregame celebrations). **[D]** *(Revised: 1/14/97, 9/12/03)*

13.10.2.5 Introduction of Prospective Student-Athlete. An institution may not introduce a visiting prospective student-athlete at a function (e.g., the institution's sports award banquet or an intercollegiate athletics contest) that is attended by media representatives or open to the general public. **[D]** *(Revised: 1/14/97)*

13.10.2.6 Intent to Enroll. A member institution shall not publicize (or arrange for publicity of) a prospective student-athlete's intention to accept its offer of financial assistance. **[D]** *(Revised: 1/14/97)*

13.10.2.7 Photograph of Prospective Student-Athlete. It is permissible for an institution to photograph a prospective student-athlete during a campus visit to be used in the institution's permissible publicity and promotional activities (e.g., press release, media guide), but the photograph may not be provided to the prospective student-athlete. **[D]** *(Adopted: 1/16/93, Revised: 1/11/94, 4/24/03 effective 8/1/03, 3/26/04, 11/17/04, 1/19/13 effective 8/1/13)*

13.10.3 Publicity After Commitment. There are no restrictions on publicity related to a prospective student-athlete after he or she has signed a National Letter of Intent or the institution's written offer of admission and/or financial aid or after the institution has received his or her financial deposit in response to its offer of admission, except as set forth in Bylaw 13.10.1. **[D]** *(Revised: 1/14/97, 4/29/04 effective 8/1/04, 8/25/04, 1/19/13 effective 8/1/13)*

13.11 Tryouts.

13.11.1 Prohibited Activities. A member institution, on its campus or elsewhere, shall not conduct (or have conducted on its behalf) any physical activity (e.g., practice session or test/tryout) at which one or more prospective student-athletes (as defined in Bylaws 13.11.1.1 and 13.11.1.2) reveal, demonstrate or display their athletics abilities in any sport except as provided in Bylaws 13.11.2 and 13.11.3. **[D]** *(Revised: 8/5/04, 1/17/09)*

13.11.1.1 Definition of "Prospective Student-Athlete" for Tryout-Rule Purposes—Sports Other Than Men's Basketball. In sports other than men's basketball, for purposes of the tryout rule, the phrase "prospective student-athlete" shall include any individual who has started classes for the ninth grade and is not enrolled in the member institution at the time of the practice or test therein described. *(Revised: 1/11/89, 1/17/09)*

*****

13.11.1.4 Competition Against Prospective Student-Athletes—Bowl Subdivision Football. [FBS] In bowl subdivision football, an institution's varsity and subvarsity intercollegiate teams shall not compete against any team that includes prospective student-athletes. **[D]** *(Adopted: 1/16/10 effective 8/1/10, 4/29/10 effective 8/1/10; a contract signed by 8/14/09 may be honored)*

13.11.1.4.1 Exception—National Service Academy Subvarsity Team. A national service academy's subvarsity team may compete against a two-year college team, a high school team or a preparatory school team, provided no payment or other inducement (e.g., guarantee) is provided to such a team and no recruiting activities occur with members of such a team in conjunction with the competition. **[D]** *(Adopted: 1/15/11 effective 8/1/11)*

13.11.1.5 Competition Against Prospective Student-Athletes—Championship Subdivision Football. [FCS] In championship subdivision football, an institution's varsity intercollegiate team shall not compete against a high school or preparatory school team. An institution's varsity intercollegiate team may compete against a two-year college team and its subvarsity team may compete against a two-year college team, a high school team or a preparatory school team, provided no payment or other inducement (e.g., guarantee) is provided to such a team and no recruiting activities occur with members of such a team in conjunction with such competition. **[D]** *(Adopted: 4/29/10 effective 8/1/10; a contract signed before 8/14/09 may be honored)*

13.11.1.6 Competition in Conjunction with a High School, Preparatory School or Two-Year College. In basketball, football, gymnastics and volleyball, member institutions shall not permit competition between or among high schools, preparatory schools or two-year colleges to be conducted in conjunction with an intercollegiate athletics event (see Bylaw 13.15.1.5). **[D]** *(Revised: 1/10/90, 1/10/95, 8/5/04)*

13.11.1.6.1 Criteria. An intercollegiate contest may be scheduled on the same day as a high school, preparatory school or two-year college contest (without being considered to be scheduled "in conjunction" with that event) only if the college and high school, preparatory school or two-year college events are conducted in separate sessions, separate tickets are sold for the events, and the playing facility is cleared between the contests. *(Revised: 1/10/90, 1/10/95)*

*****

13.11.1.10 Nonscholastic Practice or Competition—Bowl Subdivision Football. [FBS] In bowl subdivision football, an institution [including any institutional department (e.g., athletics, recreational/intramural)] shall not host, sponsor or conduct a nonscholastic football practice or competition (e.g., seven-on-seven events) in which football prospective student-athletes participate on its campus or at an off-campus facility regularly used by the institution for practice and/or competition by any of the institution's sport programs. **[D]** *(Adopted: 1/14/12; a contract signed before 8/15/11 may be honored)*

*****

13.11.1.13 Use of Institutional Facilities for Noninstitutional Camps or Clinics—Bowl Subdivision Football. [FBS] In bowl subdivision football, the use of institutional facilities for noninstitutional camps or clinics that include prospect-aged participants shall be limited to the months of June and July or any calendar week (Sunday through Saturday) that includes days of those months (e.g., May 28-June 3) and to periods of time other than dead periods. **[D]** *(Adopted: 1/14/12; a contract signed before 8/15/11 may be honored, Revised: 2/24/12)*

13.11.1.14 Tryout Events. A member institution or conference may not host, sponsor or conduct a tryout camp, clinic, group workout or combine (e.g., combination of athletics skill tests or activities) devoted to agility, flexibility, speed or strength tests for prospective student-athletes at any location. An institution or conference shall not host, sponsor or conduct any portion (e.g., instructional clinic) of an event that also includes agility, flexibility, speed or strength tests for prospective student-athletes that are conducted at a separate location. In sports other than bowl subdivision football, a member institution's staff members may only attend (subject to sport-specific restrictions) such an event sponsored by an outside organization if the event occurs off the institution's campus and is open to all institutions (see Bylaws 13.1.7.9.4 and 13.1.7.9.5). **[D]** *(Adopted: 1/10/92, Revised: 8/5/04, 1/9/06 effective 8/1/06, 9/18/07)*

13.11.1.14.1 Exception—National Team Tryout Events. In sports other than basketball and bowl subdivision football, it is permissible for an institution to host national team tryout events conducted by the applicable national governing body (see Bylaws 13.11.1.7, 13.11.1.8, 13.11.1.9 and 13.11.1.10). *(Adopted: 12/12/06, Revised: 3/13/12)*

*****

13.11.2.2 Preseason Practice and Competition. A student-athlete who is not enrolled, but who has been accepted for admission to the institution in a regular full-time program of studies, shall be permitted to engage in preseason practice and competition in fall sports or practice occurring in midyear between terms on the academic calendar, provided such practice is not used to determine whether aid is to be awarded. **[D]**

13.11.2.3 Recreational Activities. A prospective student-athlete visiting a member institution may participate in physical workouts or other recreational activities during a visit to an institution's campus, provided such activities: **[D]** *(Revised: 1/11/94)*

(a) Are not organized or observed by members of the athletics department coaching staff; and

(b) Are not designed to test the athletics abilities of the prospective student-athlete.

13.11.2.3.1 Exception—After National Letter of Intent Signing. A prospective student-athlete who has signed a National Letter of Intent (or a four-year college-transfer prospective student-athlete who has signed a written offer of financial aid and/or admission) may participate in voluntary weightlifting or conditioning activities (e.g., conditioning on the track) on the institution's campus in the presence of the institution's strength and conditioning coach, provided such activities are not prearranged, the strength and conditioning coach is performing normal duties and responsibilities in the supervision of the weight room or facility in use (e.g., track) and he or she does not work directly with the prospective student-athlete. **[D]** *(Adopted: 8/26/10)*

13.11.2.4 Local Sports Clubs. In sports other than basketball, an institution's coach may be involved in any capacity (e.g., as a participant, administrator or in instructional or coaching activities) in the same sport for a local sports club or organization located in the institution's home community, provided all prospective student-athletes participating in said activities are legal residents of the area (within a 50-mile radius of the institution). In all sports, an institution's coach may be involved in any capacity (e.g., as a participant, administrator or in instructional or coaching activities) in a sport other than the coach's sport for a local sports club or organization located in the institution's home community, provided all prospective student-athletes participating in said activities are legal residents of the area (within a 50-mile radius of the institution). Further, in clubs or organizations involving multiple teams or multiple sports, the 50-mile radius is applicable only to the team with which the institution's coach is involved; however, it is not permissible for the coach to assign a prospective student-athlete who lives outside the 50-mile area to another coach of the club. A coach also may be involved in activities with individuals who are not of a prospective student-athlete age, regardless of where such individuals reside. (In women's volleyball and women's sand volleyball, see Bylaws 13.1.7.12 and 13.1.7.13, respectively, for regulations relating to a coach's involvement with a local sports club and the permissible number of evaluation days.) **[D]** *(Revised: 1/10/90, 1/16/93, 9/6/00, 4/25/02 effective 8/1/02, 5/11/05)*

13.11.2.4.1 Exception. The 50-mile radius restriction shall not apply to a prospective student-athlete who resides outside a 50-mile radius of the institution, provided the institution documents that the local sports club is the closest opportunity for the prospective student-athlete to participate in the sport. *(Adopted: 1/9/06 effective 8/1/06)*

13.11.2.4.2 Legal Resident. A prospective student-athlete who relocates to an area within a 50-mile radius of the institution on a temporary basis (e.g., to participate on a club team or attend an institution while maintaining a permanent residence outside the 50-mile radius) is not a legal resident of the area regardless of whether the prospective student-athlete meets legal standards of state or local residency for governmental purposes. *(Adopted: 9/18/07)*

13.11.2.4.3 Institutional Sponsorship of Local Sports Club. Neither an institution's athletics department nor an institution's athletics booster group may sponsor a local sports club that includes prospective student-athletes. It is permissible for a department of the institution that operates independent of the athletics department (e.g., physical education department, recreation department) to sponsor a local sports club that includes prospective student-athletes, provided no athletics department staff member is involved with the club team. **[D]** *(Adopted: 1/16/93, Revised: 1/11/94)*

13.11.2.4.4 Women's Volleyball—Additional Restrictions. In women's volleyball, during a dead or quiet period, institutional coaching staff members may not coach a local sports club team at an off-campus competition where prospective student-athletes are present. However, it is permissible for an institution's coach to coach his or her own local sports club team in practice activities. **[D]** *(Adopted: 4/28/05 effective 8/1/05)*

13.11.2.5 Sports Camps and Clinics. An institution's coach may be employed in sports camps, coaching schools and clinics per Bylaw 13.12 without violating the tryout rule.

13.11.2.6 Medical Examinations.

13.11.2.6.1 During Campus Visit. During a prospective student-athlete's official or unofficial visit to campus, a member institution, through its regular team or other designated physician, may conduct a medical examination to determine the prospective student-athlete's medical qualifications to participate in intercollegiate athletics, provided no athletics department staff member other than the athletic trainer is present, the examination does not include any test or procedure designed to measure the athletics agility or skill of the prospective student-athlete and the results of the examination are not used by the institution to deny admission of a prospective student-athlete who is otherwise qualified for admission under the institution's regular admissions criteria. **[D]** *(Revised: 10/30/03 effective 8/1/04)*

13.11.2.6.1.1 Exception—National Service Academies. National service academies are not subject to the restrictions on medical examinations during a prospective student-athlete's visit to campus, set forth in Bylaw 13.11.2.6.1.

13.11.2.6.1.2 Exception—On-Campus Evaluation—Basketball. In basketball, additional athletics department staff members (e.g., coaches) may be present during a medical examination that is conducted as part of an on-campus evaluation (see Bylaw 13.11.2.1) and the medical evaluation may include tests or procedures designed to measure the athletics agility or skill of the prospective student-athlete. *(Adopted: 1/14/12, Revised: 1/19/13)*

13.11.2.6.2 After Signing or Acceptance for Enrollment. It shall be permissible to administer medical examinations at any time to prospective student-athletes who either have signed the National Letter of Intent with the involved institution or have been accepted for enrollment in a regular full-time program of studies at that institution, provided the examinations occur during an official paid visit, attendance at summer school per Bylaw 15.2.8 or a visit to the institution at the prospective student-athlete's own expense for any purpose. Such an examination may take place before or after, but not during, a prospective student-athlete's visit to the campus to attend a general orientation session pursuant to Bylaw 13.15.2.4. **[D]** *(Revised: 1/14/97, 6/10/04)*

13.11.3 Tryout Exceptions.

13.11.3.1 Open Events. Participation by a prospective student-athlete in open events conducted by or held on the campus of a member institution shall not be considered tryouts. Competition shall be considered open if the competitive event itself is not classified by age group or level of educational institution represented, and the selection of participants is not limited except by number, by geographical area or on the basis of some objective standard of performance (see Bylaw 13.11.1.8). **[D]**

13.11.3.2 Activities Not Involving Institution's Staff. The use of a member institution's facilities for physical activities by a group that includes prospective student-athletes shall not be considered a tryout, provided the institution's athletics department staff members or representatives of its athletics interests are not involved in the conduct, promotion or administration of the activity (other than activities incidental to supervising the use of the facilities) and are subject to all applicable NCAA recruiting legislation. This exception does not apply to activities and events that are prohibited per Bylaws 13.11.1.7, 13.11.1.8, 13.11.1.9, 13.11.1.10 and 13.11.1.14. **[D]** *(Revised: 1/9/06 effective 8/1/06, 8/12/10, 5/22/13)*

13.11.3.3 State, Regional, National or International Training Programs. Participation by an institution's athletics department staff member in recognized state, regional, national or international training programs or competition organized and administered by the applicable governing body shall not be considered tryouts, provided the athletics department staff member is selected by the applicable governing body and the participants are selected by an authority or a committee of the applicable governing body that is not limited to athletics department staff members affiliated with one institution. A member institution's coaching staff member may not participate only in noncoaching activities (e.g., consultant, on-site coordinator, participant selection), except as provided in Bylaws 13.11.3.3.1, 13.11.3.3.2 and 13.11.3.3.3. **[D]** *(Revised: 1/9/96, 11/10/97, 4/28/11 effective 8/1/11)*

*****

13.11.3.3.2 Coach/Prospective Student-Athlete Competition. It is permissible for an institution's coach to participate with or against prospective student-athletes in recognized state, regional, national or international training programs or competition, provided the competition is regularly scheduled under the authority of an outside sports organization and both the coach and the prospective student-athlete are eligible to enter the competition. **[D]**

13.11.3.3.3 Administration of State Games. A member institution serving as the site of state games is permitted to involve its staff members in the administration of the event but may not be involved in the selection or assignment of participants and coaches participating in the event. **[D]** *(Adopted: 1/10/91)*

13.11.3.4 High School, Preparatory School and Two-Year College Contests. High school, preparatory school and two-year-college athletics contests or matches, conducted by a member institution or sponsored jointly with an outside organization and held on the campus of a member institution, shall not be considered tryouts, provided the following conditions are met [see Bylaw 13.2.2-(c) for restrictions related to the provision of awards at such contests]: **[D]** *(Revised: 1/15/11)*

(a) **Team Sports.**

(1) The opportunity to participate in the event is not limited to specific educational institutions and all educational institutions in a specific geographical area are eligible to compete (limited only by number, by institutional classification or on the basis of some objective standard of performance);

(2) Each participant represents his or her educational institution in the event (no nonscholastic team representation); and

(3) No financial compensation (e.g., transportation, expenses, guarantee, percentage of income) from the event may be provided to the educational institutions;

*****

13.11.3.5 Officiating. An institution's coach may officiate competition that involves prospective student-athletes, provided the competition is regularly scheduled under the authority of an outside sports organization. **[D]**

*****

13.11.3.7 Voluntary Summer Conditioning—Football. [FBS/FCS]

13.11.3.7.1 Voluntary Summer Conditioning—Bowl Subdivision Football. [FBS] In bowl subdivision football, a prospective student-athlete may engage in voluntary summer workouts conducted by an institution's strength and conditioning coach with department-wide duties and may receive workout apparel (on an issuance and retrieval basis), provided he has signed a National Letter of Intent or, for those institutions not using the National Letter of Intent or in the case of a four-year college prospective student-athlete, the prospective student-athlete has signed the institution's written offer of admission and/or financial aid or the institution has received his financial deposit in response to its offer of admission. **[D]** *(Adopted: 4/24/03 effective 5/1/03, Revised: 4/29/04, 5/31/06, 12/15/06, 1/14/08, 8/26/10, 1/19/13 effective 8/1/13, 10/21/13)*

13.11.3.7.2 Voluntary Summer Conditioning—Championship Subdivision Football. [FCS] In championship subdivision football, a prospective student-athlete may engage in voluntary summer workouts conducted by an institution's strength and conditioning coach with department-wide duties or a countable coach who is a certified strength and conditioning coach, and may receive workout apparel (on an issuance and retrieval basis), provided he has signed a National Letter of Intent or, for those institutions not using the National Letter of Intent or in the case of a four-year college prospective student-athlete, the prospective student-athlete has signed the institution's written offer of admission and/or financial aid or the institution has received his financial deposit in response to its offer of admission. **[D]** *(Adopted: 4/24/03 effective 5/1/03, Revised: 4/29/04, 5/31/06, 12/15/06, 1/14/08, 5/4/09, 8/26/10, 1/19/13 effective 8/1/13, 10/21/13)*

13.11.3.7.3 Mandatory Medical Examination. [FBS/FCS] Prior to participation in any weight-training or conditioning workouts, a prospective student-athlete who will be a first-time participant shall be required to undergo a medical examination or evaluation administered or supervised by a physician (e.g., family physician, team physician). The examination or evaluation shall include a sickle cell solubility test unless documented results of a prior test are provided to the institution or the prospective student-athlete declines the test and signs a written release. The examination or evaluation must have been administered within six months prior to participation in any weight-training or conditioning activity. **[D]** *(Adopted: 1/8/07 effective 5/1/07, Revised: 4/29/10 effective 8/1/10)*

13.11.3.7.4 Strength and Conditioning Coach First Aid/CPR Certification and Authority of Sports Medicine Staff. [FBS/FCS] A strength and conditioning coach who conducts voluntary weight-training or conditioning activities is required to maintain certification in first aid and cardiopulmonary resuscitation. In addition, a member of the institution's sports medicine staff (e.g., athletic trainer, physician) must be present during all voluntary conditioning activities (running, not lifting) conducted by the institution's strength coach. The sports medicine staff member must be empowered to have the unchallengeable authority to cancel or modify the workout for health and safety reasons, as he or she deems appropriate. **[D]** *(Adopted: 4/24/03 effective 5/1/03)*

*****

13.11.3.10 Required Summer Athletic Activities—National Service Academies—Incoming Freshmen—Bowl Subdivision Football. [FBS] In football, a national service academy may designate eight weeks (not required to be consecutive weeks) of the summer during which incoming freshmen student-athletes who are enrolled in required summer on-campus military training may engage in required weight-training, conditioning and review of practice and game film. Participation in such activities shall be limited to a maximum of eight hours per week with not more than two hours per week spent on film review. **[D]** *(Adopted: 10/30/13)*

13.11.3.10.1 Mandatory Medical Examination. [FBS] Before participating in any required summer athletic activities, a prospective student-athlete shall be required to undergo a medical examination or evaluation administered or supervised by a physician (e.g., family physician, team physician). The examination or evaluation shall include a sickle cell solubility test unless documented results of a prior test are provided to the institution or the prospective student-athlete declines the test and signs a written release. The examination or evaluation must have been administered within six months before participation in any athletic activity. **[D]** *(Adopted: 10/30/13)*

13.12 Sports Camps and Clinics.
13.12.1 Institution's Sports Camps and Clinics.

13.12.1.1 Definition. An institution's sports camp or instructional clinic shall be any camp or clinic that is owned or operated by a member institution or an employee of the member institution's athletics department, either on or off its campus, and in which prospective student-athletes participate. *(Adopted: 1/11/89, Revised: 1/10/90, 4/26/01 effective 8/1/01)*

*****

13.12.1.1.2 Purposes of Camps or Clinics. An institution's sports camp or clinic shall be one that:

(a) Places special emphasis on a particular sport or sports and provides specialized instruction or practice and may include competition; *(Adopted: 1/11/89, Revised: 1/10/90, 5/9/06)*

(b) Involves activities designed to improve overall skills and general knowledge in the sport; or

(c) Offers a diversified experience without emphasis on instruction, practice or competition in any particular sport.

13.12.1.1.3 Football. [FBS/FCS] In bowl subdivision football, an institution's football camp or clinic may be conducted only during two periods of 15 consecutive days in the months of June and July or any calendar week (Sunday through Saturday) that includes days of those months (e.g., May 28-June 3). The dates of the two 15-day periods must be on file in the office of the athletics director. In championship subdivision football, an institution's camp or clinic may be conducted only during the months of June, July and August or any calendar week (Sunday through Saturday) that includes days of those months (e.g., May 28-June 3). **[D]** *(Revised: 4/28/05 effective 8/1/05, 1/9/06 effective 8/1/06, 1/8/07, 1/16/10, 4/29/10)*

****

13.12.1.2 Location Restriction—Basketball and Football. In basketball, an institution's camp or clinic shall be conducted on the institution's campus or within a 100-mile radius of the institution's campus. In football, an institution's camp or clinic shall be conducted on the institution's campus, within the state in which the institution is located or, if outside the state, within a 50-mile radius of the institution's campus. *(Revised: 4/29/10; for men's basketball camps, a contract signed before 9/17/08 may be honored; for women's basketball camps, a contract signed before 9/16/09 may be honored)*

13.12.1.3 Attendance Restriction. A member institution's sports camp or clinic shall be open to any and all entrants (limited only by number, age, grade level and/or gender). (See Bylaw 13.4.3.2.2.) *(Revised: 1/11/89, 1/10/91, 1/11/94, 12/12/06, 9/24/09)*

*****

13.12.1.5 Recruiting Calendar Exceptions. The interaction during sports camps and clinics between prospective student-athletes and those coaches employed by the camp or clinic is not subject to the recruiting calendar restrictions. However, an institutional staff member employed at any camp or clinic (e.g., counselor, director) is prohibited from recruiting any prospective student-athlete during the time period that the camp or clinic is conducted (from the time the prospective student-athlete reports to the camp or clinic until the conclusion of all camp activities). The prohibition against recruiting includes extending written offers of financial aid to any prospective student-athlete during his or her attendance at the camp or clinic (see Bylaw 13.9.2.2), but does not include recruiting conversations between the certifying institution's coach and a participating prospective student-athlete during the institution's camps or clinics. Other coaches wishing to attend the camp as observers must comply with appropriate recruiting contact and evaluation periods. In addition, institutional camps or clinics may not be conducted during a dead period. *(Revised: 4/3/02, 4/26/12)*

13.12.1.6 Advertisements. Restrictions relating to advertisements of an institution's sports camps and clinics in recruiting publications are set forth in Bylaw 13.4.3.2. Such restrictions do not apply to sports camp and clinic advertisements in nonrecruiting publications (e.g., a member institution's game program). **[D]** *(Revised: 8/5/04)*

13.12.1.7 Employment of Prospective Student-Athletes/No Free or Reduced Admission Privileges.

13.12.1.7.1 General Rule. An institution, members of its staff or representatives of its athletics interests shall not employ or give free or reduced admission privileges to a prospective student-athlete who is an athletics award winner or any individual being recruited by the institution per Bylaw 13.02.13.1. An institution may offer discounted admission to its camps and clinics based on objective criteria unrelated to athletics abilities (e.g., registration prior to a specific date, online registration, attendance at multiple sessions, group discounts), provided such discounts are published and available on an equal basis to all who qualify. **[R]** *(Revised: 3/10/04, 4/20/09, 9/24/09)*

13.12.1.7.1.1 Exception—Employment After Commitment. An institution may employ a prospective student-athlete in a camp or clinic, provided he or she has signed a National Letter of Intent or the institution's written offer of admission and/or financial aid or the institution has received his or her financial deposit in response to its offer of admission. Compensation may be paid only for work actually performed and at a rate commensurate with the going rate in the locality for similar services. Such compensation may not include any remuneration for value or utility that the student-athlete may have for the employer because of the publicity, reputation, fame or personal following that he or she has obtained because of athletics ability. A prospective student-athlete who only lectures or demonstrates at a camp/clinic may not receive compensation for his or her appearance at the camp/clinic. *(Adopted: 1/19/13 effective 8/1/13)*

13.12.1.7.2 Payment of Expenses. A representative of an institution's athletics interests may not pay a prospective student-athlete's expenses to attend a member institution's sports camp or clinic. **[R]**

13.12.1.7.3 Concession Arrangement.

13.12.1.7.3.1 Prospective Student-Athlete. An institution may not permit or arrange for a prospective student-athlete, at the prospective student-athlete's own expense, to operate a concession to sell items related to or associated with the institution's camp. **[R]** *(Revised: 8/5/04)*

13.12.1.7.3.2 Enrolled Student-Athlete. A student-athlete, at the student-athlete's own expense, may not operate a concession to sell items related to or associated with his or her institution's camp to campers or others in attendance because such an arrangement would be considered an extra benefit. However, the institution may employ the student-athlete at a reasonable rate to perform such services for the camp. **[R]** *(Revised: 8/5/04)*

13.12.1.7.4 Awards. Prospective student-athletes may receive awards from a member institution's sports camp or clinic with the understanding that the cost of such awards is included in the admissions fees charged for participants in the camp or clinic.**[R]** *(Adopted: 1/10/92, 8/5/04)*

13.12.1.8 Educational Session. An institution's basketball sports camp or clinic must include an educational session presented in-person or in a video format detailing NCAA initial-eligibility standards and regulations related to gambling, agents and drug use to all camp and/or clinic participants. *(Adopted: 1/14/97, Revised: 1/13/03)*

13.12.2 Employment at Camp or Clinic.

13.12.2.1 Student-Athletes. A student-athlete may be employed in any sports camp or clinic, provided compensation is provided pursuant to the criteria of Bylaw 12.4.1. A student-athlete who only lectures or demonstrates at a camp/clinic may not receive compensation for his or her appearance at the camp/clinic. *(Revised: 4/24/03 effective 8/1/03, 1/19/13 effective 8/1/13)*

13.12.2.1.1 Self-Employment. A student-athlete with remaining eligibility is not permitted to conduct his or her own camp or clinic. **[R]** *(Revised: 4/24/03 effective 8/1/03)*

13.12.2.2 High School, Preparatory School, Two-Year College Coaches or Other Individuals Involved With Prospective Student-Athletes. A member institution (or employees of its athletics department) may employ a high school, preparatory school or two-year college coach or any other individual responsible for teaching or directing an activity in which a prospective student-athlete is involved at its camp or clinic, provided: **[R]** *(Adopted: 1/11/89, Revised: 1/11/94, 6/25/08, 8/12/10)*

(a) The individual receives compensation that is commensurate with the going rate for camp counselors of like teaching ability and camp experience; and

(b) The individual is not paid on the basis of the value he or she may have for the employer because of his or her reputation or contact with prospective student-athletes. (See Bylaw 13.12.3.)

13.12.2.2.1 Prohibited Compensation. A member institution may not compensate or reimburse a high school, preparatory school or two-year college coach, or any other individual responsible for teaching or directing an activity in which a prospective student-athlete is involved based on the number of campers the individual sends to the camp. **[R]** *(Revised: 4/20/11)*

13.12.2.2.2 Employment as a Speaker in an Institutional Camp or Clinic—Basketball. An institution shall not employ (either on a salaried or a volunteer basis) a speaker in any basketball camp or clinic (including a coaches clinic or a camp or clinic involving nonprospects) who is involved in coaching prospective student-athletes or is associated with a prospective student-athlete as a result of the prospective student-athlete's participation in basketball. Such an individual may be employed as a camp counselor (except as prohibited in Bylaw 13.12.2.2.3), but may not perform speaking duties other than those normally associated with camp counselor duties (e.g., skill instruction). *(Adopted: 1/17/09, Revised: 8/26/10)*

13.12.2.2.3 Individual Associated With a Recruited Prospective Student-Athlete—Men's Basketball. In men's basketball, an institution or staff member shall not employ (either on a volunteer or paid basis) an individual associated with a recruited prospective student-athlete at the institution's camp or clinic. *(Adopted: 8/26/10)*

13.12.2.3 Athletics Staff Members. A member institution's athletics staff member may be involved in sports camps or clinics unless otherwise prohibited in this section (see Bylaw 11.3.2.6). **[D]** *(Revised: 8/5/04)*

13.12.2.3.1 Camp/Clinic Providing Recruiting or Scouting Service. No athletics department staff member may be employed (either on a salaried or a volunteer basis) in any capacity by a camp or clinic established, sponsored or conducted by an individual or organization that provides recruiting or scouting services concerning prospective student-athletes. This provision does not prohibit an athletics department staff member from participating in an officiating camp where participants officiate for, but are not otherwise involved in, a scouting services camp. **[D]** *(Adopted: 1/11/89, Revised: 1/10/90, 1/10/92, 8/5/04)*

13.12.2.3.2 Institutional/Noninstitutional, Privately Owned Camps/Clinics—Basketball. In basketball, an institution's coach or noncoaching staff member with responsibilities specific to basketball may be employed only at his or her institution's camps or clinics. Participation in such camps or clinics is limited to the months of June, July and August or any calendar week (Sunday through Saturday) that includes days of those months (e.g., May 28-June 3). It is not permissible for a basketball coach or a noncoaching staff member with responsibilities specific to basketball to be employed at other institutional camps or clinics or at noninstitutional privately owned camps or clinics. **[D]** *(Adopted: 4/28/05 effective 4/28/05 for men's basketball, 8/1/05 for women's basketball, Revised: 1/9/06 effective 8/1/06)*

13.12.2.3.3 Noninstitutional, Privately Owned Camps/Clinics—Bowl Subdivision Football. [FBS] In bowl subdivision football, an institution's coach or noncoaching staff member with responsibilities specific to football may be employed (either on a salaried or volunteer basis) in any capacity (e.g., counselor, guest lecturer, consultant) in a noninstitutional, privately owned camp or clinic at any location, provided the camp or clinic is operated in accordance with restrictions applicable to an institutional camp or clinic (e.g., open to any and all entrants, no free or reduced admission to or employment of athletics award winners). However, employment in such a camp or clinic is limited to two periods of 15 consecutive days in the months of June and July or any calendar week (Sunday through Saturday) that includes days of those months (e.g., May 28-June 3). The dates of the two 15-day periods must be on file in the office of the athletics director. **[D]** *(Adopted: 1/16/10)*

13.12.2.3.4 Noninstitutional, Privately Owned Camps/Clinics—Championship Subdivision Football. [FCS] In championship subdivision football, an institution's coach or noncoaching staff member with responsibilities specific to football may be employed (either on a salaried or volunteer basis) in any capacity (e.g., counselor, guest lecturer, consultant) in a noninstitutional, privately owned camp or clinic at any location, provided the camp or clinic is operated in accordance with restrictions applicable to an institutional camp or clinic (e.g., open to any and all entrants, no free or reduced admission to or employment of athletics award winners). However, employment in such a camp or clinic may occur only during the months of June, July and August or any calendar week (Sunday through Saturday) that includes days of those months (e.g., May 28-June 3). **[D]** *(Adopted: 1/16/10)*

*****

13.12.2.3.7 Noncoaching Athletics Staff Members With Department-Wide Responsibilities. A noncoaching athletics staff member with department-wide responsibilities may present an educational session at a noninstitutional, privately owned camp/clinic that is not operated under the restrictions applicable to institutional camps/clinics, provided the staff member does not make a recruiting presentation. **[D]** *(Adopted: 4/29/04 effective 8/1/04, Revised: 8/5/04)*

13.12.2.3.8 Noninstitutional Fundamental Skills Camp/Clinic. An institution's athletics department personnel may serve in any capacity at a noninstitutional camp or clinic conducted under the following conditions: **[D]** *(Adopted: 1/13/03, Revised: 8/5/04)*

(a) The camp or clinic is designed to develop fundamental skills in a sport (rather than refine the abilities of skilled participants in the sport);

(b) The camp or clinic is open to the general public (except for restrictions in age or number of participants);

(c) The camp or clinic is conducted primarily for educational purposes and does not include material benefits for the participants (e.g., awards, prizes, merchandise, gifts);

(d) Participants do not receive a recruiting presentation; and

(e) All participants reside in the state in which the camp/clinic is located or within 100 miles of the camp/clinic.

13.12.3 Notification of Ineligibility and Consequences of Violation—Men's Basketball. In men's basketball, if a violation specified below occurs, the institution shall declare each involved prospective student-athlete ineligible. Within 30 days of becoming aware of the violation, the institution shall provide written notification to each involved prospective student-athlete that the actions of the institution affected the prospective student-athlete's eligibility. The written notification shall also include an explanation of the consequences of the violation for the prospective student-athlete. *(Adopted: 8/12/10)*

(a) A violation of Bylaw 13.12.2.2-(b) in which an institution or men's basketball staff member employs (either on a salaried or a volunteer basis) an individual associated with a recruited prospective student-athlete at the institution's camp or clinic.

(b) A violation of Bylaw 13.12 in which an institutional boys' basketball camp offers a participation registration, procedure, fee structure, advertisement and/or logistical experience (e.g., lodging, meals, transportation or awards/mementos) that differs from other institutional boys' basketball camps.

13.13 High School All-Star Games.

13.13.1 Coach Involvement. A member institution shall not permit any coach or athletics department staff member directly involved in the recruiting of prospective student-athletes to participate (directly or indirectly) in the management, coaching, officiating, supervision, promotion or participant selection of any all-star team or contest involving interscholastic participants or those who, during the previous school year, were members of high school athletics teams. **[D]** *(Revised: 4/24/03 effective 8/1/03, 3/26/04)*

13.13.1.1 Previous Contractual Agreement. If a coach has made a contractual commitment to coach in a high school all-star game prior to being employed by a member institution and then becomes a member of the institution's staff before the game is held, the coach shall be obligated to observe this provision and disassociate himself or herself from the all-star game. **[D]** *(Revised: 4/24/03 effective 8/1/03)*

13.13.2 Use of Institutional Facilities. A member institution's facilities shall not be made available for a high school all-star game unless the provisions of Bylaw 13.11.3.2 are met. **[D]** *(Revised: 8/5/04)*

13.13.3 Use of Institutional Equipment. It is not permissible for an institution to provide its athletics equipment to a prospective student-athlete (e.g., for use in a high school all-star game). **[D]** *(Revised: 8/5/04)*

13.14 Use of Recruiting Funds.

13.14.1 Institutional Control. All funds for the recruiting of prospective student-athletes shall be deposited with the member institution, which shall be exclusively and entirely responsible for the manner in which such funds are expended.

13.14.2 Visiting a Prospective Student-Athlete. A member institution's athletics department staff member may visit a prospective student-athlete or the prospective student-athlete's relatives or legal guardians at any location for recruiting purposes. However, on any such visit, the staff member may not expend any funds other than the amount necessary for his or her own personal expenses.

13.14.3 Recruiting or Scouting Services.

13.14.3.1 Basketball and Football. In basketball and football, an institution may subscribe to a recruiting or scouting service involving prospective student-athletes, provided the institution does not purchase more than one annual subscription to a particular service and the service: **[D]** *(Adopted: 1/1/02, Revised: 8/5/04, 1/16/10, 4/14/10, 1/14/12, 7/26/12, 1/15/14)*

(a) Is made available to all institutions desiring to subscribe and at the same fee rate for all subscribers;

(b) Publicly identifies all applicable rates;

(c) Disseminates information (e.g., reports, profiles) about prospective student-athletes at least four times per calendar year;

(d) Publicly identifies the geographical scope of the service (e.g., local, regional, national) and reflects broad-based coverage of the geographical area in the information it disseminates;

(e) Provides individual analysis beyond demographic information or rankings for each prospective student-athlete in the information it disseminates;

(f) Provides access to samples or previews of the information it disseminates before purchase of a subscription;

(g) Provides information regarding each prospective student-athlete in a standardized format that ensures consistent distribution to all subscribers; and

(h) Does not provide information in any form (e.g., oral reports, electronic messages) about prospective student-athletes beyond the standardized, consistent information that is provided to all subscribers.

13.14.3.1.1 Video-Only Services. An institution is permitted to use or subscribe to a video service that only provides video of prospective student-athletes and does not provide information about or analysis of prospective student-athletes. Use of a subscription to such a service is subject to the provisions of Bylaw 13.14.3.1, except for subsections (c) and (e). **[D]** *(Adopted: 1/15/11, Revised: 1/14/12)*

*****

13.14.3.3 Subscription Limited to Approved Services—Basketball and Football. In basketball and football, an institution shall not subscribe to a recruiting or scouting service unless the service has been approved by the NCAA pursuant to an annual approval process. **[D]** *(Adopted: 1/14/12 effective 6/1/12)*

13.14.4 Slush Funds. An institution shall not permit any outside organization, agency or group of individuals to use, administer or expend funds for recruiting prospective student-athletes, including the transportation and entertainment of, and the giving of gifts or services to, prospective student-athletes or their relatives, legal guardians or friends.

13.14.4.1 Pooled Resources. The pooling of resources for recruiting purposes by two or more persons shall constitute such a slush fund. However, this provision shall not apply to persons upon whom a prospect may be naturally or legally dependent.

13.14.4.2 Company Funds. The use of a company's funds to pay the expenses incurred in transporting a prospective student-athlete to the campus constitutes the use of pooled resources.

13.14.5 Alumni Organizations. Bona fide alumni organizations of an institution may sponsor luncheons, teas or dinners at which prospective students (athletes and nonathletes) of that immediate locale are guests. A member institution's area alumni organization may be considered a bona fide part of that institution, provided such an organization is accredited by the president or chancellor of the institution and meets these additional terms and conditions: *(Revised: 3/8/06)*

(a) A staff member of the institution periodically shall inspect the financial records of the alumni organization and certify that the expenditures comply with the rules and regulations of the NCAA and the conference(s), if any, of which the institution is a member; and

(b) A club official shall be designated by the president or chancellor as the institution's official agent in the administration of the club's funds, and said club official shall file regular reports to the institution relating the manner in which the club funds have been spent in the recruiting of student-athletes. *(Revised: 3/8/06)*

13.14.5.1 Subject to NCAA Rules. If an alumni organization is certified by the president or chancellor as being a bona fide part of the institution, said organization becomes subject to all of the limitations placed upon the member institution by NCAA legislation. A violation of such legislation by any member of the alumni organization shall be a violation by the member institution. **[D]** *(Revised: 8/5/04, 3/8/06)*

13.15 Precollege Expenses.
13.15.1 Prohibited Expenses. An institution or a representative of its athletics interests shall not offer, provide or arrange financial assistance, directly or indirectly, to pay (in whole or in part) the costs of the prospective student-athlete's educational or other expenses for any period prior to his or her enrollment or so the prospective student-athlete can obtain a postgraduate education. **[R]** *(Revised: 8/5/04)*

13.15.1.1 Extent of Prohibition. The provisions of Bylaw 13.15.1 apply to all prospective student-athletes, including those who have signed a National Letter of Intent or an institutional offer of admission or financial aid.

13.15.1.2 Fundraising for High School Athletics Program. An institution may not provide funding, directly or through paid advertisements, to benefit a high school athletics program. **[D]** *(Adopted: 1/10/92, Revised: 4/26/01)*

13.15.1.2.1 Involvement by Local Representatives of Institution's Athletics Interests. A representative of an institution's athletics interests may provide funding to benefit a high school athletics program located in the community in which the athletics representative resides, provided: *(Adopted: 1/10/92)*

(a) The representative acts independently of the institution;

(b) The funds are distributed through channels established by the high school or the organization conducting the fundraising activity; and

(c) The funds are not earmarked directly for a specific prospective student-athlete.

13.15.1.3 College Use of High School Facility. An institution may not contribute to a high school or its athletics booster club any funds realized from an athletics contest played or a practice held at a high school facility, except actual and necessary expenses for rental of the facility.

13.15.1.4 State High School Association Use of Member Institution's Facilities. An institution may permit a state high school association to use its facilities to host state high school championship events at a reduced rate. *(Adopted: 4/28/05)*

13.15.1.5 High School Contest in Conjunction with College Competition. A high school contest held in conjunction with an institution's intercollegiate contest shall be governed by the following: *(Revised: 1/10/90, 1/10/95)*

(a) It shall involve a sport other than basketball, football, gymnastics or volleyball;

(b) It shall be regularly scheduled and approved by the appropriate state high school authority;

(c) The member institution shall not provide the high school with any financial compensation, including transportation expenses or a guarantee or percentage of the income realized from the contest; and

(d) The only expenses the member institution may incur are the operating and maintenance costs associated with its facility's use for the high school contest.

13.15.1.6 Donation of Equipment.

13.15.1.6.1 Athletics Equipment. A member institution may not provide athletics equipment to a high school. However, a member institution is permitted to provide athletics equipment to bona fide youth organizations (e.g., the YMCA, YWCA, Boy Scout troops, Girl Scout troops, a summer recreation league) that may consist of some prospective student-athletes, provided the issuance of equipment is in accordance with the institution's regular policy regarding the discarding of equipment. **[D]** *(Revised: 4/26/01, 4/26/12 effective 8/1/12)*

*****

13.15.1.6.1.2 Donation of Used Athletics Equipment to Foundation. An institution may donate used athletics equipment to a nonprofit foundation established to distribute such equipment to high schools, provided the request for such donations is initiated by the foundation and the institutions have no part in selecting the high schools that are to receive the equipment. *(Adopted: 1/11/94)*

13.15.1.6.2 Nonathletics Equipment. A member institution may provide nonathletics equipment (e.g., a computer) to a high school, provided there is no athletics department involvement and the equipment is not used to benefit only the high school's athletics program. *(Adopted: 1/10/91)*

13.15.1.7 Ticket Sales. It is not permissible for a member institution to compensate a high school, preparatory school or two-year college for selling tickets to the institution's athletics contests. Specifically, the member institution may not provide such forms of compensation as a guarantee, a percentage of the income realized from the sale of the tickets or any other form of commission for providing such services.

13.15.1.8 Conference-Sponsored Sportsmanship Initiatives. A conference may provide actual and necessary expenses that are directly associated with implementing a conference-sponsored sportsmanship initiative as described in Bylaws 13.1.10, 13.4.3.4 and 13.10.2.3. *(Adopted: 4/26/07 effective 8/1/07)*

13.15.1.9 Academic Services. An institution shall not provide academic expenses or services (e.g., tutoring, test preparation) to assist a prospective student-athlete in completing initial-eligibility or transfer-eligibility requirements or in improving his or her academic profile in conjunction with a waiver request. **[R]** *(Adopted: 4/23/08)*

*****

13.15.2 Permissible Expenses.

13.15.2.1 ACT and SAT Scores. An institution may pay a fee required by the appropriate testing agency to obtain a prospective student-athlete's official ACT or SAT scores. *(Adopted: 1/10/90)*

13.15.2.2 Collect and Toll-Free Telephone Calls. Institutional coaching staff members (see Bylaw 13.1.3.4.1) may accept collect and toll-free (e.g., 1-800, 1-888) telephone calls placed by prospective student-athletes and prospective student-athletes' parents and legal guardians pursuant to Bylaw 13.1.3.6. **[R]** *(Adopted: 1/10/91 effective 7/1/91, Revised: 1/10/92, 1/11/94, 12/12/06, 4/28/11 effective 8/1/11)*

13.15.2.3 Institution Providing Items to Athletics Youth Groups for Fundraising. An institution may provide items to assist in the fundraising efforts of athletics youth groups composed of individuals who have not started classes for the ninth grade without causing such individuals to become prospective student-athletes per Bylaw 13.02.12. *(Adopted: 1/10/95)*

13.15.2.4 Student Orientation Sessions. An institution may pay on-campus expenses (e.g., meals, lodging) for prospective student-athletes to attend institutional orientation sessions conducted for all students. However, an institution may provide on-campus expenses to student-athletes to attend orientation sessions for a particular group of students selected on a basis unrelated to athletics ability only if the institution is providing expenses on a uniform basis to all members of that particular group. An institutional staff member may provide transportation from and to the nearest bus or train station or major airport to the campus on the occasion of the prospective student-athlete's arrival or departure from the institution to attend the institution's required new-student orientation, provided the prospective student-athlete has been accepted for admission to the institution. **[R]** *(Adopted: 1/10/95, Revised: 1/9/96, 4/26/01 effective 8/1/01)*

13.15.2.5 Use of Bands Comprised of Prospective Student-Athletes. An institution may hire a band (e.g., marching band, pep band) comprised of prospective student-athlete-aged individuals to perform at its regular-season home contests and/or postseason home or away-from-home contests, provided the band is paid commensurate with the going rate in that locale for similar services and the organization providing the band is located within 150 miles of the competition site. *(Adopted: 11/1/01 effective 8/1/02)*

13.16 U.S. Service Academy Exceptions and Waivers.
13.16.1 Contacts.

13.16.1.1 During Junior Year in High School. Authorized athletics staff members of the U.S. Air Force, Military, Coast Guard, Merchant Marine and Naval Academies, where congressionally required institutional procedures applying to all prospective cadets and midshipmen, regardless of athletics ability, are in conflict with the Association's legislation governing telephonic and off-campus recruiting contacts, may make in-person, telephonic and off-campus contacts during a prospective student-athlete's junior year in high school. Sport-specific recruiting calendar restrictions apply to off-campus contacts, except, in football, authorized staff members may make in-person off-campus contact with a prospective student-athlete during the spring evaluation period of the prospective student-athlete's junior year in high school, including contact at the prospective student-athlete's educational institution. The total number of contacts, including those after the prospective student-athlete's junior year, shall not exceed the number permitted in the applicable sport. *(Revised: 4/24/08)*

13.16.1.2 After National Letter of Intent Signing Date. There shall be no limit on the number of recruiting contacts with the prospective student-athlete, the prospective student-athlete's relatives or legal guardians made by a national service academy to which the prospective student-athlete has applied for admission after the National Letter of Intent signing date in the sport. *(Revised: 1/19/13 effective 8/1/13)*

13.16.1.3 Freshmen at Summer Enrollment Programs. Freshmen entering the official summer enrollment program of one of the four national service academies (U.S. Air Force, Coast Guard, Military and Naval Academies) shall be considered student-athletes of a senior collegiate institution and may not be contacted by other member institutions without permission from the athletics director of the service academy.

13.16.2 Evaluation Days—Football. In football, each national service academy is limited to 54 evaluation days (see Bylaw 13.02.7.2) during the fall evaluation period. *(Adopted: 4/14/08)*

13.16.3 Air Force, Military and Naval Academies Exception. A nonprofit, outside organization representing the interests of one of the service academies may collect contributions from alumni and other friends of the academy for the purpose of assisting candidates in obtaining a preparatory education, provided the following conditions are met: *(Revised: 11/1/07 effective 8/1/08, 7/30/10)*

(a) The organization's arrangements with the preparatory school(s) shall provide that the organization's contributions shall be turned over to the preparatory school for the school's administration without interference or dictation from the organization or the academy;

(b) The preparatory school shall have sole jurisdiction in determining the recipient of financial assistance and the terms and conditions of the award;

(c) The organization may recommend candidates to the preparatory school; athletics staff members of the academy may not; and

(d) Such a foundation shall provide preparatory education assistance for prospective candidates who do not have specialized athletics abilities as well as those who do. The number of candidates with recognized ability assisted each year as the result of the organization's program shall be in equal ratio to the number of student-athletes on the regular intercollegiate squads of the academy compared with the total enrollment of the academy.

13.16.4 Precollege Expenses/Preparatory School Assistance—Waiver. The Legislative Council Subcommittee for Legislative Relief may approve waivers of Bylaw 13.15, provided such waivers are limited to procedures involving preparation for entrance into one of the U.S. service academies. *(Revised: 11/1/07 effective 8/1/08, 7/30/10)*

13.17 Recruiting Calendars.

*****

13.17.4 Football.

13.17.4.1 Bowl Subdivision Football. [FBS] The following periods of recruiting activities shall apply to bowl subdivision football: *(Revised: 1/10/90 effective 8/1/90, 1/10/91 effective 8/1/91, 4/25/02 effective 8/1/02, 2/24/03, 10/3/03, 1/11/94 effective 8/1/94, 10/12/94, 8/12/95, 4/27/00 effective 8/1/00, 9/6/00, 1/10/05, 12/5/05, 12/15/06, 1/14/08 effective 8/1/08, 2/22/08, 4/14/08, 5/27/09, 1/16/10 effective 8/1/10, 7/30/10, 10/30/13, 11/25/13)*

(a) June 1 through the last Saturday in November [except for (1) and (2) below]:

— Quiet Period

(1) A 14-day period that begins on the last Monday in June unless July 1 falls on a Monday. If July 1 falls on a Monday, a 14-day period that begins on July 1:

— Dead Period

(2) Forty-two (54 for U.S. service academies) evaluation days (see Bylaw 13.02.7.2) during the months of September, October and November selected at the discretion of the institution and designated in writing in the office of the director of athletics; authorized off-campus recruiters shall not visit a prospective student-athlete's educational institution on more than one calendar day during this period:

— Evaluation Period

(b) The Sunday following the last Saturday in November through the Saturday prior to the initial date for the regular signing period of the National Letter of Intent except for (1) and (2) below. Six in-person off-campus contacts per prospective student-athlete shall be permitted during this time period with not more than one permitted in any one calendar week (Sunday through Saturday) or partial calendar week:

— Contact Period

(1) The Sunday prior to the dead period surrounding the initial date of the midyear junior college transfer National Letter of Intent signing period (applicable only to junior college prospective student-athletes who intend to enroll midyear):

— Quiet Period

(2) Monday of the week that includes the initial date of the midyear junior college transfer National Letter of Intent signing period through the Wednesday of the week of the annual convention of the American Football Coaches Association [applicable to all prospective student-athletes (see Bylaw 13.02.5.5.2)]:

— Dead Period

(c) The Sunday prior to the dead period surrounding the initial date for the regular signing period of the National Letter of Intent:

— Quiet Period

(d) Monday through Thursday of the week that includes the initial date for the regular signing period of the National Letter of Intent:

— Dead Period

(e) Friday following the initial date for the regular signing period of the National Letter of Intent through April 14:

    — Quiet Period

(f) One hundred sixty-eight evaluation days (216 for U.S. service academies) (see Bylaw 13.02.7.2) (excluding Memorial Day and Sundays) during April 15 through May 31 selected at the discretion of the member institution and designated in writing in the office of the director of athletics [as provided in (1) below]:

    — Evaluation Period

    (1) An authorized off-campus recruiter may use one evaluation to assess the prospective student-athlete's athletics ability and one evaluation to assess the prospective student-athlete's academic qualifications during this evaluation period. If an institution's coaching staff member conducts both an athletics and an academic evaluation of a prospective student-athlete on the same day during this evaluation period, the institution shall be charged with the use of an academics evaluation only and shall be permitted to conduct a second athletics evaluation of the prospective student-athlete on a separate day during this evaluation period.

(g) Those days in April/May not designated in (f) above for evaluation opportunities.

    — Quiet Period

13.17.4.2 Championship Subdivision Football. [FCS] The following periods of recruiting activities shall apply to championship subdivision football: *(Revised: 1/10/90 effective 8/1/90, 1/10/91 effective 8/1/91, 4/25/02 effective 8/1/02, 2/24/03, 10/3/03, 1/11/94 effective 8/1/94, 10/12/94, 8/12/95, 4/27/00 effective 8/1/00, 9/6/00, 1/10/05, 12/5/05, 12/15/06, 1/14/08 effective 8/1/08, 2/22/08, 4/14/08, 5/27/09, 1/16/10 effective 8/1/10, 7/30/10, 10/30/13, 11/25/13)*

(a) June 1 through the last Saturday in November [except for (1) below]:

    — Quiet Period

    (1) Forty-two evaluation days (see Bylaw 13.02.7.2) during the months of September, October and November selected at the discretion of the institution and designated in writing in the office of the director of athletics; authorized off-campus recruiters shall not visit a prospective student-athlete's educational institution on more than one calendar day during this period:

    — Dead Period

(b) The Sunday following the last Saturday in November through the Saturday prior to the initial date for the regular signing period of the National Letter of Intent except for (1) through (7) below. Six in-person off-campus contacts per prospective student-athlete shall be permitted during this time period with not more than one permitted in any one calendar week (Sunday through Saturday) or partial calendar week:

    — Contact Period

    (1) The Sunday prior to the dead period surrounding the initial date of the midyear junior college transfer National Letter of Intent signing period (applicable only to junior college prospective student-athletes who intend to enroll midyear):

    — Quiet Period

    (2) Monday through Thursday of the week that includes the initial date of the midyear junior college transfer National Letter of Intent signing period [applicable only to junior college prospective student-athletes who intend to enroll midyear (see Bylaw 13.02.5.5.2)]:

    — Dead Period

    (3) The Friday following the initial date of the midyear junior college transfer National Letter of Intent signing period through the Sunday of the week of the annual convention of the American Football Coaches Association [subject to the dead periods (5) and (7) below in applicable years (applicable only to junior college prospective student-athletes who intend to enroll midyear)]:

    — Quiet Period

    (4) The Sunday after the third Saturday in December:

— Quiet Period

(5) The Monday following the third Saturday in December through January 3:

— Dead Period

(6) Sunday during the week of the annual convention of the American Football Coaches Association.

— Quiet Period

(7) Monday through Thursday during the week of the annual convention of the American Football Coaches Association:

— Dead Period

(c) The Sunday prior to the dead period surrounding the initial date for the regular signing period of the National Letter of Intent:

— Quiet Period

(d) Monday through Thursday of the week that includes the initial date for the regular signing period of the National Letter of Intent:

— Dead Period

(e) Friday following the initial date for the regular signing period of the National Letter of Intent through April 14:

— Quiet Period

(f) One hundred sixty-eight evaluation days (see Bylaw 13.02.7.2) (excluding Memorial Day and Sundays) during April 15 through May 31 selected at the discretion of the member institution and designated in writing in the office of the director of athletics [as provided in (1) below]:

— Evaluation Period

(1) An authorized off-campus recruiter may use one evaluation to assess the prospective student-athlete's athletics ability and one evaluation to assess the prospective student-athlete's academic qualifications during this evaluation period. If an institution's coaching staff member conducts both an athletics and an academic evaluation of a prospective student-athlete on the same day during this evaluation period, the institution shall be charged with the use of an academics evaluation only and shall be permitted to conduct a second athletics evaluation of the prospective student-athlete on a separate day during this evaluation period.

(g) Those days in April/May not designated in (f) above for evaluation opportunities.

— Quiet Period

*****

APPENDIX I: NCAA D-1 ACADEMIC "SLIDING SCALE"

(enrollees after August 1, 2016)

GPA	SAT	ACT
3.550	400	37
3.525	410	38
3.500	420	39
3.475	430	40
3.450	440	41
3.425	450	41
3.400	460	42
3.375	470	42
3.350	480	43
3.325	490	44
3.300	500	44
3.275	510	45
3.250	520	46
3.225	530	46
3.200	540	47
3.175	550	47
3.150	560	48

PARENT'S GUIDE TO COLLEGE FOOTBALL RECRUITING

GPA	SAT	ACT
3.125	570	49
3.100	580	49
3.075	590	50
3.050	600	50
3.025	610	51
3.000	620	52
2.975	630	52
2.950	640	53
2.925	650	53
2.900	660	54
2.875	670	55
2.850	680	56
2.825	690	56
2.800	700	57
2.775	710	58
2.750	720	59
2.725	730	60
2.700	740	61
2.675	750	61
2.650	760	62
2.625	770	63

APPENDIX I: NCAA D-A ACADEMIC "SLIDING SCALE"

GPA	SAT	ACT
2.600	780	64
2.575	790	65
2.550	800	66
2.525	810	67
2.500	820	68
2.475	830	69
2.450	840	70
2.425	850	70
2.400	860	71
2.375	870	72
2.350	880	73
2.325	890	74
2.300	900	75

ACADEMIC REDSHIRT:

GPA	SAT	ACT
2.299	910	76
2.275	910	76
2.250	920	77
2.225	930	78
2.200	940	79
2.175	950	80

GPA	SAT	ACT
ACADEMIC REDSHIRT:		
2.150	960	81
2.125	960	82
2.100	970	83
2.075	980	84
2.050	990	85
2.025	1000	86
2.000	1010	86

Below 2.0 Core GPA: NOT ELIGIBLE for D-1

APPENDIX J: HELPFUL WEBSITE ADDRESSES

(no endorsement or affiliation)

<u>NCAA</u>

NCAA HOMEPAGE

http://www.ncaa.com/

NCAA FOOTBALL

http://www.ncaa.com/sports/football

NCAA RECRUITING (Rules, Calendars, etc.)

http://www.ncaa.org/student-athletes/resources/recruiting-calendars?division=d1

NCAA GUIDE FOR THE COLLEGE BOUND ATHLETE

http://www.ncaapublications.com/productdownloads/CBSA.pdf

NCAA PUBLICATIONS (free downloads of Manuals (D-1, D-2 and D-3) including respective recruiting *Bylaw 13*, rules of the game of football, etc.)

https://www.ncaapublications.com/

NCAA ELIGIBILITY CENTER

www.eligibilitycenter.org

<u>NAIA</u>

NAIA HOMEPAGE

http://www.naia.org/

NAIA FOOTBALL

http://www.naia.org/

NAIA GUIDE FOR THE COLLEGE BOUND STUDENT ATHLETE

http://www.playnaia.org/d/NAIA_GuidefortheCollegeBoundStudent.pdf

NAIA ELIGIBILTY CENTER

http://www.playnaia.org/

D-2 AND D-3

D-2 TEAMS, LINKS TO EACH TEAM WEBSITE, AND OTHER INFORMATION

www.d2football.com/

D-3 TEAMS, LINKS TO EACH TEAM WEBSITE, AND OTHER INFORMATION

www.d3football.com/

Junior College Football (JUCO)

JUNIOR COLLEGE ORGANIZATION

http://www.njcaa.org/

SCOUT RECRUITING DEVOTED TO J.C.

http://jcfootball.scout.com/

RIVALS RECRUITING DEVOTED TO J.C.

http://jcgridiron.rivals.com/

High School Team Quality

MASSEY H.S. TEAM MATCHUPS

http://www.usatodayhss.com/massey-matchups/

Football Combines, Camps & Training

U.S. ARMY ALL-AMERICAN NATIONAL COMBINE

http://usarmyallamericanbowl.com/bowl-week-events/national-combine2

FOOTBALL CAMPS, U.S. NATIONAL TEAM

http://usafootball.com/trials-registration?gclid=CO75ndGSnLwCFSISMwod9AgAgg

NATIONAL UNDERCLASSMEN COMBINES

http://www.nucsports.com

NIKE COMBINES

http://www.studentsports.com/nike-football-sparq-combine-registration/

KOHLS KICKING, PUNTING, LONG SNAPPER CAMPS

http://kohlskicking.com/

FOOBALL UNIVERSITY CAMPS

http://www.footballuniversity.org/

NIKE FOOTBALL TRAINING CAMPS

[apparently no single website; word search on the internet for information]

MAXPREPS FOOTBALL CAMPS LISTING

http://www.maxpreps.com/directories/camps/list.aspx?sportid=902661 65-8674-43c3-9ffd-f5a8ecef79fc

Commercial Services & Goods

HUDL VIDEO CREATION & DISTRIBUTION

www.hudl.com

PLAYCED COLLEGE FOOTBALL TEAMS DATABASE

https://www.playced.com/

NCSA ATHLETIC RECRUITING SERVICES & FILM

http://www.ncsasports.org/

RECRUITING TAPE, *TOLAND* TECHNOLOGIES

http://www.recruitingtape.com

VIZUAL EDGE EYE MUSCLE AND REFLEX TRAINING

www.vizualedge.com

VERTIMAX JUMP TRAINING EQUIPMENT

http://www.vertimax.com/

Federal Pell Grants

http://www2.ed.gov/programs/fpg/index.html

Recruiting Websites (part free; part pay)

ESPN

http://espn.go.com/college-football/recruiting

RIVALS

http://footballrecruiting.rivals.com

SCOUT

http://recruiting.scout.com

247Sports

http://247sports.com/

Miscellaneous

USA FOOTBALL

http://www.usafootball.com/

COLLEGE TEAMS OVERSIGNING RECRUITS

www.oversigning.com

GLOSSARY

247Sports: The commercial football recruiting website found at http://247sports.com/. *See* Chapter 6.

3-4: A defensive formation having three linemen (one tackle, two ends) and four linebackers. The "defensive ends" in this formation, as compared to a 4-3, tend to be larger, more in the nature of defensive tackles.

4-3: A defensive formation having four linemen (two tackles, two ends) and three linebackers.

5-10-5: *See* "Shuttle Run".

Academic Index (AI): A single number used by Ivy League schools to evaluated academic admissibility for sports recruiting. It is based on a semi-secret formula believed to be:

$$AI = (\text{Two-part SAT score})/10 + (\text{"Converted Rank Score"})$$

The Converted Rank Score is a number that is determined by tables, taking in to account your son's class rank and the size of his high school class. A perfect AI score is 240, summing 160 points from the SAT (1600 / 10) and 80 points for being valedictorian at a big school. Currently, the *absolute minimum* AI score is thought to be about 171 to get admitted to an Ivy, although most Ivy League recruits must have a higher score.

Academic Redshirt (D-1): A student: (a) who's high school core 16 GPA was between 2.0 and 2.299; and/or (b) who did not complete 10 of 16 of their core 16 cores before their high school senior year. They may practice and may receive a D-a scholarship, but cannot play in games as a freshman. Successful remedial class work in college is thereafter required to play as a sophomore. You also will lose a year of playing eligibility, unless you complete at least 80% of your degree requirements before your fifth year in college. *Compare,* "Partial Qualifier" in D-2 football.

ACT Score: The standardized college test, and for NCAA purposes using the *sum* of the four (4) parts (English, math, reading and science). This is *not* the average of those scores (the so-called "composite" ACT score) which is commonly used by college admissions offices.

Agent: Persons who befriend student-athletes and frequently distribute impermissible benefits with plans to represent the student-athlete in the future, when the athlete turns professional, for a fee or commission.

Air (as in "On air"): A situation where no opposing player is present. This may occur, for example, in an offensive practice without defenders present. Pejorative: "He can't even catch the ball on air".

Amateur: Not a professional athlete, namely not a member of a team that declares itself to be professional or provides any player more than "actual and necessary" expenses (as defined by the NCAA) for participation on the team.

Arm length: The distance (inches) from the tip of one's fully extended middle finger to the "point" of the shoulder, which is the highest protruding bone near the outside of his shoulder when one's arm is fully extended to the front.

Arm span: The distance (inches) from one's left middle finger tip to their right middle finger tip when both arms are fully extended to each side.

Athlete: A very fast player whose diverse skills and athleticism allow him to play, and thus be recruited, at a variety of football positions.

Athleticism: Overall speed, agility, balance and coordination.

Back counting: The practice of having a recruit be an early enrollee and counting him towards the previous year's limit of 25 new D-1 scholarships rather than towards the present year's 25 scholarship limit.

Base: The normal or default formation that a team uses. For example, a team may have a 3-4 as its "base" defense.

BCS: The now defunct "Bowl Championship Series" previously used to determine which teams played in the 5 major bowl games including the FBS National Championship Game. It was replace by the College Football Playoff (CFP) .

Bending: Having good flexibility in the hips, knees, ankles and back to get low by bending at the knees rather than bending at the waist.

Bigs: Offensive or defensive linemen.

Big eaters: Offensive or defensive linemen.

Big skill (players): Larger skill positions, typically, fullbacks, H-backs, tight ends, linebackers and sometimes defensive ends.

Big uglies: Offensive or defensive linemen.

Blitz: A rush across the line of scrimmage (typically a pass rush) from a linebacker or a defensive back.

Blocking zone: An imaginary rectangle centered on the ball at the snap and extending five (5) yards to each side and extending three (3) yards forward and backward. Sometimes confused with a different concept, the "box" or "Tackle box".

Blood lines: Relating to a prospect whose father was a notable coach or player in college or the NFL.

Blue Chip: An elite or top rated prospect.

Blue-Shirting: The process of having an un-recruited (no official visits; no home visits) prospect enroll as a walk-on player, and then promptly offering and providing a scholarship after they begin practice. Unlike gray-shirting, the player is immediately eligible to play that season; but, like gray-shirting the scholarship is counted against the *following* year's recruiting class limits. This is viewed as a loophole to get around the D-1 25-signee per year limit.

Board: A college team's listing, typically by position group, of who they would like to commit to their team in rank order of their priority. Also known as it's "Recruiting board".

Boundary: The out of bounds sideline, normally referring specifically to the one on the short side of the field (based on where the ball is placed before the snap).

Broad Jump (standing): A test wherein the person's leaping distance forward from a standing start is measured in feet and inches.

Camp: Gatherings during the summer where coaches teach football skills and evaluate prospects. They are either one-day or multi-day. *See* Chapter 6. *Compare*, "Training camp".

CARA: *See* Countable Athletically Related Activities

CFP: The "College Football Playoff" system used to determine, via a selection committee, which teams play in the 6 major bowl games including the FBS playoff bracket. It replaced by the Bowl Championship Series (BCS).

Clearinghouse: Former name for what is now the NCAA "Eligibility Center" pertaining to academic and amateur eligibility.

Clustering: When a college team's members tend to cluster, or enroll, in disproportionately high percentages in academic majors that are easy and/or of questionable value and/or are not consistent with the player's post-graduation (non-football) aspirations.

Combine: Gatherings where prospects are tested on a variety of events, such as 40-yard dash, shuttle run, vertical jump, and others. Often, football skills are also showcased.

Commit: *Verb*: Either a non-binding verbal commitment or a signing a binding Letter of Intent. *Noun*: A prospect who has committed to a college. *Compare*, Soft Commit.

Contact: Any time a coach has any face-to-face contact with a prospect or the prospect's parents off the college's campus and says more than hello. A contact also occurs if a coach has any contact with the prospect or his parents at the prospect's high school or any location where the prospect is engaging in competition or practice, such as during an "evaluation".

Contact period: The time when a college coach may have in-person contact with a prospect and the prospect's parents on or off the college's campus. The coach may also watch the prospect play or visit his or her high school. The prospect and the parents may visit a college campus, and the coach may write and telephone during this period.

Coordinator: Usually the second highest ranking coaches on a staff, beneath the head coach. Typically these are the offensive coordinator and the defensive coordinator. However, sometimes teams have "co-coordinators" splitting such duties. For example, one co-coordinator on offense may be the "run game" coordinator whereas the other is the "pass game" coordinator. *Compare*, Recruiting coordinator.

Cover [number]: (*e.g.* "Cover 2") A designation of defensive pass coverage, generally with the number (0, 1, 2, 3 etc.) indicating the number of defensive backs in zone pass coverage at the deepest part of the field. "Cover 0" is man-on-man pass coverage.

Core Courses: A list of 16 required high school academic courses to be eligible to play D-1 or D-2 football. The lists are slightly different as between D-1 and D-2.

Countable Athletically Related Activities: Per NCAA rule, the number of hours a team may require a player to devote per day or per week to certain listed activities. This is misleading, however, because while only 20 'CARA' hours per week are allowed during football season, in fact the time required of players (legally) under those rules is typically about 40-50 hours per week during season.

D-1: Shorthand for "Division-I", the NCAA athletics highest levels that includes *both* FBS and FCS level football.

D-2: Shorthand for "Division-II", the NCAA athletics level that includes the third highest level of football.

D-3: Shorthand for "Division-III", the NCAA athletics level that includes the fourth highest level football. Athletic scholarships are not permitted at this level.

Dead period: A time when the college coach may not have any in-person contact with a prospect or the prospect's parents at any time. The coach may write and telephone during this time.

Depth Chart: The listing on a college football team, position by position, of who is first string, second string, and so on.

Division-I: Also known as "D-1", the NCAA athletics highest levels that includes *both* FBS and FCS level football.

Division-IA: The former name for what is now called FBS (Football Bowl Subdivision) football.

Division-IAA: The former name for what is now called FCS (Football Championship Subdivision) football.

Division-II: Also known as "D-2", the NCAA athletics level that includes the third highest level of football.

Division-III: Also known as "D-3", the NCAA athletics level that includes the fourth highest level football. Athletic scholarships are not permitted at this level.

Duck: A badly thrown pass that is high and wobbly.

Early enrollment: When a high school senior graduates early and enrolls in college classes in December or January of his senior year so as to participate in winter workouts and spring football. Synonymous with green shirting.

Eligibility Center: The website used to collect information about a prospects academic and amateur eligibility, for the NCAA found at:

www.eligibilitycenter.org

and, for the NAIA found at:

http://www.playnaia.org/

These allow for a prospect to register for academic and amateur eligibility at a single (website) location for the NCAA and another for the NAIA, and for colleges to confirm that at those websites. This reduces duplication if a prospect had to fill out this information separately for each school.

Equivalent (scholarship): A scholarship that has the dollar value of one full ride scholarship but which can be split among multiple players. *Compare* "Head count" scholarship.

Evaluation: An activity by a coach to evaluate off-campus a prospect's academic or athletics ability. This would include visiting the high school or watching the prospect practice or compete in a game. It may or may not include an in-person "contact".

Evaluation period: The time a college coach may watch a prospect play or visit the high school but cannot have any in-person conversations with him or his parents off the college's campus. The prospect his parents can visit a college campus during this period and a coach may call or write during this period.

Explosive: Having the ability to powerfully and quickly lunge forward from a standing start. This usually is the byproduct of powerful, fast (white) twitch leg muscles and fast reaction time. It is frequently tested by the vertical jump and the standing broad jump.

Eyeball test: A coach seeing a prospect up close and in person, with his own eyes. Used to confirm height and weight, and to evaluate "frame", personality, and other attributes.

Fade: A passing route typically to the back corner of an end zone. This can test the soft touch and precision of a quarterback's passing.

False step: A player's initial step taken in a direction (usually backwards) other than the direction that they should be heading.

FBS: "Football Bowl Subdivision", namely the highest level of NCAA college football. It is a *sub*-division of Division-I (aka "D-1). This used to be called Division-IA. The FBS schools are eligible to participate in bowl games.

FCS: "Football Championship Subdivision", namely the second highest level of NCAA college football. It is a *sub*-division of Division-I (aka "D-1"). This used to be called Division-IAA.

Film: *see* Highlight Film; Game Film.

Frame: The size, shape and thickness of a prospect's skeletal structure.

Full ride scholarship: A scholarship that pays all tuition, room and board, books and permissible fees. Formally called, "Grant in Aid". *Compare,* "Head Count" scholarship, "Equivalent" scholarship, "Pell grants".

Game Film: Footage, often on DVD, of an entire football game. Also called "full game film".

Get off: Reaction time of a player from the snap to when they move (typically about 0.2 second).

Going up for it: The ability of a tight end or other pass receiver to jump up and catch a highly thrown pass, typically while in traffic.

Graduate assistant: An entry level job on a college football coaching staff who is not a full-fledged "coach". He is like an assistant, assistant coach. He cannot recruit off campus but assists the coaching staff on campus.

Grant in Aid: The formal NCAA term for a scholarship for playing football. If "full", this pays for all tuition, room and board, books and fees, but is not allowed for anything else. Such scholarships are, by NCAA rule, limited to one-year, but are renewable each year at the determination of the coach/university. *Compare*, "Pell grant".

Gray-shirting: Withholding a scholarship to an offered recruit who has signed a Letter of Intent until a semester following normal enrollment. Thus, rather than enrolling in the summer or fall, the player misses that football season and enrolls the following January. *See* Chapter 10. *Compare* Blue-shirting.

Green-Shirting: When a high school senior graduates early and enrolls in college classes in December or January of his senior year so as to participate in winter workouts and spring football. Synonymous with early enrollment.

Guide for the College Bound Student-Athlete: A free and very helpful publication by the NCAA that summarizes recruiting rules, eligibility rules, and other information for D-1, D-2 and D-3 sports. It is available online at:

http://www.ncaapublications.com/productdownloads/CBSA.pdf

Separately, the NAIA also has a guide by this title.

Hand in/on the dirt: Playing in a 3-point or 4-point stance, namely as an offensive or defensive linemen.

Hand size: The measurement of the hand in inches with the hand laid fully open from the tip of the thumb to the tip of the pinky finger.

H-Back: An offensive backfield position that is a hybrid between fullback and tight end.

Head count (scholarship): A full ride scholarship which cannot be split among multiple players.

Head hunter: A football player, typically on defense, who is particularly aggressive and hard hitting.

Highlight Film: A collection of video clips, usually on DVD or internet, of a player's best high school varsity game plays. Typically it is 4-7 minutes in duration.

High Point: Pertains to catching (or intercepting) the ball, and more specifically to timing one's jump and arm reach to catch the ball at the highest elevation possible. It is like rebounding in basketball.

Hold the edge: The ability of a defender, (normally a defensive end or outside linebacker), to contain the ball carrier from getting outside around the defense.

Hold the point: The ability of a defender on a run play to not be pushed away from the point of attack.

Hot: A short pass route, or a receiver running such route, that the quarterback can quickly pass the ball to in response to a blitz so as to avoid being sacked.

Impermissible benefits: *See* NCAA formal definition, Appendix H, Bylaws 13.2.1.1 and 13.2.1.2.

JUCO: Junior college. *See* website:

http://www.njcaa.org/ .

Juke: A rapid cut or change in direction by a ball carrier to make a would-be tackler miss him.

Junior Day: A one-day recruiting event on-campus hosted by coaches and other football staff for H.S. junior prospects. It almost always require an invitation. It typically include a tour of facilities, one or more talks or presentations, food (since it is not an "official visit", you are required by NCAA rule to pay), and a meet and greet gathering with coaches and other recruits. They typically occur in February or March.

Key: *see* "Read".

Letter of Intent: The document a prospect signs when he or she agrees to attend the designated college or university for one academic year. Upon signing other NCAA schools must cease recruitment of a prospect. *Compare* NCAA formal definition, Appendix H, Bylaw 13.02.10.

Leverage: A vague term in football having been used in so many contexts that it lacks clear, universal meaning. It generally implies playing low and in a good position to force an opponent to go where he does not want to go. One specific use of the term is a player maintaining an advantageous *outside* position with his head across his opponent (blocker or defender) and toward where the ball carrier is going. For example, a linebacker may create leverage by forcing himself under (ripping) one side of a lead blocker to force the running back to cut back inside towards the majority of other defenders. Ironically, another (arguably opposite) example is where a defender positions himself *inside* with the ball carrier between him and the sidelines, thereby using the sideline to create 'leverage' to trap the ball carrier.

Loop: A defensive stunt, usually involving one defensive lineman and one linebacker, where the lineman slants towards the linebacker and the linebacker blitzes around the slanting linemen when the ball is snapped to confuse blockers. *Compare*, Twist.

Loose hips: Having good flexibility in the muscles and joints of the hips and groin to allow the player to readily swivel, rotate, open up, turn around and/or change direction.

Majoring in eligibility: The practices of having a player take too many: (a) remedial classes (due to high school shortcomings) which the NCAA counts toward playing eligibility requirements yet do not count towards a university degree; and/or (b) easy classes scattered across various majors that, short term, could be among degree worthy classes but, long term, collectively do not count towards any one degree requirement; and/or (c) "clustering" (defined above) classes.

Mechanics: The detailed movement of a quarterback during passing, taking into account the positions and motions of most every body part, including feet, hips, shoulders, eyes, elbow, wrists, hands and fingers.

Medical Red Shirt: Slang for "Medical Hardship Waiver" per NCAA Bylaw 14.2.4, giving a player one more year of eligibility to play due to illness or injury. One must petition the NCAA showing the following four conditions are met: (1) the student-athlete may not have participated in more than two contests or dates of competition or 20 percent (rounded up) of the team's completed contests/dates of competition; (2) the injury or illness must occur prior to the completion of the first half of the season; (3) the injury or illness does not have to occur during practice/competition, but it must be incapacitating; and, (4) appropriate medical documentation must exist and be provided. *Compare*, "Red shirting".

Mike: Middle linebacker.

Move the chains: To get first downs.

Move the pile: A ball carrier hitting tacklers so hard and/or with leg drive so as to push them backwards.

Motor: Hustle and effort during play.

National Letter of Intent (or "NLI"): *See* "Letter of Intent".

National signing day: The first day that recruits may sign a binding Letter of Intent, normally the first week in February of a recruit's senior year. They may, but rarely do, sign for about two months following. Also, if a recruit is an early enrollee, (Green-shirt), then he may sign sooner in time to enroll in college during January.

Nickel: A defensive formation against an expected pass play, having an extra (5th) defensive back, offset by one less linebacker or defensive lineman than normal.

North-south: the direction directly toward the end zone. Usually used to describe a running back's style of running straight ahead with power, as opposed to with sideways fakes and cuts.

Offer: An offer from a college coach to play football for his team. It can be verbal, and beginning in September of your son's junior year it can be in writing. It may be for a full ride scholarship or something less. It is non-binding and the college can withdraw it.

Official Visit: A prospect's visit (upon invitation) to a college campus paid for by the college. They may not occur during a dead period. The college can pay for transportation to and from the college, room and meals (three per day) while visiting and reasonable entertainment expenses, including three complimentary admissions to a home athletics contest. NCAA recruiting bylaws limit the number of official visits a recruit may take to five. An FBS school may only extend 56 football official visit invitations.

On the hoof: *See* Eyeball test.

Over-signing: When a college program has more recruits sign Letters of Intent than it has Roster limit spots (85) on the team for them. *See* Chapter 10.

Pad level: The height of a player's shoulder pads, particularly during impact. Low is better.

Partial Qualifier (D-2): A student that did not meet all of the D-2 academic requirements, but who graduated high school and met at least one of: (a) high school core 16 GPA was at least 2.0; and/or (b) had a combined SAT of 820 or ACT sum score of 68. They may practice and may receive a D-2 scholarship, but cannot play in games as a freshman. Maintaining collegiate academic eligibility thereafter allows him to play as a sophomore. A similar concept in D-1 is called, "Academic Redshirt".

Pass efficiency (also, "Passer efficiency" or "Passer rating"): A number (PR) pertaining to quarterbacks blending passing yards, touchdowns, completions, interceptions and pass attempts. In college football it is calculated by the formula:

$$PR = \frac{(8.4 \text{ X yds}) + (330 \text{ X TD}) + (100 \text{ X Comp}) - (200 \text{ X Int})}{(\text{\# of pass attempts})}$$

The single season record (as of 2014) in college is 191.8. The *NFL* uses a different formula.

Preferred Walk-on: *See* Recruited Walk On.

Package: A designated group of players (offense or defense) for a particular situation. Also sometimes refers to a formation, normally deploying that group of players. Often on offense, this is defined by two digits, *e.g.* "21", with the first digit being the number of running backs and the second digit being the number of tight ends.

Pell grants: A federal program that provides need-based grants (not loans needing to be repaid) to low-income students to promote access to postsecondary education. As of 2015, one could receive up to $5,730 per year. This is not limited to football, or even athletics, but may be awarded even to low-income students that also receive a Full ride scholarship. *See* website:

http://www2.ed.gov/programs/fpg/index.html .

Period: One of four (4) categories of dates on the NCAA Recruiting Calendar which dictate when coaches can engage in various form of recruiting. Those categories are: (1) dead period; (2) quiet period; (3) evaluation period; and, (4) contact period.

Personnel groups: *See* "Package".

Phone Booth: At or pertaining to the crowded, interior most part of the interior offensive line, namely the location of the center and two guards.

Point of attack: The location on the field where, based on the play called, a running back is intended to cross the line of scrimmage.

Pop on the ball: In a quarterback's passing, the attribute of throwing a quick, crisp pass.

Position coach: A coach that coaches a particular position group. The position coaches tend to report in the chain of command to their respective coordinator (offensive or defensive). However, such coordinators and even the head coach frequently also double as a position coach.

Position groups: Groups of similar football players on a team. They are normally grouped by position coach (which varies somewhat between teams), for example: (a) quarterback; (b) offensive line; (c) tight ends; (d) wide receivers; (e) running backs; (f) defensive line; (g) linebackers; (h) defensive backs; and, (i) special teams.

Pro-Agility: *See* "Shuttle Run".

Prospect: A student who has entered ninth grade, or earlier in a few other situations. *See* NCAA formal definition, Appendix H, Bylaw 13.02.11.

Prospective student-athlete: *See* "Prospect".

Quiet period: Times when the college may not have any in-person talk with the prospective student-athlete or the parents off the college's campus. The coach may not watch the prospect play or practice. The prospect can visit college campuses during this time and a coach may write or telephone.

Read: *Verb*: to analyze and react (quickly) to an event or what another player is doing during play. *Noun*: the event or other player that one is supposed to analyze and react to.

Recruit: A prospect that is being recruited. *Compare* NCAA formal definition, Appendix H, Bylaw 13.02.12.1.

Recruited Walk On: A player enrolling in the college and invited on the team who was recruited as such but does not have a football scholarship.

Recruiting: The process by a college of evaluating a prospect's eligibility and athletic ability, and while such prospect has an offer from that college, their attempting to persuade him to sign a Letter of Intent with them. *Compare* NCAA formal definition, Appendix H, Bylaw 13.02.12.

Recruiting board: A college team's listing, typically by position group, of who they would like to commit to their team in rank order of their priority. Also known as it's "Board".

Recruiting coordinator: A college football coach, other than the head coach, who organizes and coordinates the team's recruiting efforts.

Representative (of a college for purposes of NCAA rules): Includes but is not limited to person's who have made financial contributions, participated as a varsity athlete, been involved in promoting athletics, provided employment for the college's student athletes, and/or assisted or requested to assist in recruiting a prospect, as well as boosters and/or season ticket holders. Once a person is a "representative", they retain that status forever. *See* NCAA formal definition, Appendix H, Bylaw 13.02.13.

Red Shirting: When a college player does not play at all (not even one play) during any game during a season, and thus does not use one of his four (4) years of playing eligibility. *Compare* Medical Red Shirt.

Rivals: The commercial football recruiting website found at http://footballrecruitng.rivals.com *See* Chapter 6.

Roster limit: The cap set by NCAA rules for the number of players on a team's roster during Training Camp, namely for FBS 85 scholarship players and 20 non-scholarship (walk-on) players. *See* Chapter 1, Table 1.

Runner: Individuals who, is an intermediary between a sports agent and a student-athlete, befriend student-athletes and frequently distribute impermissible benefits.

Runs (Plays) well in his pads: A football player who has sufficient overall strength that his speed and agility are not degraded much while wearing football pads and helmet, as compared to when he is not wearing them.

Sand is his pants: Having sufficient body weight to anchor oneself against being pushed around during blocking.

Sack: A TFL (tackle for loss) of a quarterback attempting to pass. Note that in terms of football statistics one sack is also, at the same time, both one tackle and one TFL.

SAT Score: The standardized college test using the summed two (2) part (math and reading), *not* the three (3) part (math, reading and writing) score.

Sam: Strong side outside linebacker.

Scholarship: Either a "Full ride scholarship" (typical for most D-1 FBS football programs) or a partial scholarship, more common in D-2, NAIA and JUCO programs. D-3 and Ivy League programs are not allowed to give *athletic* scholarships. *See also*, "Pell grants".

Scout: The commercial recruiting website found at http://recruiting.scout.com. *See* Chapter 6. Also, a person that reviews and analyzes player's abilities on film and/or live.

Shake 'n bake: The ability of a ball carrier to quickly cut or "juke" to fake a would-be tackler and then rapidly accelerate running speed.

Shuttle Run: A test, also known as the short shuttle, pro-agility, or 5-10-5, that is a timed and measures agility. *See* Figure 1 in Chapter 6.

Sign: To sign a Letter of Intent.

Silent Commit: A recruit that has committed to a program but who has not publicly disclosed the commitment.

Sixth year: The rare granting by the NCAA of a petition for a player to have a sixth (school) year in which to complete his fourth (4th) year of playing eligibility. This happens, for example, in unusual injury or sickness situations.

Skill player(s): The positions of quarterback, running back, receiver, safety and cornerback. Compare "Big skill" and "Specialists".

Sleeper: A high school prospect who is unknown or at least has not been evaluated.

Slobber-knocker: An especially hard and violent hit.

Soft Commit: A prospect who has verbally committed to a school but is actively visiting and considering other schools.

Soft hands: The quality of being able to catch most or all passes without bobbling the ball, and in particular doing so when the ball is thrown fast.

Training camp: The intense, uninterrupted multi-week series of college football practices and meetings in August preceding the first game. Normally, D-1 players and coaches are together in a single dormitory throughout.

Special Admits: Recruits that are admitted and eligible to play D-1 football despite falling below the school's normal academic admission minimums.

Specialists: Kickers, punters and long snappers. Sometimes includes punt and kickoff returners.

***SPARQ* score:** A number calculated on a website by *Nike* (per an unpublished formula) as a standardized score indicating athleticism. It is an acronym for speed, power, agility, reaction and quickness. *See* Chapter 2.

Speed score: A number (SS) blending speed and weight calculated by the formula:

$$SS = (200 \times weight) \div (40\ time)^4$$

When used this typically pertains to running backs. *See* Chapter 2.

Spread: An offensive formation (or style) having numerous (3-5) receivers spread out widely so as to spread out the defense. This formation tends to rely more on speed than on power.

Spread Option (or Spread Read-Option): A "spread" offense where the quarterback is a key ball carrier as part of the running game and with at least one other running back with whom the quarterback optionally gives (or keeps) the ball.

Stunt: Where various defenders make a planned move other than their normal, expected movement to confuse the offense. These include: slanting; two defenders twisting or looping (crisscrossing with respect to each other); linemen dropping into pass coverage; and, blitzing.

Tackles (total): The sum total of: (a) solo tackles; and, (b) assisted tackles. Both categories also include sacks and TFL's (tackles for loss), including any safeties.

Technique (as in "3-Technique"): The position, ranging from "0" to "9", where a defensive lineman is located before the snap. The lower the number, the closer to the offensive center. For example, "5-technique" means being lined up across from the outside shoulder of the offensive tackle.

Telegraph: The tendency of a player (often a quarterback) to reveal in advance what they are about to do, thereby losing the element of surprise.

TFL: Tackle for loss, namely a sack or other tackle behind the line of scrimmage. Note that in terms of football statistics one TFL is also, at the same time, one tackle.

Trainer: Member of football staff who works on injuries and pre-practice taping of players.

Training Table: The place and time where the college football team eats meal(s), typically apart from the general student body and with more and better food.

Two deep: The first and second string player positions, collectively, on a team. A player "in the two deep" is either first or second string at his position.

Two-stepper: A fast runner with strides long enough to cover the span between 5-yard stripes on a football field in two steps.

Twist: A defensive stunt, usually involving at least one defensive lineman, where two or more defenders crisscross with respect to each other when the ball is snapped to confuse blockers. *Compare,* Loop.

Under the radar: A high school player who is relatively unknown or underappreciated in the recruiting process. This may be due to lack of exposure and/or to late development. *See also,* "Sleeper".

Unofficial visit: Any visit by a prospect and/or their parents to a college campus paid for by them. The only expense the prospect can receive from the college is three complimentary admissions to a home athletics contest (or 5 tickets if the parents are divorced or separated). The prospect may make as many unofficial visits as he or she likes and may take the visits at any time. The only time the prospective student-athlete cannot talk with a coach during an unofficial visit is during a dead period.

Verbal Commitment: A prospect indicating to a program that has offered him that he intends to sign a Letter of Intent with them. It is not binding on the prospect or the college.

Vertical Jump: A test wherein the person's vertical jumping height (inches) from a standing start is measured. It is a differential test, namely subtracting: (a) the height of the middle finger extended upward while stationary; from, (b) the height touched while jumping. However, sometimes the differential is measured by precisely timing from when the jumper is off and then back on an electronic timer landing pad. Based on that time, the height is computed using the physics of gravity.

Walk On: A player in the college and on the team but does not have a football scholarship. He may be awarded a scholarship at some point in the future.

War daddy: An elite level football player, most commonly used in the context of an offensive or defensive lineman.

Will: Weak side outsider linebacker.

Zebra: Referee or other such official in a game.

INDEX

The e-book reader version of this book does not have pages or page numbers, and thus has no index. However, most e-book readers will allow you to word search for terms.

ABOUT THE AUTHOR

Dan Lueders is an avid student of the game of football, reading most everything that he can find on the subject. In working on this book, in addition to the experiences with his son's recruitment, he read eight other books about college recruiting. He has been a youth football coach for many years. His profession is patent and trademark litigation and law, having an engineering degree from Northwestern University and a law degree from Indiana University. He has also served as an adjunct professor of law at his alma mater, and also was a volunteer deputy prosecutor in his county. His hobbies include fly-fishing, waterfowl hunting, woodworking, photography, travel, friends, one mountain, and of course, football. His favorite quote is from the Greek philosopher Athanasios Filis, "Life is about making memories."

49279928R00177

Made in the USA
Lexington, KY
31 January 2016